THE INSIDE STORY OF BRIGHTON & HOVE ALBION'S JOURNEY FROM DESPAIR TO TRIUMPH AND THE PREMIER LEAGUE

BRIGHTON UP

NICK SZCZEPANIK

First published in Great Britain in 2017 by
Biteback Publishing Ltd
Westminster Tower
3 Albert Embankment
London SE1 7SP

ISBN 978-1-78590-239-0

10 9 8 7 6 5 4 3 2 1

A CIP catalogue record for this book is available from the British Library.

Set in Minion Pro

Printed and bound in Great Britain by
CPI Group (UK) Ltd, Croydon CR0 4YY

To Nigel Beal, Roy Chuter, Sarah Watts, Paul Whelch and all dedicated fans of Brighton & Hove Albion who never got to read the next chapter.

CONTENTS

FOREWORD

When I became the manager of Brighton & Hove Albion in January 2015, my immediate task was to steer the club away from the wrong end of the Championship.

But it was clear that the long-term goal at Brighton was to reach the Premier League, and I could tell that everything was in place at the club for that to happen.

We nearly managed to realise that dream the following season, but as everybody knows, we fell just that little bit short.

However, we had proved that we had a team with potential and I knew that the players were motivated to go one step further.

The fans had given us fantastic support that we knew would continue the next season.

And the club had shown its true quality as the whole community came together after the tragedy of the Shoreham airshow crash in August 2015.

Thankfully, with great efforts from everyone on and off the field, and that little bit of luck that you always need, we were able to achieve our ambition in 2017, and the scenes after we beat Wigan to clinch promotion will live long in the memory.

This book is the inside story of those two seasons, the lows as well as the highs, told by an experienced journalist and lifelong Albion fan. I hope you enjoy reliving them.

Chris Hughton
Lancing, May 2017

PREFACE

When I began thinking about writing this book, I could have decided to concentrate on the 2016/17 season alone, or to go back as far as 1997 or beyond; either would have had merit. But I opted for a tale of two seasons and the contrast of the glorious failure of 2015/16 with the success of a year later.

I had two main reasons: first, because they were Chris Hughton's first full seasons in charge; and second, because the Shoreham air crash and the games against Middlesbrough and Sheffield Wednesday affected the club and the players so much that what promotion meant can only be fully explained by understanding what came before.

Naturally, any attempt to build up suspense would be doomed to failure, because everyone knows that the story has a happy ending. And if it had not, the book would not have been written – few publishers would have held out much hope of selling a story of two successive seasons that ended badly.

Instead I have tried to take you inside the club as Chris Hughton and his players pushed to reach the Premier League by, as far as possible, letting the people most closely involved put into their own words their tales of despair and triumph.

Nick Szczepanik
Brighton, May 2017

ACKNOWLEDGEMENTS

This book could not have been attempted without the assistance of Brighton & Hove Albion, who allowed me generous access to players, staff and coaches. Thanks to Paul Camillin and his media team, Tony Bloom, Paul Barber, Chris Hughton, Dick Knight, Alan Mullery, Bruno Saltor, Sam Baldock, Lewis Dunk, Anthony Knockaert, Solly March, Glenn Murray, Liam Rosenior, Steve Sidwell, David Stockdale, Íñigo Calderón, Ben Roberts, Colin Calderwood, Paul Trollope and Paul Winstanley. Also to Brian Horton, John Baine, Paul Samrah and Alan Wares.

Special appreciation to club historian Tim Carder for access to his invaluable and exhaustive Albion Almanac. Thanks also to local and nationally based colleagues in the football media including Andy Naylor, Steve Bailey, Paul Hayward, Ian Winrow, Tony Banks and Mike Walters.

Pictures: BHAFC/Paul Hazlewood

INTRODUCTION

16 MAY 2016

As the final whistle blew on Brighton & Hove Albion's 2015/16 season, some players dropped to the turf of the American Express Community Stadium. Others stood, heads bowed and hands on hips. Grown men cried like children, on the field as well as in the stands.

Eventually, those on the ground dragged themselves to their feet for a weary lap of the pitch, acknowledging the applause of the home crowd, most of whom had stayed to cheer a team who had come so close to delivering so much yet fallen so agonisingly short.

Away to their left as they trudged off the field, they could hear Sheffield Wednesday and their fans celebrating their 3–1 aggregate win in the Championship play-off semi-finals, gleefully anticipating the Wembley final – the £100 million match, as the media called it, reflecting the riches on offer in the Premier League to the winner. Riches that Brighton would have to wait at least another year to claim, if they would ever manage it.

As the Brighton players slumped in the dressing room, it was no consolation to reflect that almost no other team had ever amassed so many points without achieving automatic promotion. Or that they themselves, tipped for relegation before the season, had shocked much of the football world by beginning the campaign with a twenty-one-match unbeaten run and coming so very close to reaching the Premier League.

Tony Bloom, the chairman, came down from the directors' box to thank the players and coaching staff for their efforts, but his words must have sounded hollow.

The received wisdom is that the team fell short of promotion by two goals, but actually it was one.

One more goal, one single, solitary goal, either in the 3–0 home defeat by Middlesbrough that ended that run of invincibility, or in the 1–1 draw in the final game of the regular season, away to the same opponents; a wrongly disallowed goal at home to Ipswich correctly given or one kept out in games where leads were surrendered late on at Bolton, Derby or QPR – and it would all have been different.

Eleven months later, it was.

CHAPTER 1

SUMMER 2015

As most Brighton & Hove Albion fans know only too well, there are far worse things in football than losing play-off finals.

In spring 1997, Brighton were at the lowest point of their history.

Chairman Bill Archer, a Blackburn-based businessman with no historic connection to the Albion, had sold the Goldstone Ground, the club's traditional home, to property developers. Supporters had fought a long battle to oust him and his chief executive, David Bellotti. A new board of directors led by advertising man Dick Knight, a lifelong supporter, had now taken over, but too late to save the crumbling stadium.

On Saturday 26 April, the team played the last game there, beating Doncaster Rovers 1–0. The following season, the fans and directors faced a groundshare with Gillingham, seventy miles away, and knew that they would have to fight again to bring the team home to Sussex.

But that was not the worst of it. The team had to play one more game that season, away to Hereford United, and defeat would mean relegation from the Football League. If that happened, would there be the appetite among enough fans to keep battling? To save a homeless non-League club?

This was the level to which a proud club had sunk, a club that had played four seasons in the top flight, regularly attracted crowds of 30,000-plus and come within one kick of winning the FA Cup. The game at Hereford finished in a draw, but the jubilation and relief at staying in the League was quickly tempered by the sobering certainty of tough times ahead.

At times like these, losing a Championship play-off semi-final would have sounded more like an aspiration than a disappointment. Back then, as the few thousand fans who still cared enough set off the following season on those 140-mile round trips to watch their team play dreadful fourth-tier home games in north Kent, the prospect of getting within two games of the glamour of the Premier League was beyond some fantastic and distant horizon.

Dick Knight and the fans persuaded Brighton & Hove City Council to let the club come home in 1999 and play at Withdean Stadium, a converted athletics venue with a fraction of the Goldstone's capacity. And for the next decade they lobbied local and national government for permission to build a proper, permanent stadium.

Somehow the team won four promotions (and suffered two relegations) while at their cramped temporary accommodation. Even on the best of those days, the idea of watching the team play for a place in the big league in a sold-out, world-class 30,000-capacity stadium would have represented luxury beyond expectation.

But a sense of historical perspective only helps so much the morning after defeat in a play-off semi-final. The victors are the ones talking about Wembley on the back pages. The losers can only think about the summer holidays, then possibly rebuilding and going one or two better next time.

That empty feeling in 2016 was nothing new for Brighton. They had known it in 2013 and in 2014 too. On each occasion they had had to dust themselves down and go again, with the added complication of having to bed in a new manager.

Gustavo Poyet, the former Uruguay, Chelsea and Tottenham Hotspur midfield player, had been in charge when they had lost to Crystal Palace, their greatest rivals, in 2013. He left in controversial circumstances within weeks. He was replaced by Óscar García, once Barcelona's B team head coach, who worked wonders in taking a less talented squad to the same stage in 2014 but saw his men outclassed by Derby County. García surprised the club by resigning soon afterwards, and the club surprised everyone else by appointing Sami Hyypiä, the former Liverpool and Finland defender, to replace him.

If defeat in the play-offs is painful, then fighting a relegation battle is worse, and that was where Hyypiä's team found themselves. He walked away in December 2014 and was replaced by Chris Hughton, who had been out of management since being sacked by Norwich City five games from the end of the previous season. It was seen as a good omen that he was a former Spurs player, like Poyet – who had masterminded the club's previous promotion, from League One in 2011 – and Alan Mullery, the only man who had previously led Brighton to the top flight, in 1979.

Hughton, then fifty-six, was a highly respected figure in the game. He also had an excellent record at Championship level. He had led Newcastle United to the division title in the 2009/10 season and taken Birmingham City into the play-offs in 2011/12 despite the enormous distraction of a Europa League campaign.

His immediate priority at Brighton was very different. He was forced to grind out results over the remainder of the 2014/15 season and do enough to get the points required for safety. It was not pretty, it was seldom entertaining, and there were few indications that any renaissance was over the horizon.

Perhaps it was hardly surprising in the circumstances that expectations for Brighton as they prepared for the 2015/16 season were not high. *FourFourTwo* magazine, in fact, predicted relegation in twenty-third place for the Seagulls – and Wolves to go up as champions.

Hughton thought differently.

'When I first came, we were in the bottom three and there is always a reason for that,' he said.

'The team was very different from the team that Óscar or Gus had. A new manager can always come in and add something different, so I was always confident that we would get out of the bottom three and stay out, and then it was a question of the summer. The only way the team was going to improve that next season was for us to recruit well. I also wanted to play a completely different way to the way that Sami did. It was a question of simplifying the roles they had and getting them to do things a different way.'

The second half of the 2014/15 season had largely been a question of making the most of the squad he had inherited. 'I hadn't expected to change everything immediately,' he said.

'Although I came in on the first of January and we would work hard to see what we could possibly bring in during the transfer window, I don't think many managers take a job thinking they are going to sign lots of players to make a team better. You think you will get more out of the players you have got. That has to be the first principle.

'Sami played 4–3–3 and we still had to play it at times after he went because of the players we had. We didn't have the wide players we have now – Kazenga LuaLua was very much in and out with injuries, and we had to use Sam Baldock on the left. I very much wanted some consistency and it was really just getting the best out of the players we had. Sometimes I look back and the team is almost unrecognisable.'

As he set about the task of transforming Brighton from strugglers to challengers, Hughton knew he could salvage the nucleus of a new team from the squad that had struggled.

David Stockdale, the goalkeeper, had played in the Premier League with Fulham and been called into the full England squad by manager Fabio Capello. Bruno, the right-back, had played in La Liga and the Champions League with Valencia, and his understudy, Íñigo Calderón, was a popular and whole-hearted performer. In the centre of defence, club captain Gordon Greer brought experience, and local boy and youth team product Lewis Dunk immense promise.

In midfield, dynamic Israel international Beram Kayal and Dale Stephens, a talented ball-player who was now fully recovered from a long-term ankle injury sustained a few months after his transfer from Charlton Athletic in January 2014, looked a promising pairing, with England under-21 prospect Jake Forster-Caskey, raw youngster Rohan Ince and experienced Andrew Crofts as back-ups. Wide men Kazenga LuaLua and Solly March could unlock any defence on their day. And forward Sam Baldock had proved that he could score goals, albeit mainly at League One level.

The gaps were obvious. For several seasons, the club had not had a first-team left-back, relying instead on a series of loan signings, including former England star Wayne Bridge, to fill in. Cover in defence and on the wings was thin. But the most glaring absence was a proper, line-leading, goal-scoring centre forward.

After losing out in the 2014 play-offs, the club had sold the big, mobile Argentinian Leonardo Ulloa to Leicester City, and his nominal replacement, Chris O'Grady, although a hard worker, had fallen short of requirements. He would be sent out on loan.

Hughton needed to fill those gaps with players who were good enough to allow his team to compete in one of the toughest and most competitive leagues in world football.

The Championship is a gruelling marathon in which twenty-four clubs battle their way through forty-six games knowing that finishing first or second will put them literally in a different league. The Premier League is arguably the most glamorous domestic competition in sport, attracting star players from every nation, all bankrolled by television deals that alone guarantee each of the twenty clubs a minimum of £100 million.

But what made it harder for Brighton to get there was that clubs relegated into the Championship from the Premier League received parachute payments to soften the financial impact of going down. For Burnley, Hull City and Queens Park Rangers, the three clubs coming down that summer, the payments amounted to £64 million over four years, with £24 million of that up front. So Hughton's men were competing against wealthier clubs with Premier League-quality players.

And a final unfair twist was Financial Fair Play (FFP), a system devised with the best of intentions, to ensure that clubs did not risk bankruptcy by spending beyond their means. Clubs were not allowed to spend more than a certain percentage of their revenue on transfer fees and wages, or they would face fines and transfer embargoes. The rules had been widely ignored and then watered down, but even if Brighton owner Tony Bloom, who had taken over from Knight in 2009, had wanted to splash out an unlimited amount of cash on big-money signings, he would have been prevented from doing so.

Nevertheless, Bloom made available the largest playing budget in its history for the coming season. 'The previous season was my biggest disappointment as chairman,' Bloom said.

'It didn't work out for Sami Hyypiä, some players we thought were coming fell through, we were a bit unlucky at times. These things happen. Chris came in and kept us up, but our points total was very poor. I knew it would be different the next season, we'd have a better squad and promotion was the aim, although it wouldn't be easy.

'In the Championship, if you want a team that has a realistic chance, you have to spend a lot of money. Every team, apart from perhaps those with parachute payments and the odd club that sells a player for a lot of money, will make significant losses – the Championship losses are huge and they're only going to go up now the FFP rules have been relaxed. The reason that people spend so much is because the rewards of being in the Premier League and the TV revenues are so large, and everyone wants to get there. The reality is that, if you want a team that has a realistic chance of going up to the Premier League, it will cost you at least £10 million a year unless you've got parachute payments.'

However, the club did have considerable other assets when it came to attracting players. Bloom had funded not only the award-winning 30,000-capacity American Express Community Stadium (usually known as the Amex) at Falmer, on the north-eastern outskirts of Brighton, at an estimated cost of £93 million, but also a new training headquarters at Lancing, a few miles west of the city of Brighton & Hove and a long goal kick away from the sea, which cost a further £30 million.

Stadiums catch the eye of the general public and the fans who pay to watch games, but training grounds are footballers' workplaces, and the facilities there matter to prospective new signings. 'We went to look at training grounds at Arsenal, Manchester United, Tottenham and Chelsea and the FA headquarters at St George's Park, so you can tell where we set our sights,' Martin Perry, the managing director, who oversaw the project, said. 'We think it's up there with them. The level of provision and facilities is the equal of anything you'd see in the Premier League, if not better. It is a statement of the club's ambition.'

The players had previously been used to sharing breezeblock changing rooms and muddy pitches with students at the University of Sussex sports centre, also at Falmer, not far from the Amex. For them, moving into the American Express Elite Football Performance Centre – to give the training ground and academy headquarters its full title – in summer 2014 was like being taken from a squat into a five-star hotel.

'I couldn't quite believe it, to be honest,' Lewis Dunk said. 'Growing up and doing my scholarship at Falmer, coming from there with the Portakabins and coming to this humungous training ground with everything you could possibly want to be the best you can be, I couldn't quite believe it that we had come this far as a club.'

He remembered the surreal sight of Vicente Rodríguez, a former Spain international winger who had played in the Champions League with Valencia, experiencing a type of injury treatment facility at Falmer that was very different from what he had been used to at one of the leading clubs in La Liga.

'Vicente was in one of the cabins getting his physio and his rubs – that was a bit of a change for him, from Valencia in the sunshine to a cold, wet winter in a Portakabin,' Dunk said. 'It could get breezy, although it gets chilly at Lancing too with the wind coming straight off the sea, but you don't mind when it's such a nice place.'

Lancing has thirteen pitches, including two that are identical to the stadium's in size and turf quality, and a half-size indoor surface.

The Y-shaped two-storey main building houses changing rooms, gyms, pools, medical and physiotherapy facilities, video rooms, a media centre and offices for the staff. The first team are based in the west wing, the academy in the east.

It is regarded as one of the best training facilities anywhere in the country and was praised by Gareth Southgate, the England head coach, who used it when manager of the England under-21 squad. 'You only have to walk around to see how carefully everything has been thought through,' he said. 'You couldn't want for anything more really and it is obvious the club is really geared up to be successful.'

'The day I walked in I'd been told of the set-up here,' Hughton said.

'The training ground is now three years old but the players still feel grateful to be working at such a good facility. So the chairman feels that there has been a reason why he's paid for it. It's an exciting place to come and work, and the players are highly motivated. It's our responsibility as a staff to keep that going.'

The first floor of the west wing at Lancing is a long, airy corridor flanked by glass-fronted offices. One of these on the north side, overlooking the South Downs and the Gothic chapel of Lancing College, is the base of Paul Winstanley, the club's head of recruitment. He had worked as an analyst under Paul Jewell at Wigan Athletic and Derby County, staying on at Pride Park under Nigel Clough and Steve McClaren, before being head-hunted by the Albion in September 2014. By the time Hughton arrived, Winstanley had established the processes that enabled him to present the manager with potential transfer targets.

'We have a master list and Chris only sees the top end of it, although he sees the process,' Winstanley explained. Targets are identified by combining statistical research with traditional methods.

'Master list names will always be covered by every aspect of scouting. We will have ticked every box in terms of objective and subjective reports.

'Players work their way up the stages for him to be aware of, but we're covering 200 players a week, so it's impossible for him to be aware of all of them as well as focusing on the first team. Some we eliminate and the better ones move up – the ones that are gettable. But we're constantly talking and I'll let him know when one of them is on TV, for example, so he can check on them.'

'The problem with being a manager in the Championship is that there are so many games to play and that has to be your focus,' agreed Hughton.

'But I am kept in the loop of players that we like or are monitoring that little bit more carefully. I will get involved, or I will say these are the positions that we are looking for and this is the type of player that I would like. And there isn't anybody who comes in that I don't sanction.

'There might be some that I haven't seen as much of as some of the other recruitment people, but that's only because it's impossible to see them live. After the season you use the opportunity to go out and watch players. But during the season it's very difficult. Then I'm watching a lot of video. But trying to reach the Premier League is so important that you have to put so much of your efforts into getting there that you don't have time to do everything you would like to.'

When a target is identified and permission is received from the selling club to speak to the player, Hughton and Bloom will sell Brighton to him. 'It is massive to have Chris and the chairman personally involved, in Europe especially,' Winstanley said. 'We have a good reputation at the minute and everyone knows that the chairman is a lifelong fan and in Europe they are very passionate about that. Players love that story rather than foreign investors coming in and it helps massively.'

Winstanley and Hughton would have a busy summer.

• • •

The need to strengthen the squad after such a disappointing 2014/15 season was obvious, and the most glaring requirement for a team that had averaged fewer than one goal a game was a striker. The top scorer had been Portugal under-21 midfield player João Teixeira, on loan from Liverpool and now back on Merseyside, with six goals. Central defender Dunk was second with five. Forwards Baldock, Adrián Colunga and O'Grady had only seven between them.

But quality defensive cover was also needed, and the first arrival reflected that, as Albion captured Liam Rosenior, an experienced and versatile player who had been released by Hull City on their relegation from the Premier League and whose father, Leroy, had, coincidentally, once been interviewed for the Albion manager's job that eventually went to Mark McGhee in October 2003.

Rosenior was nominally a right-back, but could also play in midfield or at left-back. 'When I came, I expected to be the best right-back in the division,' he said later. 'Then I saw Bruno at close quarters and I realised I wasn't even the best right-back in the club.'

The fans noted with interest that their counterparts in Hull were shocked and outraged by their club's decision to let the player go, and were also impressed that Rosenior wrote an open letter to those fans in the *Hull Daily Mail* telling them how much he had enjoyed his time by the banks of the Humber and valued their support. This spoke of a man of character, and everything the articulate and intelligent Rosenior said on his arrival reinforced that early impression.

He revealed that his father bore no grudges about being turned down for the job that Hughton now held. 'As soon as I found out about Brighton's interest, I called my dad,' Rosenior told Sky Sports.

'He told me to drive down now.

'I'm quite lucky that my dad played with Chris Hughton before at West Ham. Chris is just a good man and an honest man. Also, his record as a coach and a manager speaks for itself. He's someone that I've always wanted to play for and I'm just pleased it's happened now.'

After five years in Hull, Rosenior was ready for a change of scenery. 'It's like being in a different country down here – nice and hot,' he said.

'There were clubs who called my agent and told me to hold off and not sign so early in the window. But when I came down to Brighton, it just felt right.

'I brought my wife along and she loved it. That made my decision because it's not just me that signs for a football club. I've got four children and a family too. As soon as I stepped into the club and spoke to the manager, I knew this was the perfect place for me.

'The stadium is fantastic. I'm not sure everyone has seen the training facility here but it's up there with the best in the country. I'm talking Champions League standard. Now it's about making sure we fulfil our potential on the pitch. Hopefully I can be a big part of that.'

Where he would fit in with Bruno ahead of him in his best position, he admitted, remained to be seen. 'Bruno is a player that I've always rated. I voted for him as the Championship right-back of the year in the season that I was promoted with Hull,' he said. 'Technically, he's a fantastic right-back. But the club has so much ambition and potential they want a squad that's strong enough to get to the

Premier League. So I'm not worried about the strength of the competition. Instead, I thrive on it and want to help the club grow.'

Next in was a forward, Tomer Hemed. The Israel striker was not a well-known name, but had played in Spain's top division with Real Mallorca and Almería, the club from which Brighton had signed Ulloa. The Israeli journalist Ouriel Daskal described Hemed as a 'run-through-brick-walls centre forward', and it helped that he was close to Beram Kayal, his Israel teammate, who had joined Brighton from Celtic in January.

They had come through the youth system at Maccabi Haifa together and although there was no shortage of journalists keen to highlight the cross-cultural friendship between the Jewish Hemed and Muslim Kayal, Hemed disagreed with the suggestion that it was in any way unusual. 'In Maccabi Haifa, there are many Israeli Arab players,' Hemed says. 'There is a good feeling. You don't feel something weird.'

But there were rumours of a more headline-grabbing signing. The club's former striker Bobby Zamora, who had been one of the most popular Brighton players since their days in the top flight, was a free agent after leaving Queens Park Rangers, and Albion were looking to add forward options. Plenty of people were happy to put two and two together and make any number they liked.

The club played down the rumours, but continued to do transfer business early in the window, in contrast to previous years. Leaving signings until late in the hope of bargains as prices dropped had bitten them before Winstanley's arrival. They had indulged in brinkmanship and lived to regret it in the case of Wolves defender Stephen Ward. He had had a successful season at the Amex in 2013/14 as the latest in a series of loan left-backs and was due to sign on a permanent basis that summer of 2014, but at the last moment

Premier League Burnley stepped in and offered both Wolves and Ward more money.

If anyone thought that Rosenior was earmarked for that perennial problem position of left-back, then the arrival of Gaëtan Bong changed their minds. The twelve-time Cameroon international signed on a free transfer after leaving Wigan Athletic, and his CV also included experience with Metz, Tours, Valenciennes, and Olympiakos, where he had played in the Champions League. It worried some that Wigan had been relegated from the Championship despite Bong's presence, but if Hughton, a former left-back, approved his signing then he had to be good enough.

The squad then left for a training camp at Tignes in the French Alps, in the mood to improve on the previous season's results. 'Being under pressure at the bottom at the start of the year, the harshness of that made the group more determined,' Hughton's long-time assistant manager Colin Calderwood said. 'So that when the next season started, it was all about moving on to some sort of achievement, and what they could do.

'When we set our targets, the staff talked about the play-offs and possibly pushing for automatic promotion. But the boys wanted to win the title. They had a very clear goal of trying to win the league, which was interesting – very, very interesting. So although some people would have thought it was impossible after where they'd been the previous season, that was their goal. And they knew that to achieve that they'd have to be at the very top of their game in most matches. But with what we saw in the training camp, with our experience we knew that, if we could believe what we were seeing, we would be competitive. Because their attitude was excellent.'

New players continued to arrive. Finland's Niki Mäenpää came in to challenge David Stockdale for the goalkeeper's jersey. And another signing from Spain, on 23 July, was Jack Harper, a Scotland under-19 international from Real Madrid.

The fact that a Scot played for Real was news to most. Harper's parents had moved from Scotland to Spain and he had been born in Málaga, eventually attracting the attention of the giants from the capital. Initially he would play for the under-21 team but expected to be pressing for a first-team place by the turn of the year.

Hemed scored his first Albion goal three minutes into the opening pre-season friendly away to FC Meyrin of Geneva, Hughton fielding different teams in the first and second halves of a 6–1 win. The manager did the same in a behind-closed-doors match against Southampton at their Staplewood training ground on the borders of the New Forest, which the Premier League side won 1–0 with a late goal. He also rang the changes regularly in a goalless draw at Lewes, but the teams in a 3–0 victory at Crawley and a 1–0 loss in a testimonial away to Aberdeen looked more like a side that might begin the Championship season.

The formation was 4–4–2 rather than the 4–3–3 that had finished the previous campaign. The back four in front of Stockdale would be Bruno, Greer, Dunk and Bong. The centre of midfield would be Kayal and Stephens. On the wings would be LuaLua and either March or Rosenior, and Hemed and Baldock would form the spearhead of the team.

'A form of 4–4–2 is a system I prefer,' Hughton said.

'I like my wide players to be hard-working. They don't have a free licence to do whatever they want. They have a responsibility to work without the ball and to work back. You can have two types of wide player – the winger type with pace like Kazenga or Solly, or more of a wide midfield player. But whoever played there would have the same responsibilities; the roles are the same.'

The system puts pressure on the two central midfield players to perform both attacking and defensive duties. Kayal had been Hughton's first permanent signing in January, but Stephens had surprised him after his return from injury. 'I knew Dale from his time at Charlton, but not well,' Hughton admitted.

'If I'd been asked to tell you all of his qualities, I probably couldn't. But they are both multi-functional players. There isn't one that you would regard as a specific holding player. Sometimes it's about the qualities of each player. You might get a player who is higher-energy, who naturally breaks forward a little bit more, but I prefer ones who can do a little bit of everything, and that's what they both were.'

'4–4–2 was the way we played at Newcastle, and at Birmingham, and more of a 4–4–1–1 at Norwich,' Calderwood said.

'But the main thing was that we played with wide players – Anthony Pilkington, Robert Snodgrass and Elliott Bennett at Norwich, Chris Burke and John Beausejour at Birmingham, Jonás Gutiérrez and Ryan Taylor at Newcastle. And at Brighton, Rosenior, Solly March and eventually Knockaert. And two central midfielders who are comfortable making tackles but who can pass it too.'

'The last three managers before me all played possession-based football, so I inherited players who were comfortable on the ball,' Hughton said. 'I wanted to tweak it so that we got the ball forward a little quicker and played more in the opposition's half. I knew we would have enough good footballers.'

But would those footballers score enough goals? The fans were not convinced. Baldock had been signed for a seven-figure sum in 2014 after scoring twenty-six goals the previous season for Bristol City. But he had struggled so far at Brighton, scoring only three times in the league. And although the bench looked strong in some ways, with Mäenpää, Rosenior and the popular Calderón joined by Ince, Forster-Caskey and Crofts, forward options were thin on the ground.

On Sunday 2 August, Baldock and Hemed began encouragingly enough, combining for the only goal of the final pre-season friendly, against Sevilla, the reigning Europa League champions, at the Amex. It came when Baldock's pass found Hemed, who was baulked by two defenders. The penalty award was, perhaps, soft, but Hemed put away the first of many spot kicks he was to convert. The team wore the dazzling new 'Volt' yellow away shirts that were to appear in some key games in the coming season, and which were on sale at the club shop along with a red third shirt.

The shop occupies a key site at the stadium, where fans arrive from the railway station and the car parks and gather before matches, and its exterior is effectively a giant advertising placard, where the club sends a message as well as showing off its wares. Gone now was a 20-foot-high image of a rather nervous-looking Jake Forster-Caskey, replaced by a similar-sized but more resolute quartet of Rosenior, Stephens, Greer and Kayal in the full range of kits on sale within.

There was also a new slogan, '#Together', instead of the rather vague 'One Club, One Ambition' of the previous campaign. It was not particularly original, having been used similarly or in variations by Arsenal, Manchester City, Preston North End and the Wales national side. But it was to take on real meaning over the next eighteen months.

• • •

Slogans, though, were forgotten the next day when Zamora returned after an absence of twelve seasons. During that time he had played Premier League, European and international football with Tottenham, West Ham, Fulham, QPR and, on two occasions, England. 'I said when I left that I would love to come back one day and this seemed like the right time,' he said.

He had first joined the club on loan from Bristol Rovers before signing permanently in 2000 for £100,000, plus a 30 per cent sell-on clause. He scored eighty-three goals in 136 Brighton appearances, winning two promotions as a dynamic central striker, but now, at thirty-four, he was returning as a free agent on a one-year contract, and with a reputation for being injury-prone.

That, he said, had been overstated, although he admitted that his workload in training and on the field would have to be carefully monitored. 'I was available for 93 per cent of the games [last season],' he said.

'I missed the last two with a little injury, but we were already relegated and if we had needed something from them I probably would have played. Other than that, I caught a bug that had been going round and I had some back spasms.

'Here, it is just management of my fitness and workload. It's just a matter of getting me available for Saturdays. I'm more than happy to come on for twenty minutes to help out whenever I'm called upon.'

Even that would not happen immediately, as he had missed pre-season training, but supporters with an eye on the season as a whole recalled that Zamora had twice scored the winning goal in play-off finals to take first West Ham and then QPR into the Premier League.

However many or few minutes Zamora was to play, most supporters were ecstatic to have one of the greatest Albion players of recent seasons back in blue-and-white stripes, and although some dismissed the signing as a cynical exercise aimed at selling replica shirts, many more were happy to head for the club shop to oblige. And that created a minor difficulty of its own, as chief executive Paul Barber explained a few days later.

'The deal was done quite late on Monday night, and everybody was looking pleased when it occurred to me that Z is not a letter we stock in the shop very much, so I sent a message to Ben Price, our retail manager, to get some in,' he said. 'Of all the shirts since Bobby joined us, 80 per cent have involved a Z on the back!'

Zamora had been synonymous with success at Withdean Stadium and now fans hoped that he would thrive at the Amex, which had been a distant promise in his previous stay. 'We told Bobby Zamora when we signed him in 2000 that he would be playing in this fantastic stadium one day,' life president Dick Knight recalled. 'We didn't think it would take until 2015 for it to happen.'

Zamora agreed that the club was very different, although there were still some familiar faces around. Derek Allan was still the club secretary and his former teammates Paul Rogers, Nathan Jones and Paul Watson were commercial manager, coach and physio respectively.

'The talk back then was always of the new stadium, although I loved it at Withdean,' Zamora told Bleacher Report.

'But it is here now, and what a ground it is. And I've been around and played in all four divisions, but this is the best training ground I've seen.

'[Getting to] the Premier League can be a question of fine margins, but there can't be any excuses from the players in terms of the facilities – and players will use any excuse if they can get away with it. But everything is here for us.

'It was strange that when I signed, Derek Allan, the secretary who did my first signing, was still here. It seems pretty much the same club. The catchment area is the same, and the fans are still brilliant at filling the stadium.

'The aim is to be able to sustain Premier League football, and I think the club is in a good area to be able to do that. The owners have taken it slow and steady, and that's certainly the best way. At QPR, a lot of money was spent to try to get the instant fix. It doesn't always work, although it can help.'

The club website showed the first new image of Zamora in the stripes, the camera panning upward to the man himself saying: 'I'm back.' But despite the euphoria, his signing now rather than at the beginning of pre-season training suggested to many that a different target must have fallen through.

On 6 August, the eve of the new season, Bloom addressed the issue of the disappointing previous season at a fans' forum. 'When things go badly, I think it's how one reacts to that that's key,' he said. 'There are always going to be bad seasons and events, and it's what we can learn from it and the resilience we show.' Those words would prove prophetic.

Sky Sports had more faith in Brighton than some, and selected the home game with Nottingham Forest to open their live coverage of the season on Friday 7 August, the first of many matches whose dates and kick-off times would be moved to suit the satellite broadcaster over the next two campaigns.

The changes infuriated supporters who had booked cheap advance rail tickets or who could not make the rearranged games for work reasons. But the club were bound by the League's television contract and also benefited financially from live coverage, especially of home games. A total of 24,623 were at the Amex, most of them delighted to see Zamora presented to the crowd before kick-off.

Forest showed first, Henri Lansbury clipping the outside of an upright from 30 yards following a free kick. Then Kayal's shot in free play from just outside the penalty area made slightly firmer contact with the Forest post. And new man Hemed forced a spectacular save from Forest goalkeeper Dorus de Vries with a header from a cross by Solly March on the right.

Five minutes into the second half, Albion made the breakthrough with a goal from LuaLua. The winger was an unquestioned fan favourite and had been ever since he had arrived at the club, initially on loan, from Newcastle United in February 2010. The brother of former Premier League striker Lomana Trésor LuaLua, Kazenga is a wide player blessed with large amounts of raw pace.

Rather than use the speed of a ball passed to him, nine times out of ten he will stop it and confront the full-back, matador-like. By 2015, there could not have been a right-back in the Championship who did not know what was coming next: LuaLua would explode past him on the outside and either hit a fierce shot with his left foot or cross the ball. But the problem was doing anything about it.

A history of persistent injury is all that has prevented him from being more successful than he has been. So many comebacks began with him returning to the bench that he began to be seen as a permanent impact substitute. This frustrated him, but he often made less impression on matches when starting than after sixty minutes building up resentment that he had not been playing, which he could then take out on the opposition defence.

'You don't just want to come on as sub, you want to be in the starting eleven every game,' he said. 'I don't view myself as just an impact player, and I know that I can play ninety minutes of football. Every manager has their own opinions and you have to respect them.'

Hughton, who described LuaLua as a player who can 'create and score goals and gives the club something different', knew him from their days at Newcastle and, after a full pre-season, trusted him to start against Forest. And now, receiving the ball from Stephens, LuaLua took the ball up to Forest right-back Eric Lichaj, touched it past him and hit an angled shot low across de Vries and in off the foot of the far post. There followed his trademark somersault celebration, the same one that his brother had been told to stop after breaking a bone in his foot when with Portsmouth.

It proved to be the winner, the first goal of the new season, and put Albion on top of the table after one game, sending the fans home in good spirits. A much-changed team then beat Southend United at Roots Hall on the Tuesday in the first round of the Capital One Cup, LuaLua again winning the game but in the final minute this time.

The season might have begun, but the transfer window was open until the end of August, and next day came another addition to the defence: German centre half Uwe Hünemeier. The 29-year-old had played for Borussia Dortmund and Energie Cottbus before joining SC Paderborn in 2013. He had captained them to promotion to the Bundesliga, a miraculous achievement for the small club from Westphalia, who had a 15,000-capacity stadium and one training pitch, where the caretaker's flat doubled as changing rooms. Locals concerned by noise even managed to get evening kick-off times changed so that games finished by 10 p.m.

However, Paderborn lasted only one season in the German top flight and Hünemeier sought a fresh challenge. 'It was a great feeling to lead Paderborn into the Bundesliga,' he said.

'And it was a great experience for us to play against teams like Borussia Dortmund and Bayern Munich, who had some of the best players from Germany and world football.

'Sometimes it was very hard to play against them because they are such good players, but we did our best and we can be proud of what we achieved last season. I hope they have a good season and I wish them all the best. As captain of the club, it wasn't an easy decision to leave, but it's definitely the right one. It will be a great experience for me to play in England and hopefully I can help Brighton achieve what we did there.'

At the time, that was probably wishful thinking. He would later admit in a programme interview that reaching the Premier League was not really on his radar after Albion's struggles the previous season. Now he added: 'I heard about the interest from Brighton about three weeks ago. It was surprising for me. It is a good chance for me to play in English football and that is something I always wanted to do. I'm glad I'm here and hopefully I'll have a great time.'

The pursuit of Hünemeier, who knew only the big names of British football, revealed an area of the club's player recruitment that could be improved. 'Uwe had never heard of Brighton,' Winstanley said.

'So, with the help of the media team, we put together a recruitment video that could showcase Brighton as a football club – the facilities, the stadium, the manager, the chairman, the history, the philosophy of the team, everything. So when I'm watching players and we're getting serious about putting this player in front of the manager, we can make the player well aware of what Brighton is about. When Uwe saw the video, it was like: "Wow, this is incredible." I use the video a lot now so that the player representatives across the world know about us.

'The video shows Cup Final goals but also highlights the dark days of the history, including the fans going on demonstrations and showing their passion for the club. The Amex and the Lancing training facility – the players' workplace most days – feature heavily. The attractions of the city and surroundings are also well to the fore, but also a reminder of the close proximity of Gatwick Airport and the quick transport links to London. The reaction we get is very positive.'

Next to arrive was 25-year-old former Scotland under-21 winger Jamie Murphy from Sheffield United, who also had experience as a second striker. He was to become a valuable and consistent performer who was capable of scoring and creating goals, but he did not figure in the next league game, away to Fulham.

Craven Cottage was becoming a lucky ground and it proved to be so again. In an otherwise unchanged team, Hünemeier made his debut in place of Dunk, who had been a contender for the man-of-the-match award against Forest. That led to speculation that Bloom was thinking of accepting an offer for the home-grown defender, with Fulham one of the clubs interested.

Albion began well, Hemed hitting the bar and March and LuaLua making ground down the wings. So it was no surprise when Bruno's cross was knocked home by Baldock on the half-hour. In contrast, a shot from Fulham's Tom Cairney that screamed past Stockdale came from nowhere and for a time the team's confidence was shaken. Fulham grew into the game in the second half and Hughton seemed to have settled for a point when he introduced Rosenior, Ince and Forster-Caskey for March, Baldock and Stephens late in the game. Ince is primarily a defensive midfield player, while Forster-Caskey, although looking as if he might be a potent attacking force early in his career, was now regarded as a specialist in keeping possession.

But as the match moved into added time, Forster-Caskey's pass sent LuaLua speeding into the penalty area. Whichever side of the 18-yard line he was brought down by Fulham's Shaun Hutchinson, referee Neil Swarbrick awarded a penalty, and Hemed, in front of the Albion fans at the Putney End, converted after the stuttering run-up that was to become so familiar.

That kept Albion on top of the fledgling league table. And they looked certain to stay there when Kayal put them ahead with a 20-yard left-foot shot in the opening minute of the next game, away to Huddersfield Town on the Tuesday evening. An unchanged starting line-up dominated the first half but failed to press home their advantage. That allowed Jacob Butterfield to level after fifty-four minutes, beating Stockdale at his near post with an angled shot. But even though Hughton made another defensive-looking change, bringing Ince on for Hemed, Albion could still have won it if March, Baldock or LuaLua had taken late chances.

The rumours that Dunk was to be sold only intensified after the signing of Connor Goldson, another central defender, from Shrewsbury Town for a reported fee of £800,000 the day after the Huddersfield match. Already a veteran of 110 league games at twenty-two, he did not seem to have come to play for the development squad. One West Midlands-based journalist claimed that Goldson was 'Championship-ready'. But all such debate faded into insignificance by comparison to what would happen later that day.

CHAPTER 2

SHOREHAM

Saturday 22 August 2015 was a scorching summer day, with temperatures reaching 28°C. The build-up to Albion's home match against Blackburn Rovers was well under way when news began to reach the stadium of severe delays on the A27 west of the city, caused by an incident at an airshow at Shoreham Airport.

It was announced that kick-off would be delayed by fifteen minutes to give supporters coming from that direction extra time to take their seats, but soon the full horror of what had taken place began to be revealed on news bulletins and social media.

At 1.22 p.m., a vintage Hawker Hunter jet flown by 51-year-old Andy Hill, an experienced pilot, had opened the afternoon session of the airshow with an aerobatic display. But Hill failed to pull out of an inside loop in time and crashed onto the busy A27 running to the north of the airport, killing eleven men and injuring sixteen other people. Some of the victims had been standing at the roadside to watch the airshow; others had been in their cars at what is known as the Sussex Pad junction. Hill was somehow thrown to safety.

Information was sketchy at the stadium at first. 'I remember warming up for the Blackburn game and we were told there had been a big disaster and we weren't sure what had happened,' Liam Rosenior said. 'I sneaked into the toilets ten minutes before kick-off to call my family just to make sure they were all right. We weren't aware of the gravity of what had happened until afterwards.'

Murphy made his first start and LuaLua scored with a shot from a pass by Baldock, but as further details of the Shoreham crash continued to emerge, three more points gained in the Amex sunshine seemed incidental.

The tragedy would turn out to have hit close to home in every sense. The club's training ground is so near to the site of the incident that the large white roof of the indoor pitch was clearly visible in the background of many images of the crash scene. The stretch of road where the jet came down, part of the main east–west link along the Sussex coast, was familiar to most players, coaches and staff who drove in from Brighton or Hove. And two of the victims were intimately connected with the club.

Matt Grimstone, an assistant groundsman at the training ground, and Jacob Schilt, an Albion fan, two friends who had played in the same school team as Lewis Dunk, had been on their way from Brighton to play for Worthing United in a Southern Combination Premier League home match against Loxwood. When they failed to arrive at Worthing's Lyons Way ground, some three and a half miles along the A27 from the crash site, officials feared the worst.

Goalkeeper Grimstone and midfield player Schilt had been in Grimstone's silver Vauxhall Corsa driving westward towards Worthing when it became the first vehicle hit by the plane, and they would have died instantly.

Grimstone, twenty-three, had started working for Albion as a member of the match-day event team at Withdean seven years previously. Schilt, also twenty-three, had played on three occasions in the annual charity match between supporters of Brighton and rivals Crystal Palace in aid of the Robert Eaton Memorial Fund (REMF), which commemorates another Brighton supporter who perished when death came unexpectedly from the skies, in the 9/11 terrorist attacks on the World Trade Center in New York in 2001. The Brighton fans' team in the match in April had been coached by Albion chief executive Paul Barber.

'It was a terrible weekend,' Barber said.

'At about quarter to two, I got a message from Adrian Morris, our safety officer, about an incident on the A27 that was going to delay people. The natural assumption was that it was a car accident. Then within a few minutes he called back and said no, a plane had crashed. Within twenty minutes social media were showing pictures of this fireball with our training ground in the background.

'My immediate message to Rose Read, our head of human resources, was to do a head count to make sure all our people were accounted for. Rose did a great job of ticking off everyone who was due to be at the stadium and everyone who had been looking after academy fixtures at the training ground. The one gap was the staff who had been granted leave that day, which included Matt because he was playing for Worthing.

'Later that evening I got a call from Rose, who said that Matt was unaccounted for and his family hadn't been able to get in touch with him. And he'd been in the area and on that road. My heart and stomach did a sort of convulsion. I felt suddenly very sick and about an hour later Paul Camillin, our head of media, picked up a video on the internet that showed what looked like Matt's car. One small frame showed the number plate and we were able to match it with Matt's car on our system. We still weren't 100 per cent sure that Matt was in it, but we knew he had been and Jacob Schilt was with him, who I knew because he'd played in the REMF team just a couple of months before.

'Jacob's family were actually travelling behind them on the A27, which was a terrible thing because they knew he was ahead of them, they couldn't get through the traffic that had backed up and knew this thing had happened and had been trying to call him and couldn't reach him. As the night went on, it became obvious that they had been in the car.'

In a club statement, Barber said:

'Matt's been a very popular member of our groundstaff team and has proved to be an absolute credit to the club and his boss, Steve Winterburn. I also got to know Jacob as one of the REMF squad during the coaching sessions we held leading up to this year's charity match against Crystal Palace. As well as being a very good footballer, Jacob is [*sic*] a popular and impressive young man.

'It is hard to find the right words to express the full extent of our shock and sadness at this time, but Matt and Jacob's family and friends are very much in our thoughts, along with all those who've been affected by this terrible tragedy.'

Dunk remembered their days at Varndean secondary school in north Brighton. 'We shared some great memories,' he said.

'Many of those were created playing football for the school team. Year 9 was our most memorable, when we won the treble of the Brighton & Hove Schools' Cup, the Division One title and the County Cup final. Both Jacob and Matt played a big part in that success, with Jacob being a true leader as captain and Matt saving the day on many occasions between the sticks. The memories of that team and the games we played will stay with me for ever.'

Barber made the training ground and its facilities available as a base for the emergency services both in the immediate aftermath and in the days that followed as the crash scene was painstakingly investigated. 'I also thought it was the right thing to do to go and visit Matt's and Jacob's parents,' he said.

'On the Sunday, Rose and I went to see the Grimstones and it was pretty harrowing. I'd never done anything like that before. It was heartbreaking because the raw emotion of it was just terrible. Then a couple of days later I went to see the Schilt family, again with Rose. What I'll always remember is how dignified the families were. Brave is the wrong word, but maybe unjudgemental. They weren't looking to blame anyone.

'The impact on the staff was enormous because Matt was well-known and well-liked. Jacob [was] less well-known but some people did know him because he had played in the club's colours for the REMF team and they had trained at Lancing. And by then the scale of the disaster had hit the community. Fans knew people who had been killed, people in Shoreham and Lancing had seen the fireball, fans going to the Blackburn game knew that something terrible had happened. My daughter had been on that stretch of road going from Hove to see her boyfriend in Lancing. Another hour and she'd have been there. We had to deal with the grief and emotion of the groundstaff and the grief and shock of the community as a whole.'

The eleven deaths represented the greatest loss of life in a single incident in Sussex since the Second World War, and not only local but also national and international media descended on the area. 'It was the first time we'd had national news people who weren't sports-based in our media centre,' Barber said. 'It added to the scale and gravity of the disaster. Chris and I were suddenly having to take questions from ITN and BBC news on subjects neither of us had ever spoken about before.'

On the Monday, Grimstone's colleagues on the groundstaff

visited the old wooden toll bridge over the nearby River Adur that had quickly become the location for impromptu floral shrines to the eleven dead. 'We all loved Matt dearly and he will be sorely missed,' head groundsman Steve Winterburn said.

'He was a gentleman in the true sense. It's extremely upsetting. No one expects something like this to happen. We are feeling it a lot. Matt didn't just work for the club, but supported it as well. He was an exceptional young man. You couldn't wish to meet a nicer person.'

Footballers are often regarded as living in a cosseted bubble, cut off from some of the grimmer realities of life, but the Albion players were now confronted with this particular reality every day, and counsellors were brought in for any players or staff who needed them.

'The police were in the academy canteen, so you got to know faces and to say hello,' David Stockdale said.

'They appreciated coming here and, knowing the effect it had on us, imagine the effect it must have on them. We were seeing them come in tired after doing hard work, trying to piece together what had happened and we were just doing not-so-hard work at the training ground kicking footballs about. In a good way, it made us want to fight on the pitch for a community, not just a football team.

'It was a weird, weird chain of events, the way you heard about it straight after a game and you heard that Brighton fans were in it. I know other people were involved, but Jacob and Matt, because they were fans, and on their way to a game of football, and you've been playing and it was in the same area, and near the training ground – it was somehow different. The club is massive in the community and Matt actually worked here. I spoke to him a few times because he was a goalkeeper.'

'And what hit us was driving in to training every day along that road, every day,' Rosenior said.

'To see the police response unit working from the training ground hits you in a way you can't explain, how devastating that was to the area, to the community. To lose people in the prime of their life, who supported the club, who worked for the club, Matt and Jacob. It was a sad, sad time and we said that, as players, if we can make people just a little bit happier then that's what we've got to do.'

Stockdale felt he wanted to do more. '[Club ambassador and former manager] Alan Mullery said he was going to go and see the families and I said I'd like to come and see Matt's family,' he said. 'That was one of the toughest times I'd been through as a footballer. I was stunned by how it affected the family. Nothing you do as a player prepares you for that, nothing.

'I couldn't do anything but if me just being there made them feel better in any way … Alan Mullery was unbelievable. He chatted about anything, he managed to keep the spirits high, looking at photos, we had a cup of tea. There were a lot of family there and I got to know Matt's family quite well.'

'That was just David as a person,' Rosenior said.

'That's the type of people we have in the dressing room, and I don't think that's by accident. If you look at the work that has been put into the club in terms of identity and recruitment, there's a massive emphasis on character, the type of player and person that you want. That is carrying us a long way.'

• • •

The club asked permission for a minute's silence to be observed before the Tuesday's Capital One Cup match away to Walsall, in which a below-strength Brighton team made a low-key exit, and the Football League went further, requesting the same mark of respect at all games in the competition that week. Stockdale had 'Matt' and 'Jacob' stitched into his goalkeeping gloves and wore their initials on his warm-up top for the next league match, away to Ipswich Town, the jersey also bearing the words 'In memory of Matt and Jacob' along with '#Together'. All the players wore black armbands.

Amid all the emotion, the team could have been forgiven if they had given a below-par performance at Portman Road against the only team above them in the table. Instead, they put on an outstanding attacking performance in a thrilling 3–2 victory, their twenty-one efforts on goal easily eclipsing their hosts' eight and making them deserving Championship front-runners by the final whistle.

LuaLua continued his rich vein of scoring form with a left-foot shot across goalkeeper Dean Gerken and just inside the far post after only nine minutes, and Dale Stephens's free kick after a foul on LuaLua two minutes later took the faintest of touches off the head of Hemed on its way into the net. With the yellow-shirted Brighton players enjoying themselves, a big win looked on, but Hünemeier had been shown a yellow card and was living dangerously so Hughton decided to withdraw him at the interval.

Stephens saw his 20-yard shot hit a post, and a third goal then might have made it a rout, but the defence was now shaky. Dunk, on in Hünemeier's place, got away with a handling offence that the referee failed to spot before Freddie Sears put Ipswich back in the game after Brett Pitman's shot had come back off an upright. And after Bruno was deemed to have fouled Ryan Fraser, David McGoldrick equalised from the penalty. However, Hughton's men came back to win it when Hemed glanced home LuaLua's deflected cross.

There could have been more goals, but the main source of delight for the travelling fans was the introduction of Zamora as a late substitute, making his first appearance for the club since May 2003.

'It's been a sad moment for everyone involved at the club,' LuaLua said afterwards. 'Obviously we wanted to win the game against Walsall for them [the victims of the air crash] but we couldn't, so I'm glad we did it today. The win, and especially my goal, was for them. The most important thing was to win for them.'

Stockdale and Hughton also dedicated the team's 3–2 victory at Portman Road to Grimstone and Schilt, and the club announced that it would remember its two fans and the other nine victims officially before the next home match, against Hull City. Barber also offered the Schilt and Grimstone families the use of suites at the stadium for their sons' wakes, which the club paid for.

Before then, Worthing United would play their first match since the tragedy, an FA Vase tie at home to East Preston. It was soon clear that the match would attract an unusually large crowd as people flocked to pay their respects, so Albion offered to assist with ticketing and security that would be needed and which went beyond the Worthing club's experience. Hughton, Bloom, Barber, Stockdale and other players and staff attended Grimstone's funeral on the Monday.

'If I felt highly about our club before the events of last week then I certainly feel more now,' Hughton said.

'The club have been absolutely excellent in everything they have done. That's as regards the incident itself, the family [of Matt Grimstone], what they have done for the authorities. The police are using our training ground as a base and the club have been really excellent. It has been a tough time but what you have seen is a club and a community pulling together.'

On the morning of the Hull match, a sponsored walk was held

by REMF from Shoreham to the Lyons Way ground, symbolically completing the journey that Grimstone and Schilt never finished. The proceeds were donated in their names to the Worthing United youth scheme.

At the Amex that afternoon, soprano Donna-Marie Hughes sang 'Abide with Me' on the pitch as two giant versions of Grimstone's and Schilt's Worthing United shirts were carried on by their team-mates. Grimstone's colleagues on the groundstaff lined up in the goalmouths. First responders, representatives of the emergency services and hospital staff wearing Worthing United scarves were presented to the crowd, and Hughton and Hull manager Steve Bruce laid wreaths provided by the respective supporters' clubs before a minute's applause. Cards held up by spectators in the lower tier of the East Stand spelt 'TOGETHER'. The marketing slogan had become a statement of club identity and would appear on tweets by players and supporters alike.

'The reason we'd launched the "#Together" theme that summer was because the previous season had been so difficult and we'd struggled,' Barber said.

'We'd avoided relegation but there'd been a fracture between the club and part of its fanbase, which is inevitable in a relegation struggle, and so we felt that "together" was the right word. We had to regroup, get back to where we were in the previous two play-off seasons. To be honest, it was no more and no less than that at that point. And then of course Shoreham happened and "#Together" became a much stronger and more meaningful theme. It wasn't just a marketing slogan that was designed to have a literal as well as a symbolic meaning; it took on a more emotional meaning as well.'

Alan Wares, the co-presenter of the *Albion Roar* radio programme and podcast, agrees. 'People must never underestimate the effect of the Shoreham air crash – the response of the club, the fans, the players,' he said. 'When "One Club, One Ambition" was replaced by "#Together", you rolled your eyes, but what happened added poignancy to it. There was a coming together of the hearts and minds of the club and the fans.'

After kick-off, the team continued its winning ways, beating a likely promotion candidate 1–0. The goal was scored after only five minutes when Hemed won possession in Hull's half, allowing Baldock to tee up Stephens for a shot from 22 yards. It was parried by goalkeeper Allan McGregor, but Baldock knocked the rebound forward for Hemed to sweep in from six yards. After seventy-five minutes of the second half, Zamora made his third Albion home debut, helping start a move that ended with Kayal having a goal-bound shot blocked.

To some extent, the final whistle ended the formal mourning for Shoreham, but the incident remains a wound in the memory of those directly and indirectly involved. The Air Accident Investigation Branch (AAIB) report found no evidence of mechanical failure but stated that the pilot had started the manoeuvre that led to the crash far too low for the type of aircraft he was flying and at too low a speed – although both height and speed would have been safe for a different type of jet that he had flown at a different airshow the previous weekend. The report also criticised the event organisers' risk assessment.

Permanent memorials to the victims are planned for the banks of the River Adur and the toll bridge, and both Schilt and Grimstone have joined the list of past Brightonians who have had buses in the city named after them.

But what happened will also remain in the memories of players such as Stockdale. He was given the Professional Footballers'

Association's Community Champion award at the end of the season in recognition of his efforts in the aftermath, the trophy presented at an emotionally charged section of the club's player of the year dinner by parents Phil Grimstone and Caroline Schilt. But he accepted it reluctantly and with mixed feelings.

'If someone said, "You'll get a medal for doing this," you'd think twice about doing it,' he said later.

'You wouldn't want anyone to think you were doing it for that reason. I still speak to Matt's brother now and again, and anything they need, I will do if I can. I also spoke to Jacob's mum at the game at Worthing, and we were able to dedicate a couple of games to them, Ipswich and Hull.

'If you ask me what I took from it, it's being humble about what you have. Life is more important than material things. So I dedicated the award I got from the PFA to them. It was tough for me to talk about it because, as I said at the time, I would never want to receive a medal as a result of someone else's misfortune, someone's tragic death. It was quite hard for me to accept an award that I didn't really want.'

'The Shoreham tragedy brought the club, the community and the fans together,' Barber said.

'It kind of healed some of the wounds of the previous season in a way we couldn't have imagined – or wanted, of course. We would have given anything, and would still give anything, for it not to have happened. But it did happen and gave us an opportunity to draw strength from it.

'I've maintained very close contact with the families, as has the club as a whole, and we have had them as our guests many times since that awful day. That has been an indirect source of strength and encouragement. Caroline Schilt recently sent me a photograph of a park bench that has been dedicated to Jacob near his old school and wrote: "Isn't it amazing that we're now in the Premier League? Jacob would have just loved that." And she put "#Together" at the bottom of her email, as a way of underlining, even two years later, what that period meant for the club and how, I hope, the families have drawn strength from the football since then.'

CHAPTER 3

UNDEFEATED

Two days after the Shoreham crash, there had been a piece of positive news, which, understandably, had gone largely unnoticed but which was highly significant on the playing side. Lewis Dunk, who had seemed to be on his way out of the club, had signed a new five-year contract.

The Albion have not been known for producing large numbers of home-grown players, but defenders have long been the exception. Dunk was in a tradition of locally produced back-four men that included Gareth Barry, Tommy Elphick, Joel Lynch, Steve Cook and Grant Hall. All had left to achieve their ambitions, so persuading Dunk that he could do so with his home-city club was significant.

Not that it had always been Dunk's dream to wear the stripes. Although from an Albion-supporting family, he had grown up as an admirer of John Terry and admits to supporting Chelsea as a result.

'My dad went to the Goldstone when he was proper young, getting in the North Stand and going home and being told off by his dad,' Dunk said.

'He still tells me about those times. But because John Terry was such an idol to me since I was tiny and I wanted to be like him, it made me swing towards Chelsea. I've always looked up to him. There's been a lot of top centre halves, you watch their game and see what they do, but he's always been the main one I've looked up to.

'When I was growing up, you would never really see a Brighton shirt in a park or in the street or at training or whatever. Now wherever you go kids have the shirt on, even adults, and it's unbelievable to see how far this club has come.'

Some of those shirts, of course, bear Dunk's name and number and would one day have Premier League sleeve patches. 'I can't wait to see that and I can't wait to put one on myself. It's a great feeling to know that someone wants your name on their shirt, that they like you that much and feel you're doing well.'

His father, Mark, who managed in Sussex local football, was unable to wean him off Chelsea, but influenced Lewis in other ways.

'Since I can remember, I've had a ball at my feet, running around, going to watch him manage and going to watch my brother play. It's always been in my blood to play football. I joined the club aged ten, I was at Wimbledon before but they folded and I came down here and I've seen it all, through all the Withdean days.'

He went on loan to Bognor Regis Town 'and learned a bit of men's football. Two years later, I was playing in the team here.'

He made his first-team debut in a low-key goalless draw away to MK Dons on 1 May 2010 as manager Gus Poyet took a look at his options.

'Personally, it was a great experience making my debut for my hometown club, but the game at MK was not a memorable one. It was 0–0 and there were two sending-offs just before half-time, so it wasn't the best game but it was a great time for me.'

He got his first taste of big-time football in November that year, when he had to come on as substitute for Adam El-Abd after only thirty-five minutes of a match away to promotion rivals Southampton in front of a crowd of 26,237. He played a part in keeping a clean sheet against a team including Rickie Lambert, Adam Lallana and Alex Oxlade-Chamberlain and might have come away from St Mary's a winner if Chris Wood had not missed a penalty. He started the first league game of the following season – the first match at the Amex Stadium in 2011 against Doncaster – and made thirty-six appearances in that first season as a first-team regular.

Some wondered about the signings of Hünemeier and Goldson now, and how four players fitted into two places in the team, but most were relieved and impressed by this statement of intent by the club that re-signing Dunk represented. 'We try to keep hold of our best players,' Bloom said. 'This season we wanted to build on the players we had, but these things happen and you can never say "Never", but we wanted to keep Lewis and we're delighted that he's with us and signed a new five-year contract.'

After signing his new deal, Dunk's next task was to get back in the team. Hünemeier, despite his withdrawal at half-time at Ipswich, had started the following game, the victory against Hull that had strengthened unbeaten Albion's position at the top of the table. The only changes for the next fixture, a mid-week match at home to Rotherham United, were in the wide positions, where Murphy and March replaced Rosenior and the suspended LuaLua, who had the consolation prize of being voted Championship player of the month for August. Hughton took the manager's award.

Having beaten and replaced the leaders and then the team in second place, Brighton should have seen off the bottom-placed outfit with ease, but long-time supporters knew that things seldom worked out in so straightforward a fashion. At first, though, everything went well. Murphy justified his selection with the pass from which Hemed scored the opening goal, getting away from his marker at the near post to hit the ball in off the crossbar after twenty-seven minutes. Stephens doubled the lead in the second half, shooting low after the ball had broken to him from a challenge on the edge of the penalty area.

However, slack marking from a free kick allowed Rotherham substitute Jonson Clarke-Harris to head the visitors back into the match, to the evident frustration of Bruno, who nearly had the last word with a dipping volley that was tipped over the bar by goalkeeper Lee Camp. In a way, it was typical of many games in the first half of the season: Albion failed to score as many goals as they should have and ended up hanging on instead of pulling away.

A bigger lead in the closing stages might have meant a debut for Elvis Manu, a 22-year-old Netherlands under-21 forward, signed late in the transfer window from Feyenoord. Sadly, despite experience in the Europa and Champions Leagues, he never adjusted to the physicality of British football, leaving behind him the frustration for football reporters of many unused Elvis puns.

Manu had been a fall-back signing after the club had been unable to tie up a deal to bring Boca Juniors' £10 million-rated striker Jonathan Calleri to Brighton. Barber had even flown out to Buenos Aires, but the problem in concluding a transfer, not without precedent in South America, was in the number of different parties claiming a financial stake in the player.

'It was a long journey via Madrid and I went with the agent to meet the guys from Boca and tried to get the deal done,' Barber said.

'Paul Winstanley had gone down there beforehand to meet the player, meet his family, and get a sense of what was possible. I went to see if there was a way of doing the deal, but it fell down on the ownership of the player and the complexity and value of the deal, with all sorts of characters involved, including Carlos Tevez and agents we didn't even know existed.

'We spent so long trying to negotiate that my chances of getting my return flight were getting smaller and smaller. Two of the agents involved said it was OK, let's give it one more hour to try to get it done and they'd get me back to the airport in time. We actually gave it an hour and a quarter and then they said: "Right, we've got to go, now!" So I got in the back of their car and it was like a scene from *The Italian Job*, driving through doorways and along these narrow streets and even down a set of steps at one point.'

Calleri ended up at West Ham the following season, where his poor form anywhere near goal suggested that the Albion had had a lucky escape. But even being in the hunt showed that ambition at the club was high and getting higher.

The next day, preparations began for the Amex to stage two games in the Rugby World Cup over the forthcoming weekend of 19 and 20 September: the Pool B matches between South Africa and Japan on the Saturday and Samoa and the United States on the Sunday. That meant sockets in the pitch for the rugby posts and extra press seats at the rear of the West Stand upper tier, as well as more subtle changes – the normal sponsorship and advertising was covered or removed and the stadium was referred to as 'Brighton Community Stadium'.

The club had worked and lobbied hard to be selected for matches ahead of more established stadiums such as St Mary's in Southampton. The reward for the success of their bid was greater than they could have hoped for – unprecedented coverage on almost every back page in the world as 29,290 saw Japan beat two-time champions South Africa 34–32 on the Saturday evening with a last-gasp try in the biggest upset in the history of the competition.

The Albion, however, made far less of an impact on the sports pages, with a goalless draw against Wolves at Molineux earlier in the day. They missed an early chance to go ahead when Murphy was fouled by Scott Golbourne, but Hemed's under-hit penalty and follow-up were both saved by Emiliano Martínez, on loan from Arsenal.

Hemed later made up for his failure from the spot by clearing a shot from Adam Le Fondre off the line, and when Conor Coady fouled Rosenior four minutes into the second half, referee Jeremy Simpson reached straight for his red card and Hughton's men had a clear chance to take three points. But despite mustering a total of nineteen shots, eight on target, they were unable to score. Manu came on for his debut and looked promising, which proves that first impressions can be deceptive.

Brighton were now the only unbeaten team in the division and Hughton decided that they were strong enough to be able to send Forster-Caskey out on loan to MK Dons, but the result at Molineux felt like two points dropped. Another failure to take maximum points followed on 26 September at Bolton, where Zamora made his first start in the absence of the injured Hemed, and Murphy replaced LuaLua.

Sadly, injury had hit the unfortunate LuaLua once again and he would be out until the New Year. But no one was worrying about that as Zamora pounced on an error by Trotters goalkeeper Ben Amos to set up Stephens to score against his hometown club and then Murphy turned in Rosenior's low cross from Zamora's pass to put the visitors 2–0 ahead. Bolton, though, had always been in the game and Neil Danns halved the deficit four minutes before the interval after catching Kayal in possession.

Albion still looked capable of going on to win until Bruno was forced off by injury and Murphy was shown a red card for a tackle on Danns, even though it seemed clear that the Scot had slipped as he went to make the challenge. So it was a depleted side that conceded an injury-time equaliser as Gary Madine got above Hünemeier to glance a header past Stockdale.

Despite the frustration of another two points lost, the unbeaten team still topped the table, against the expectations of most people outside the club. Within the squad, the expectations were higher. 'The league isn't won by bookmakers or pundits,' Rosenior told the *Football League Paper*.

'It's won by what happens out there on the pitch. And when we go out onto the pitch, everyone is willing to fight and tackle for each other.

'People talk about quality, but every team in this league has good players. Do they have the mentality to win games under pressure? Do they have the resilience to dig points out when things aren't going well? At the moment, we're passing those tests and, if we can keep it up, we could do something very special.'

Hughton shared those feelings, although he had not expected to be unbeaten so late in the season. 'I was confident that we would be challenging, and when I say that, I mean in seventh, eighth, ninth place – two or three points outside the play-offs,' he said.

'And that's what I wanted after the season before, so that you knew that each game you won gave you a chance to get in the top six and every game you lost took you away from it. I wanted every game to matter.

'So the unbeaten run did surprise me, yes. I knew we could get a little bit of a rhythm, but whether we could get that real level of consistency? We hadn't shown it before, so there was an element of surprise. The simple answer is that I didn't expect it, because of the league. We were in a division of such good teams, like Burnley, Hull and Middlesbrough, that it was difficult to imagine putting an unbeaten run like that together. But what we were able to do was gather momentum and then you start to think, "We've got a good chance here." Then I became more confident, but I didn't know at the beginning.'

Albion appealed against Murphy's red card on the grounds of wrongful dismissal, but although the video evidence seemed to prove conclusively that he had slipped before making the challenge, the FA upheld the red card and consequent three-match suspension. It was not to be the last time the club felt hard done by, and there was more frustration in the next game, at home to Cardiff City.

The team found itself behind for the first time in a league match after only five minutes when Bruno was caught too far forward and left-back Scott Malone's cross was met at the near post by Joe Mason. Cardiff goalkeeper Simon Moore made three excellent saves before Stephens nipped ahead of his marker to turn Kayal's cross home seven minutes before half-time.

Dunk had to clear off the line from Sammy Ameobi to prevent Cardiff from going back in front, but after that it was all Albion. Unfortunately, a blatant foul on March by former Manchester United full-back Fabio da Silva was not punished with a second yellow card, and two players combined to squander an excellent chance in the dying seconds. Stephens played an inviting cross in from the left but Manu failed to make contact and behind him the unmarked Greer, alone in front of an empty net and perhaps surprised that it had reached him, scooped the ball wide of the far post.

Even so, Albion went into the next international break unbeaten and two points clear of Middlesbrough at the top of the table. But it could, and perhaps should, have been eight.

• • •

International breaks can provide breathing space or upset momentum. In Albion's case, it turned out to be the former as they returned to record one of their best and perhaps most significant results of the season at Elland Road, Leeds.

Leeds had not won at their imposing ground for seven months and a home victory was surely due, while former Seagulls Chris Wood and Will Buckley were in their squad and a decent crowd was behind them as usual. Leeds began quickly, but Albion went ahead with almost their first attack, March going through on a clever pass inside Scott Wootton from Kayal and beating goalkeeper Marco Silvestri to score.

Unfortunately, the lead lasted less than ten minutes, Liam Cooper glancing in a header following a trick free kick eventually taken by Alex Mowatt. It got worse when Greer limped off and could have been worse still – but Wood headed wide from a similar Mowatt kick when scoring looked easier and Mowatt then charged down an attempted clearance by Stockdale and the ball hit the post.

Both teams went for the win, using up all their substitutes, so when Cooper went down injured, Leeds were reduced to ten men. Gaps began to appear and in the eighty-ninth minute Bong threaded the ball through one of them for substitute Zamora to take it in his stride and loft it gently over the advancing Silvestri. It was his first Albion goal for 4,549 days and won the three points.

Players kissing their shirt badges can be a sickening sight when everyone suspects they will probably be on their way to a richer club at the first wave of a credit card. But the sight of Zamora running towards the away fans in the West Stand kissing the Seagull emblem on his yellow shirt was very different.

His previous strike had been a penalty in a 2–2 draw away to Grimsby Town on the final day of the 2002/03 season, as the club finally succumbed to relegation at the last. That had been a day to forget, but this was an occasion to savour for fans and player. 'Everyone knows what the club means to me, and the fans, so obviously I wanted to celebrate with them,' he said.

'A few people have been asking me when it was going to come, and Nathan Jones said, "About time!"

'It was a lovely time to score, although injury time seemed to go on for ever. Bongy did well. I thought the goalkeeper would get it, to be honest, but he stood still at first and that gave me time to adjust myself and make the decision where I wanted to put it.

'The unbeaten record is a great one to have and we want to hang onto it as long as possible, and we've got another chance to keep it going on Tuesday. The boys have been doing tremendously so I'm happy to play my part, whether that's starting, or for twenty minutes or five minutes. Whenever I'm called upon, I'll try to do my part.'

Having scored the first goal after his return, Zamora had one more feat to accomplish: scoring at the Amex. And not only did he manage it at home to Bristol City four days later, but it was also another winner.

City had looked the better side early on and Derrick Williams had volleyed past Stockdale after seventeen minutes. Baldock thought he had equalised when he hooked the ball over goalkeeper Frank Fielding, only for Luke Ayling to clear. But Baldock did get the goal his running had deserved after fifty-three minutes, sliding in to poke home Bruno's low cross to the near post.

And the comeback was complete in the eighty-second minute when Stephens's shot from 20 yards rebounded off defender Aden Flint and fell for Zamora, who had come on six minutes earlier.

The ball bounced off the turf onto Zamora's left foot and he flicked it up and volleyed it past the wrong-footed Fielding. Like the goal at Leeds, it was a strike that combined instinct and technique, and Zamora ran behind the net to celebrate in front of the North Stand.

'Two goals in two games coming on as a sub is special, especially for myself at Brighton,' he told BBC Sussex. 'I don't know what to say really – it was a great occasion. It was a reaction finish. When you do shooting practice for that many years, it sort of comes as second nature or instinct, just trying to hit the target.'

Paul Samrah, a supporter who had fronted the Falmer For All campaign aimed at obtaining planning permission for the stadium, and who had doubled as the joint PA announcer at Withdean, was more effusive, as were many fans. 'When I did the PA at Withdean, I thought I had announced the last-ever Bobby Z home goal for the Albion,' he said. 'That was back in April 2003. I was wrong! Twelve years on, he's back as a super sub – and, boy, does he know where the net is. An effortless, class act, showing how scoring goals can be easy. Welcome back, Bobby, we've missed you.'

But not even Zamora could win matches on his own. An unwelcome yellow card for Kayal in the City game ruled him out for the visit of a Preston North End side who were to give Albion more than their fair share of problems over the next eighteen months. Add that to a thigh strain that sidelined Stephens and the heart of the side was absent.

Ince and Crofts, who had helped win Norwich promotion in 2011, tried their best but could not find the creative spark required against a five-man Preston midfield that also subdued the Albion wingers. And what turned out to be a long-term thigh injury sustained by Bong, who left the field on a stretcher, made for a depressing day at the Amex.

The only bright spot was the continuation of the unbeaten run, and if a point was a disappointing return, then the same outcome from the next game, away to Reading, was one that most would have settled for in advance. Kayal and Stephens were back and Rosenior took Bong's place, but it was not until the thirty-sixth minute that Hemed forced a save from Ali Al-Habsi, briefly an Albion goalkeeper on loan from Wigan.

But after fifty-one minutes, Hemed crossed low for Murphy to sweep the ball home and three points suddenly seemed possible. The last word, though, went to Reading and Czech Republic striker Matěj Vydra, who was on an expensive season-long loan at the Madejski Stadium and took advantage when Stockdale could not hold Nick Blackman's low shot.

A third successive draw followed, but given that it was against Sheffield Wednesday at Hillsborough, a ground where Albion had never won, and the unbeaten run stretched to sixteen games, equalling the club record, it should have been an acceptable result. There was also a sign that Albion were possibly emerging from under the radar, with Wednesday's best crowd of the season, 23,712, turning out on a wet and windy Sheffield evening. Dunk impressed under pressure and Stockdale seemed unaffected by his error in the previous match.

However, the fact that the team dropped from first to third in the table as both Burnley and Hull City won was a warning that draws and unbeaten records were all very well, but wins were better.

After testing matches against possible promotion rivals, Albion returned home to face what should have been an easier task against bottom-six MK Dons on their first visit to the Amex. Forster-Caskey was unable to play against his parent club under the terms of his loan deal, and when March, from 20 yards, and Murphy from closer range, put them 2–0 up after nineteen minutes, it looked as straightforward as most of the 23,661 present probably expected. But a slip by Dunk let Nicky Maynard halve the arrears.

Albion tried to restore their two-goal advantage but the third goal refused to come. Hemed hit the post, but Stockdale also had to make a save with his feet, and Dunk seemed to bring down Samir Carruthers inside the area but somehow the referee, Dean Whitestone, perhaps alone in the ground, did not see the challenge as worthy of a penalty. Karl Robinson, the visitors' manager, said the decision was 'as bad as I've seen' and few disagreed. But Albion were more concerned about a thigh injury that forced Baldock off and was to sideline him for two months.

The next fixture at the Amex was a prestige occasion, an England under-21 qualifying match for the 2017 European Championships against Switzerland. A 5.45 kick-off on a Monday evening kept the attendance down to 12,003 even though Albion's Solly March was in the starting line-up. Switzerland went ahead late in the first half through Shani Tarashaj and that goal looked to have won the points until England scored late through James Ward-Prowse, Duncan Watmore and Chuba Akpom, who had replaced March after fifty-eight minutes and was later to join Albion on loan from Arsenal. Jake Forster-Caskey also had a late cameo on his return to his home ground.

The trip to Burnley originally scheduled for Saturday 22 November was moved to the following day with a lunchtime kick-off for live TV coverage, and anyone switching on late would have missed the scoring. With Baldock out, Zamora started and put the Albion ahead after only fifty-seven seconds, reacting quickest when Burnley goalkeeper Tom Heaton deflected a shot by Hemed onto the bar. But two minutes later, Dunk was judged to have pulled Michael

Keane's shirt as the two tried to reach a corner kick and Andre Gray, Burnley's £6 million summer signing from Brentford, put the penalty just out of Stockdale's reach.

Conceding so soon after going ahead, and at a ground where few visitors won, was galling, but in the end the point was welcome, as Scott Arfield sent two shots narrowly wide in the late stages. It put the team temporarily back on top, although Hull replaced them later in the day on goal difference.

• • •

The need to add firepower with Baldock out of action led to two signings as the loan transfer window closed on 26 October. James Wilson, nineteen, an England under-21 forward who had been singled out as a star of the future by Ryan Giggs, arrived from Manchester United for the rest of the season – although with a recall clause – and Dutch winger Rajiv van La Parra, twenty-four, moved from Wolves.

Albion were reported to have beaten a number of rivals to land Wilson, who had scored four times for United in six starts and a further fourteen appearances from the bench. Two of those goals had come in his debut against Hull when Giggs was caretaker manager. 'He's a goal-scorer, a natural goal-scorer; but he's got more to his game than just that,' Giggs said. 'He can turn and run and he's a very clever player. If you give young players a chance, they will take it.'

Hughton revealed that Wilson had been the club's top target as a loan signing and fans liked the sound of Giggs's description of him as a natural goal-scorer. But Hughton surprised no one by putting him and van La Parra on the bench rather than in the starting line-up for the visit of Birmingham City, which was to be one of the best games of the season. Instead, Zamora made his first home start since his return.

Blues, in sixth place, harked back to the days of the 1970s and Bob Latchford and Kenny Burns with their retro away kit in the colours of the German flag. Albion had dropped to third place after Derby had won at Hull the previous night, but had to be at their best to beat another team that was exceeding expectations, under manager Gary Rowett.

March looked in the mood on the right, although his opening goal was created on the other flank. Murphy skipped between two defenders before passing out to the overlapping Rosenior. His cross was met on the volley by March and although his shot struck Hemed, the rebound dropped for March again and his right-foot shot beat former Albion goalkeeper Tomasz Kuszczak on his near post.

But slack marking on the left allowed Birmingham back into the game and although Stockdale blocked a goalbound shot by Jacques Maghoma, the rebound fell kindly for Jon Toral to nod into the empty net. And there was another serious injury as Rosenior powered into a challenge as he charged towards the penalty area but went flying over Maikel Kieftenbeld. For the second time in three home games, the Albion left-back left the field on a stretcher.

Calderón replaced him and Albion regained the lead early in the second half, with Murphy and March again involved. Murphy cut the ball back from the left across the penalty area to the far post, where March hit a sweetly struck first-time shot. Kuszczak parried, but only to Zamora, in the right place at the right time, who could hardly miss.

The Amex expected a third when Kayal put Wilson through, but although the substitute's shot beat the onrushing Kuszczak, the ball smacked back off the post, and it was left to Stockdale, who had earlier saved well from Demarai Gray, to have the last word, plunging to his right to save a low shot from David Davis that was bound for the bottom corner.

Zamora had now scored four goals – three winners and one worth a point in a difficult away match – and his latest put Albion back on top of the table. But Rosenior had damaged knee ligaments and would be out for many weeks. There seemed to be some curse working against the Albion left flank. The partnership of Bong and LuaLua had been a key part of the good start, but it had been disrupted and now even the back-up pairing of Rosenior and March or Murphy had been split up. Calderón was the obvious replacement for Rosenior but was right-footed.

There was still a month to go before the opening of the transfer window and the possibility of reinforcements, although the club announced that Richie Towell, a goal-scoring midfield player from Dundalk, of the League of Ireland, who had begun his career at Celtic, would be joining in January on a two-and-a-half-year contract.

Nevertheless, a second home game in succession, against a Charlton Athletic team struggling at the wrong end of the table, would surely furnish three more points. That must have been the players' opinion too until the sixth minute, by which time they were 2–0 down to goals from promising youngster Ademola Lookman and Iranian Reza Ghoochannejhad. The young London side broke repeatedly, running at a surprised defence, and only two excellent saves by Stockdale kept Albion in the match before the interval.

'By our standards, we couldn't have started any poorer than we did,' Hughton said.

'We conceded two poor goals by being caught in advanced

positions, knowing that they've got that pace. And it could have been more. We're grateful to our keeper. We certainly knew we had to make amends in the second half and I knew if we got the first goal then the momentum would change. I told them we couldn't get caught again and had to work our way back into the game. But most of all we needed to show character. They needed to show how desperate they were not to lose the match.'

Five minutes into the second half, Wilson, who started the game in place of Hemed, dribbled through the heart of the Charlton defence and mishit a shot under goalkeeper Stephen Henderson. March, head bandaged after a first-half injury, hit the post with an angled shot from 25 yards before defender Patrick Bauer was sent off for bringing Zamora down on the edge of the penalty area as he ran onto a pass from Murphy just short of the hour.

Even against ten men it seemed Albion might run out of time until Hemed came on after seventy-three minutes. He made an almost instant impact. He turned a cross from March against a post in the eighty-third minute and Zamora rapped home the rebound. And two minutes later the comeback was complete as the Israeli's powerful header from van La Parra's cross was parried by Henderson but dropped into the net.

'It was very much a question of resting Tomer, not dropping him,' Hughton said afterwards.

'He had been going through a barren spell as regards scoring goals, but nobody feels it more than him and it wasn't down to his work ethic. It was those small margins between not scoring and scoring and I think everyone was pleased for him. We again haven't lost but again we haven't won by more than a goal and that shows how hard every game is. We have had to show character and we have a very tough run ahead.'

CHAPTER 4

THE BLIP

That tough run that Hughton had spoken of began on Saturday 12 December with a trip to Derby, who had beaten Albion in five of the previous six meetings. Although a 2–2 draw sounds like a good result in the circumstances, the match was calamitous in different ways for two of the team's young players.

Solly March went down clutching his knee early on but tried to continue, and spirits soared when Wilson put the team ahead with a clever near-post volley from Murphy's cross after twenty-two minutes. However, March went down again and this time left the field on a stretcher. Anterior cruciate ligament damage was to keep him out of action for almost a year and, to add insult to injury, he was booed by the home fans, who suspected him of play-acting.

'It wasn't nice,' he said.

'In fairness, they were a bit frustrated because the game wasn't going well for them and they wanted me to get off. From the pain I think I probably knew it was bad. You don't feel that pain when you've sprained an ankle or pulled a hamstring. But it didn't really sink in until I had an X-ray and that revealed the extent of the damage.'

Bradley Johnson levelled, but van La Parra, on for March, restored the lead on the break from Stephens's pass fifteen minutes from time and a first away win in four matches appeared likely. But then Rohan Ince, sent on to help preserve the lead, ended up costing the team two points when his backpass sold Stockdale short. Even then, the ball was scrambled away for a corner, but it was not cleared and referee Lee Mason, alone in the iPro Stadium, spotted a foul by Gordon Greer on Johnny Russell. Chris Martin, so often the bane of Brighton, converted the kick.

Ince, voted the club's young player of the season in 2014, had begun his career at Brighton very promisingly after Óscar García had converted him from a central defender to a holding midfield player following his arrival on a free transfer from Chelsea. But opportunities to start in Hughton's 4–4–2 system were few, and his error had not improved his first-team chances.

But the side as a whole was beginning to creak. And as Hughton had noted after the Charlton game, although they were unbeaten, none of the wins had been by more than one goal, meaning that the team could never coast and Hughton could not take key players such as Kayal or Stephens off for twenty minutes to save their energy for the next game. The turgid stalemate against Preston had proved that that pairing was almost indispensable.

'During that season I always had the feeling that we had to fight, to battle hard to win every game,' Hughton said.

'One example of that is Sam Baldock, who played a lot of the season for us, had a great record – if you look at the results, he wasn't often on a losing team – so had a really good impact on the team, but scored only four goals. Hemed scored seventeen goals, five of which were penalties. So we were a team that didn't have a twenty-goal-a-season striker. We were a side that had to work very hard for our wins. The margins were always very fine.'

There was an immediate chance to bury the bad memories of Derby three days later at Queens Park Rangers and the away end at the glorified shoebox that is Loftus Road was full to see van La Parra make his first start for the club, with Albion surviving a brisk opening from the home side. Charlie Austin, back in the QPR side after injury, forced a save from Stockdale, as did Matt Phillips, who then beat Stockdale, only for Calderón to clear off the line.

But, having reached half-time unscathed, Hughton's men came out for the second half and almost immediately built a two-goal lead. After fifty-three minutes, van La Parra sent a corner to the far post, Dunk headed it back into the danger area, and Stephens produced an overhead kick that found its way past unsighted former England goalkeeper Rob Green. Two minutes later, van La Parra hit a shot from fully 30 yards that skidded past Green, who seemed to react late – not for the first time in his career.

If they could have held the lead for any length of time, Albion might have killed QPR off, but instead they allowed them back into the game almost immediately as Greer let Austin take a low cross from Phillips on the right, turn him and fire past Stockdale into the roof of the net.

Now QPR's tails were up and the home crowd was roaring. As the pressure mounted, Dunk picked up a yellow card for a needless foul on Phillips out on the left and well away from danger, then a second for a lunge at Alejandro Faurlín in an attempt to retrieve a situation caused by his own failure to control a long ball.

Hünemeier immediately replaced Murphy, but the disrupted defence was unable to prevent Austin from heading the equaliser from Faurlín's corner. QPR might even have won it but for a save by Stockdale and a shot by Phillips that hit the post. In retrospect, that might have better reflected the balance of play, but a point felt like meagre reward after the team had led 2–0.

Middlesbrough were now at the top of the table, and they were also the next visitors to the Amex. In other circumstances, the fixture could have been an opportunity to regain confidence by beating the new leaders. But the team's performances had been starting to decline as injuries took their toll, the defence was conceding goals at an alarming rate, and the visit of a strong and confident Boro side came at the wrong time.

Lunchtime kick-offs did not suit the team, and a 3–0 defeat before the Sky cameras was a low point for many reasons. With Bong and Rosenior injured and Dunk absent through suspension, the defence was under-strength and Kike nipped in front of Hünemeier to nod in a cross from the left after only four minutes.

Recovering from that early blow was made difficult as Boro's five-man midfield harried Kayal and Stephens, while neither Murphy nor van La Parra were able to offer much inspiration. For the fourth match in succession, the defence was to concede at least two goals and the second, just before the interval, took two deflections on its way from Daniel Ayala's header from a corner to the net.

Had they known it, Albion would have been better to settle for a 2–0 defeat and no further swing in goal difference between the two teams. But the defence was further disrupted by an injury to Hünemeier. He was replaced by Goldson, who made his Championship debut but could not stop Ayala heading goalwards again for Cristhian Stuani to score from close range.

The consensus was that Boro were the best team that Albion had faced, even if their tendency to go down 'injured' at the least contact was unnecessary. But it had still been a shattering way to experience a first defeat of the season.

The immediate consequence of the defeat was that Boro went three points ahead of the Seagulls at the top of the table, with Derby second, a point behind the Teessiders. The psychological consequences would take a little longer to evaluate.

• • •

All good things come to an end, and Albion's 21-game undefeated start to the season had set a new club record and been very good, exceeding all pre-season expectations. And there were the extenuating circumstances of the injuries, not to mention Dunk's suspension.

But it still left everyone surrounding the club feeling less than festive as the holiday season approached, even if the campaign so far had to be judged positively, especially with the January transfer window approaching.

'In a strange way, the injuries actually contributed to giving us a good squad feeling,' Hughton said.

'Because everyone wants to play and it's difficult. Injuries can give other players opportunities. The ideal situation is to use a lot of your squad but still to be winning and doing well so there is that feel-good factor in there because everyone is playing regularly.

'That season we had some bigger injuries and we had to try to cope. Perhaps in the end in the accumulation of things, the injuries were a factor. Some players had consistent seasons, Dale, Beram played a lot of games, Dunky, Bruno, Hemed, so there were some who were always there, but we didn't have the strength in depth that we needed and had later.'

A goalless draw at Brentford on Boxing Day at least stopped the defensive rot, although Stockdale being voted man of the match told another side of the story. There was also a mixed message in the stats. The draw at Griffin Park represented a new club record for away games unbeaten in all competitions in one season – ten – but also consecutive away draws (six). And, alarmingly, the team had lost a lead five times during that sequence.

And there had been yet another defensive injury at Brentford, Greer going off after seventy-eight minutes. That meant Goldson making his first start at home to Ipswich, when van La Parra would also make the last appearance of his loan spell.

With Wilson not fully recovered from a bug that had forced him off at Brentford, Hughton made a tactical change too, starting Andrew Crofts in a holding midfield role that allowed Kayal and Stephens to push forward, a 4–1–4–1 formation that had looked promising in the second half of the game at Griffin Park.

Ipswich, though, arrived in good form, looking for a fifth straight away victory, and Kévin Bru made the first impression, hitting the crossbar from distance. Albion thought they had taken the lead when Hemed dribbled past Christophe Berra on the right and crossed low for Stephens to produce a clever flick that Dean Gerken, the Tractor Boys' keeper, touched onto the crossbar. The ball dropped for Murphy to tap in, but the referee's assistant flagged him offside – incorrectly, as Berra had been closer to the goalline than Murphy throughout the passage of play.

The only goal of the match was the result of an unforced error. Dunk took his eye off a pass from Calderón and the ball rolled under his foot. Ipswich forward Daryl Murphy was onto it like a flash and struck an angled shot past Stockdale that smacked the inside of the far post and was probably already over the goalline before it hit Goldson, who was frantically trying to clear.

Bru then hit the post from three yards out when scoring seemed easier, but Albion also struck the overworked woodwork, substitute Zamora meeting a cross from Bruno with a side-footed effort that looped over Gerken but came back off the crossbar.

Goldson's debut had been a positive, as he defended competently and looked comfortable with the ball at his feet. But it had been a distinctly downbeat end to 2015. Things had to get better in the New Year. Didn't they?

CHAPTER 5

NEW YEAR 2016

What was to prove a memorable and eventful 2016 for Albion began with the news of yet another loan left-back, but a necessary signing with Bong and Rosenior sidelined. The experienced former Premier League defender Liam Ridgewell, who was back in Britain during the Major League Soccer close season, arrived from Portland Timbers. He had played for Hughton at Birmingham before leaving for West Bromwich Albion and moving on to Oregon.

But he was not available for the first match of the year, at home to Wolves in front of the Sky cameras on New Year's Day, and he might have been glad of that. It was yet another game that suggested that not only form but also luck had completely deserted the Albion.

As a Wolves fan, Connor Goldson's father must have dreamed of seeing his son score winning goals for the men in old gold and black and in this match the dream came true but in the worst possible way. The first goal scored by an Albion defender all season was at the wrong end and meant another defeat, with a fourth successive blank on the Albion side of the scoresheet.

Perhaps the signs for the attack were bad when the cameras

caught Wilson vomiting on the pitch. Clips of the incident quickly spread on social media, and although he completed the ninety minutes, there were always doubts after that as to whether he was ever fully fit.

'He played in the game at Brentford and he hadn't been well for a couple of days before that,' Hughton said.

'We spoke before that game and he did the warm-up and he said he felt fine but he obviously struggled with his recovery, hence we took him off at half-time. We left him out in mid-week, really just on that recovery period. I spoke to him again and he said he felt fine.

'This is a lad that has gone also from being very much part of a Manchester United squad, not playing so many games, to coming here and what the Championship entails. But he was fine to play and over the course of the game he was one of the more likely to get us a goal.'

Once again, Goldson showed immense promise and proved that the recruitment department was finding real talent. But own goals are an occupational hazard for any central defender, and after thirty-two minutes he swung a leg at Jordan Graham's cross and diverted the ball gently between Stockdale and the near post. There had been little danger, with no attackers waiting to pounce, but the communication and understanding that becomes second nature in a settled defence had yet to be established.

At the other end, Wilson had an early chance when he swung at a knock-down from Zamora and his looping effort forced goalkeeper Carl Ikeme to fingertip the ball over the bar. And in the second, Bruno hit the bar with a rocket shot from outside the penalty area and Ikeme made another good save, from Dunk's close-range header. But the ball refused to go in.

The Amex pitch did not appear to be helping the team's fluency, and Steve Winterburn, the head groundsman, explained the problems on the club website. 'It has been a particularly tough period through December, mainly due to the heavy rainfall, which not only affects the ongoing condition of the surface but also really hampers the grounds team's ability to get out and work on the pitch,' he said.

'It's the same at a lot of clubs up and down the country, with a lot of pitches taking a battering, and some have been affected much worse than ourselves.

'The good thing is we have some time now to work on improving the surface. The club has invested in the pitch and the grounds equipment here at the stadium, not to mention the training ground, and we will be using that and working around the clock to get the pitch into the best possible condition for the Huddersfield match later this month.'

Albion were now fourth, behind Middlesbrough, Derby and Hull and three points ahead of Burnley, and lost a key member of staff when Nathan Jones was offered the manager's job at Luton Town, the club where he had begun his professional career. The Welshman had served Brighton as a player, coach, caretaker manager and even translator, using the Spanish he had acquired when playing for Numancia and Badajoz early in his career to smooth communications for Óscar García.

He wrote a farewell message in the next match programme, becoming surely the first departing employee ever to thank contract cleaners.

> It's been a wrench to leave the Albion and to have to make this decision, and I just want to thank everyone for how they treated me in my time back at the club.
>
> I always knew that Brighton was an unbelievable club, but it's the

people that make it special. From the chairman to the cleaning company, the people are amazing and that's what I will really miss.

I'd like to thank everyone for the progression I've made. At times I've been a little bit impetuous, but the club have kept me grounded and have invested in me. I'm at a stage now that I'm ready. I've worked under three different managers and I've learned so much from all three. I was very close to Óscar; Sami and I got close; and I've taken a lot from Chris.

It would've been easy for Chris not to have trusted me as much as he has, knowing that I had ambitions myself, but I found quickly that I wanted to work for him. He's a really good man, an excellent manager and I know that the club will do well under him.

The chairman and Paul Barber have been amazing to me. Paul was the first person I met when I came back and we had a really good football talk. We hit it off straight away and the chairman I've known for quite a while. He's Brighton through and through, understated and not in your face. He's a fantastic chairman and I've loved working for him. I'd like to thank him and Paul for the faith they've put in me. It would've been easy for them to not show as much loyalty to me but I hope they saw something in me and they honed that.

Finally, I'd like to thank the fans. I've always had a great relationship with them. I wasn't a special player but I gave my all for this club. I was the first one in for training along with Danny Cullip and I was the last to leave for the five-year stint I was here. Everything I have done for the club they have given back to me, and I'd like to think the fans have seen that.

The number of messages I have received since I've left has been unbelievable. I wish everyone associated with Brighton & Hove Albion all the very best for the future. The club is in my heart and it always will be.

But the day after Jones left, there was an arrival that would prove to be one of the key acquisitions of modern Albion history. Anthony Knockaert, the former Leicester City winger, was signed from Standard Liège of Belgium for an undisclosed fee that some papers estimated at around £2 million, but which was soon rumoured to have been considerably less, the song that came to be sung about him suggesting that 'he only cost a mil'.

Even £2 million would have been a bargain for the talented wide man, a skilful dribbler but also a hard worker, who had helped Leicester win promotion to the Premier League and played for them in the top tier. How did Albion persuade him to come back to England to play in the Championship?

According to Paul Winstanley, it was a triumph for perseverance. 'We had tried to get Anthony in the summer, before he left for Standard Liège, because he was coming out on a free from Leicester,' Winstanley said.

'But he was led to Standard without knowing what offers were on the table in England, by the sounds of it. Nevertheless, we carried on watching him although he was playing off the front man there in a kind of 4–4–1–1 formation, when you know he's better on the right.

'We kept in touch with his agent at the time, and he was saying: "No, he's not happy, it's not quite working out. There might be an opportunity here. He did enjoy his time in England and wants to come back but it has got to be the right fit."

'We were doing well in the league at the time, which helps, and once Chris was aware of what could be done, we quickly thrashed a few things out and moved it forward. We got him here, showed him around, and he wanted to do it. He was impressed with the vision of the club, the chairman, Chris, and we told him straight away that we saw him playing on the right again in our system and that was where he wanted to play. We knew he was a great chance-creator but we had to be sure his character would fit into this group. We thought they would carry him and he would thrive here.'

Why were there no other suitors? 'We were so aware of him and great admirers but I think a lot of other clubs had dismissed him because of the position he was playing in for Liège and thought: "Oh, that's where he sees himself"', Winstanley said.

'But he wasn't playing good football out there and he didn't look as if he was enjoying himself. There was no taking away his ability even then but we always saw him playing back on the right. We stayed close to the agent to make sure we could figure out the lad's mindset and keep letting the player know how much we wanted him. And the fee was good.'

The fee was, in fact, a steal and the whole transfer had been a triumph for Winstanley's preferred method of keeping everything as far under the radar as possible. Transfer speculation, either on club message boards or in the print media, sometimes amazes him.

'That's how we always try to go about our business. It's very rare that I ever see any names linked with us in the press that are real to us. A lot of stuff gets put out there and I'll get the occasional email but most of the time it's wide of the mark.'

• • •

Knockaert was not risked in the next match, the FA Cup third round tie away to Hull City. It was an extra fixture that nobody wanted, bereft of any glamour for either side and incidental to the main business of attempting to get promoted. The only plus for Hughton was a chance to give game time to fringe players such as Mäenpää,

Ince, Towell, Manu and Danny Holla, all of whom started. In addition, LuaLua and Baldock were on the bench on their returns from injury and took the field for the final half-hour. Ridgewell was given a chance to pick up the pace of English football again without points at stake.

Some eyes were opened by the fact that Hull also rested players but that the men they brought in were established and experienced Premier League performers such as Tom Huddlestone and Sone Aluko. That strength in depth was enviable and showed how far Albion had to go if they wanted to build a squad that could shrug off more than a few injuries.

It was no surprise that Hull won, the only goal scored from the penalty spot by Robert Snodgrass after Dunk had brought down Harry Maguire. Mäenpää was Albion's standout performer, while the goal drought continued. Crofts's 89th-minute shot against the bar from a cross by LuaLua was as close as they came and the number of games without a win was now seven.

The winless run stretched to eight games as the season reached its nadir in a 2–0 mid-week defeat away to Rotherham. Knockaert must have wondered what he had let himself in for as the struggling Millers won without too much difficulty, profiting from two defensive errors. First Dunk slipped as he attempted to clear just before half-time, and the ball looped towards Danny Ward. As Ward shaped to volley, the chances of the spinning, dropping ball ending up anywhere but row Z of the stand seemed negligible. But he made scoring look as easy as the Albion had recently found it difficult.

Hughton read the riot act during the interval and the team improved in the second half but could not find an equaliser and, with four minutes to go, Bruno, of all people, attempted unwisely to cushion a header to a teammate in his own penalty area. He succeeded only in presenting the ball to Matt Derbyshire, who produced another first-time finish worthy of a far better team than one in twentieth place.

'We are giving away poor goals but we had nowhere near the intensity that you need in the first half,' Hughton said.

'We needed to get into the players at half-time, to set a few things straight. They were better than us, certainly in that first half. And we're finding it difficult to get goals. The margins aren't going our way. It's a big concern. But the players are aware that we cannot start a game the way we did tonight against anybody and expect to do as well as we have done.

'But of course it's different now. At the start of the season perhaps no one expected us to do well. Now there's an expectation and a pressure and other teams raise their game and we have to be able to match that. We're going to need more from everybody. We have got characters in abundance in the changing room and they're going to have to show that.'

There had been signs of promise from Knockaert and the suggestion of the beginnings of a right-wing partnership with Bruno, but too many other players had been below par, and some fans were now wondering if sixth place, where the team now found itself, was a more realistic position than the top two had been.

• • •

The team badly needed a performance that did not include basic defensive errors and to end the run of six games without a goal. They managed both in the sleet and snow at Ewood Park, Blackburn. Only three minutes had passed when two Blackburn defenders failed to cut out Stockdale's long kick, leaving Murphy with a clear shot. Goalkeeper Jason Steele turned the ball onto the post but, for once, luck was with the Albion and it ran to Zamora, who celebrated his thirty-fifth birthday with the club's first goal in 578 minutes of play.

The red-shirted Albion defence now set about defending the club's first lead since QPR a month earlier better than they had the two-goal advantage at Loftus Road. As Blackburn sent in a stream of crosses and long throw-ins, Dunk and Goldson won every header, while Zamora gave a master-class in hold-up play at the other end. He also came close to a second with a chip over the advancing Steele, the ball dropping just wide.

Blackburn's best effort came from a free kick, Ben Marshall's attempt hitting the post and Stockdale before Dunk smashed the ball clear, but Knockaert might even have doubled the lead with a shot on the turn that struck an upright.

The recovery continued with a 2–1 home victory over Huddersfield that included a Zamora goal to stand comparison with any he had scored in his first two spells in Sussex. He began the move on the Albion six-yard line with a defensive header from a corner before sprinting forward. Kayal kept it going, finding Knockaert on the right. The Frenchman checked inside and floated the ball to the far side of the penalty area, where Zamora timed his arrival perfectly, sending a controlled volley across goalkeeper Jed Steer into the bottom right-hand corner.

Huddersfield, on a five-match unbeaten run in the league, hit back with a header by Harry Bunn just before half-time, but Hughton made two positive substitutions to turn the game, sending on LuaLua for his first appearance at the Amex since his injury, and Wilson. Knockaert, impressing with his energy and ambition on his home debut, twisted and turned before crossing for Wilson to glance home a header. And LuaLua tormented right-back Tommy Smith into two yellow cards.

The FA Cup fourth round weekend was empty for Albion in the wake of their early exit at Hull, but the recruitment department was far from idle, and another astute signing was made when Steve Sidwell returned to the club. The experienced and intelligent midfield player, who had first played for Albion on loan from Arsenal at Withdean in the 2002/03 season, now came back on another loan, from Stoke City, a journey that had taken him via Reading, Chelsea, Aston Villa and Fulham.

Like Zamora, he found a much-changed club. 'Training at the university was different – taking your kit home to wash it, bringing it back the next day, being caked in mud every day,' he said.

'But that was part of it. I loved it, I loved my time there. It was a learning experience and one that makes you feel grateful for the training ground that we have now and the way we're treated.

'Who would have thought, at Withdean and Falmer, that the infrastructure the club now has would be possible? A few, perhaps, but it is all testament to the owner and everyone behind him. The town and the fans have all pushed in the right direction. They have given themselves every chance with what is in place. It is all geared up to be in the Premier League. But you don't forget your roots and what was done to get us all here today. Back in 2003, I was desperate to stay but circumstances were that Reading could afford me and Brighton couldn't. I've come full circle and it felt like unfinished business, where I wanted to be with the club.'

On the outside looking in was Manu, who went public with his frustration at being on the bench in a Dutch online newspaper, metronieuws.nl. 'The Brighton training complex is a fairy tale,' he said.

'Really, it is not normal, as the top Dutch clubs do not even come near it. I live half an hour from central London so there is plenty to do. And the salary? I have little to complain about. But I have to play. [Not playing], to me, is very disappointing. Brighton and I do not have a happy marriage.'

A move away from the club seemed inevitable after that, and it duly materialised in the form of a three-month loan to Huddersfield, while Rohan Ince moved to Fulham for the rest of the season. On the final day of the transfer window, Czech Republic and former Sparta Prague forward Jiří Skalák, twenty-three, arrived from FK Mladá Boleslav for a fee reported in his home country as £1.3 million.

But a move to bring back Glenn Murray, the forward whose goals had fired the team to League One promotion under Gus Poyet in 2011, had failed. Murray was barely figuring in AFC Bournemouth's Premier League side, and still lived in Brighton almost five years after he had last played for the club, so a return – either permanently or on loan – made sense. But Bournemouth manager Eddie Howe still wanted Murray around as the Cherries battled to stay in the top flight, and later refused to let him go during the loan window.

Hughton now surveyed a squad that had added attacking flair and experience, even if the goal-scorer the fans craved was still absent. 'I am really delighted with the work done to bring in the players we have over this period – and some was done very early in the window,' he said.

'We have good levels and good numbers in the squad. At this moment I am delighted with what I have on this final day of the window. It is for myself and this group of players to get our ultimate aim and keep pressure on those top teams and give ourselves an opportunity for promotion.'

• • •

And the first match with that refreshed squad backed up Hughton's confidence as the team recorded its first victory by more than a single-goal margin, thumping Brentford 3–0 at the Amex on Friday 5 February. The Bees arrived in tenth place and looked good early on, with Alan Judge's fierce first-time shot forcing a save from Stockdale, who leapt to his left to palm the ball away. But it was Albion who made the breakthrough after twenty-seven minutes with Knockaert's first goal for the club.

Bruno might already have scored when his shot was deflected onto the bar by Brentford defender Harlee Dean before Knockaert took Murphy's pass, tricked his way past two opponents and hit a low left-foot shot into the bottom far corner.

Just before the break, Knockaert's quick free kick gave Kayal the chance to cross from the right and Hemed, although backing away from goal, still found the power in his neck muscles to head the ball back across goalkeeper David Button and in.

And although the visitors posed some problems in the second half, the defence stood firm and Stephens sent the outstanding Murphy clear in the dying seconds to clip a shot past Button and in off the foot of the far post.

Murphy scored the first goal of the next match, at home to bottom-of-the-table Bolton, but if the supporters thought that the nail-biting was over and that the Brentford game had heralded a new period of comfortable wins, they were to be disappointed.

Murphy's goal, another low shot past an advancing goalkeeper, this time from a pass by man of the match Kayal, should have been a platform for a comfortable and efficient victory. But the Trotters were level only eleven minutes later as a penalty area full of Albion defenders failed to clear Wellington Silva's cross from the left and Emile Heskey hit a shot that struck Dunk and was deflected past Stockdale.

But in the forty-second minute came one of the goals of the season. Knockaert ran powerfully from his own half, shrugging off Jay Spearing as he charged into the area and cut a low cross back for Zamora. The Albion legend had used his experience to check his forward run and win a yard of space in which to receive the ball and now he showed his awareness and touch with a delightful backheel that nudged the ball on into the path of Hemed, who side-footed past Ben Amos.

It was a goal that deserved to win any match, but it was not to be. Five minutes into the second half, Albion made a mess of clearing a long free kick from the left, and Spearing seized on Kayal's mis-kick to drive the ball through the crowd of defenders and in. And it almost got worse as Bruno's error let Liam Feeney run through. Stockdale, though, got a strong right arm to his shot.

Hemed nearly restored the lead when he rounded Amos, but his shot from a difficult angle was cleared off the line by Dorian Dervite. And within minutes Kayal caught Mark Davies in possession, knocking the ball away from the Bolton man to Hemed. He returned the ball to Kayal, who bent a shot around Amos from 18 yards to win the game.

A very different challenge followed, away to Hull, the new leaders. Fortunately, there was none of the sloppiness shown against Bolton. Sidwell started in a five-man midfield and Calderón replaced Ridgewell, whose loan had expired, while Rosenior made a welcome return to the bench. Dunk and Goldson came under pressure but gave their opponents nothing, and Dunk even ran from his own half late on to strike a 25-yarder that was the closest Albion came to a goal. Hull had pressed and Stockdale tipped a late shot from Sam Clucas onto the crossbar, but they were shut out at home for only the second time so far.

A few days after the Hull game, the club briefly became a victim of internal politics at Old Trafford. Factions attempting to undermine Manchester United manager Louis van Gaal planted a story with a national newspaper journalist suggesting that Albion were 'angry' that van Gaal had 'revealed' that Wilson could be recalled to the Premier League club at any time and that this could unsettle the player. If the journalist had checked more carefully, he would have discovered that the recall clause was common knowledge – and a check on Wilson's recent form might have suggested that van Gaal would have had to be very short of other options to recall him.

The story was a minor annoyance to the club but no more, and certainly could not explain how a disciplined and controlled performance at Hull was followed by a collapse in Cardiff – unless the team's poor record in lunchtime kick-offs is any justification. Yet another televised fixture, at a rain-swept Cardiff City Stadium, showed Hughton's men at their worst. The only possible consolation for Albion fans was that the three points went to a team now managed by Russell Slade, who had guided the Albion to safety in League One in 2009.

Again there was a five-man midfield, but with Crofts replacing Kayal, who had a groin injury, and Skalák making his full debut. While Albion had made the most of a minority of possession in some games, here they were the team damaged by opponents breaking quickly after turnovers. Peter Whittingham got away from Sidwell to score too easily after sixteen minutes and three minutes later Stockdale's attempted clearance hit Goldson and the ball was quickly worked to Anthony Pilkington. He cut inside Dunk and his shot, although central, found its way under Stockdale's dive. On the half-hour, an interception by Goldson turned into an assist for Lex Immers. Even when lone forward Zamora escaped his markers, he could only slide a cross from Skalák wide of the goal.

In the second half, Rosenior was brought on and another cross by Skalák, one of few Albion successes on the day, created a consolation goal, headed in by Stephens, but Cardiff had the last word. Goldson slipped on the saturated turf and brought down Pilkington, Whittingham converting the penalty.

'We conceded what I regard as soft goals, which is not like us,' Hughton said.

'I can't have any complaints. It's about a team making sure you are blocking holes and we had a tough afternoon. They gave us problems and we needed to deal with it better. I don't think it was down to tactics or formation. We didn't give ourselves an opportunity to get into the game.

'We've been a good team for most of the season but you get days like today when we didn't look a good team. There will be bad days and you hope you don't concede goals but we did. Off the back of a big defeat you want to get back out there as soon as possible and we look forward to Tuesday.'

Would this be a one-off, or the beginning of another slump?

• • •

As Hughton said, a chance to put things right came quickly at Bristol City, and the players answered with a resounding victory. As in Cardiff, one team had most of the ball and the other scored four goals, but this time the Albion had things the right way round.

Hughton abandoned the 4–5–1 formation, and it helped that

Kayal and Baldock were both back in the side. After only eight minutes, Murphy pounced on Zak Vyner's failure to control a kick-out from goalkeeper Richard O'Donnell, exchanged passes with Hemed and rolled a shot past the keeper. In Albion's next attack after twenty-one minutes, Rosenior and Hemed worked the ball to Baldock and he punished his former club with a low shot into the near corner from 22 yards.

In the second half, Kayal played a pass through the defence for Hemed to slide past O'Donnell, and Stephens's far-post header from a free kick by Skalák went in off defender Mark Little. To emphasise that it was not City's night, substitute Kieran Agard hit a penalty against the crossbar after he had been felled by Kayal. It was the best possible answer to the Cardiff debacle: the biggest win of the season so far, equalling the club's best-ever away victory in the second tier.

And the team did it again six days later at home to Leeds, except that an unchanged side had equalled its goal tally at Ashton Gate by half-time. Rosenior, doing his best Jamie Murphy impression, cut into the penalty area from the left and was brought down by Scott Wootton to win the team's first penalty at home in the league for almost two seasons. Hemed made the occasion even more memorable with a cheeky conversion, allowing Marco Silvestri to dive and then dinking the ball into the centre of the empty net.

Four minutes later, Sol Bamba gave the ball away to Baldock, and after a quick one-two with Stephens, Baldock saw his shot deflected past Silvestri by Liam Cooper. Hemed then pounced on a half-clearance by the under-pressure Bamba to score with a low drive. And Dunk rose highest to nod in Stephens's corner and make it 4–0. Skalák had the best chance to add to the score in the second half but was tackled on his way round Silvestri, and nobody was complaining after back-to-back four-goal wins.

There were complaints after a goalless draw at Preston, the fourth successive double blank in matches between the clubs, but they were directed at the match officials for disallowing two Brighton goals. Replays showed that the first, late in the first half, should have counted, Murphy level with the last defender as he ran onto Knockaert's chipped pass before hooking the ball in. The second decision was more clear-cut as former England goalkeeper Chris Kirkland, making his Preston debut, had his blushes correctly spared by a flag as Hemed pounced after he had spilled Rosenior's shot.

Preston's best moment was a half-volley by Calum Woods from a cross by Adam Reach after fifty-six minutes that Stockdale somehow touched onto the crossbar, but otherwise Goldson and Dunk came off best despite several robust challenges, Goldson in particular requiring treatment twice following clatterings.

Instead of moving back up to second place, Albion stayed fourth, four points behind leaders Burnley, and there was another stalemate at home to Sheffield Wednesday. Carlos Carvalhal, their Portuguese manager, was to talk a good game at various stages about vision and ambition, but on his side's visit to Brighton, there was, at first, only a desire to get as many men behind the ball as possible and frustrate.

Kayal was only fit enough to appear on the bench and, without his drive and guile, there was no way through Wednesday's navy blue wall. Wednesday, though, could have been down to ten men after thirty-six minutes when Portugal forward Lucas João kicked out at Goldson, but referee Darren Drysdale had his back to the incident, and after taking plenty of advice via his headset, showed a yellow card to João in what seemed to be a compromise.

Nothing was seen of the visitors in attack until the fifty-first minute, but their first attempt at goal was dangerous, Barry Bannan's swerving shot from distance demanding a diving save from Stockdale. Bannan, directing operations in midfield as well as sending a series of set plays into the Brighton penalty area, tested Stockdale again after seventy-six minutes with a long shot along the slick surface, Wednesday's attacks now more frequent and certainly more incisive than Albion's previously fruitless battering at their massed defence.

Albion now had to hang on, which they did, but a fourth successive clean sheet was not much consolation in the context of hopes of a top-two finish. Hughton's team had not managed a shot on target but despite an end to a run of five home wins, he pronounced himself relieved that his team had maintained the nine-point advantage over the visitors.

Although nobody knew it at the time, Bobby Zamora's appearance as a second-half substitute was his last in a Brighton shirt, as his continuing struggles for fitness overcame him. He had made ten league starts and come off the bench sixteen times, scoring seven goals. His final figures for the club were 162 appearances in all competitions and ninety goals. Those strikes had included goals of the highest quality and it was entirely fitting that his last goal for the club had been the controlled volley against Huddersfield in front of his own fans.

Albion were now third, but so tight was the division that victory over Reading in another cagey affair three days later was enough to put them second again. The visitors showed little ambition except, perhaps, in their choice of an unusual lilac-coloured away kit, but Albion were only able to score once against them. Baldock had already created two chances, for Knockaert and Stephens, before Wilson finally profited from one of his passes in the twenty-fifth minute, shooting low across Ali Al-Habsi and in off the foot of the far post.

Matěj Vydra had had Reading's only noteworthy effort before that, but when he hit a low shot, Stockdale couldn't hold it and was fortunate that Ola John put the rebound over the crossbar. Baldock shot high from a pass by Knockaert, as did Murphy when found by Baldock, and a chance to improve the goal difference had been missed, however welcome the three points were.

Nevertheless, 7,000 fans, one of the largest away followings in the club's history, took advantage of a cheap ticket offer for the away match the following Saturday at MK Dons, creating a new attendance record at Stadium MK. Nobody much liked the idea of giving money to the hated 'Franchise FC', but there was a growing feeling that the team was back on track and that there might never be a better chance to reach the Premier League.

The *Albion Roar* radio programme and podcast often had fans as guests, and co-presenter Alan Wares was in a good position to gauge the falls and rises in enthusiasm and belief. 'At the beginning of the season, we just wanted to do better than we had the previous season,' he said.

'So after the first dozen games or so and we hadn't lost, there was an air of: "This is going really well, we're quite good. But we're drawing games that we should be winning." So there was pleasure but also frustration. Because we never won by more than one goal, we thought goal difference would be an issue and we knew the blip was coming. So when we got tonked by Middlesbrough, the feeling was that it had to end sometime.

'There was still positivity because we were challenging, and people thought: "We could do this." Any negativity was a sense that we could fall away because that's what we do. But even when the blip was over, we made the new signings and the victories became more convincing, the biggest pessimism was not about whether we'd maintain our promotion push but still that goal difference would count against us. The fact that it eventually did didn't give anyone any pleasure.'

But there were few doubts after the final whistle in the land of the concrete cows, some even taking the outcome as a sign that this would be the Albion's year.

Seven yellow cards suggested that Hughton's team had kicked their way to victory, but perhaps that total said more about referee Chris Kavanagh's erratic performance. After a little-and-medium combination of Baldock and Wilson had failed to make much impression in the first half, Hughton sent on Hemed, and his impact was swift. Seven minutes after coming on, he was brought down by Darren Potter for a penalty that he converted himself. Six minutes later, Rosenior sent Skalák down the right and Hemed climbed above Jordan Spence to meet his cross with a classic centre forward's header. Murphy and Wilson both forced saves from goalkeeper Cody Cropper and a third away goal looked likely, but some controversial decisions from referee Kavanagh changed the course of the game.

First he gave a free kick for handball against Bruno that he alone had spotted and allowed the home side to gain ten yards, Antony Kay heading home Josh Murphy's cross. Then he showed two yellow cards in quick succession to Dons defender Kyle McFadzean, which should have allowed Albion to see out the game comfortably, especially as Hemed shot wide from a pass by substitute LuaLua, and then had a goal mystifyingly disallowed.

Kavanagh's final intervention was to award a last-minute penalty to the home side for handball against Stephens as he cleared a corner by Carl Baker, on the advice of his assistant. Rosenior and LuaLua were booked for delaying the game before Baker took the kick. It grazed the outside of Stockdale's right-hand post and went behind.

Two points that might have been lost were in the bank after all. Surely the dream of promotion must now become a reality?

CHAPTER 6

THE SPRING OFFENSIVE

As Carl Baker's penalty hit the advertising hoardings at Stadium MK instead of the net, there was bedlam in the Brighton dugout and technical area. Colin Calderwood punched the air and the other Brighton coaches and substitutes went wild with delight. One figure was immobile, gazing out at the pitch before turning slowly to walk back to the bench: the dark-suited Hughton.

Hughton might have written 'Keep calm and carry on' as his own plan for life. The knee-slide down the touchline as practised by Paolo Di Canio or José Mourinho is not for Hughton, who confines his goal celebrations to an occasional fist pump – double on special occasions – and a turn before he collects himself.

Whole threads on fan message boards are dedicated to satirising his restrained reactions during matches. One began: 'He put his water bottle down so firmly that there was a ripple on the surface. Surely the FA must now take action.'

The reserve is natural, Hughton insists:

'And more so as I've become more experienced. Probably, although not to the same extent as other managers, there would be clips of me at Newcastle certainly being more emotional, jumping up in the air, but still not to the levels of an Antonio Conte.

'That's my character, that's my personality, and definitely not a lack of passion. But it has also been a conscious effort throughout my managerial career to try during the game to concentrate on the things that matter. Spending half the game berating the referee or the fourth official would be difficult for me because I can't do that and also concentrate on the game and any tough decisions I might have to make. And that's not to say anything against anyone who does things differently. Everyone manages according to their own personality. Some are very emotional people and I'm not the most emotional person anyway. So generally what you see is how I am.'

His calm demeanour in the technical area and his thoughtful and measured comments in press conferences disguise a steely resolve. 'What you see on the touchline is an accurate picture of him, but people underestimate how determined and strong he is,' Calderwood said.

'He's tough. He can be hard on the players, as hard as any manager I've dealt with. But he never comes away from his work ethic, never. And his biggest asset is his honesty to everyone. You know where you stand even if it's not what you want to hear on occasion. He tells people his team selection, what he expects of them and where he sees them, now and in the future.'

The players responded to Hughton's honesty and tough love. 'He shouts when things are going wrong,' Stephens said.

'It's great that he can do that. He's a calm character but when things are not going right, he makes it known. He's got the respect of every player and every member of staff. He has since he walked through the door, purely because of his pedigree at this level.

'We're on the training pitch every week working on how we're going to play. We don't really change for anybody. We play the way we play and what he thinks suits us. He has got us playing the way he believes and that is reaping its rewards.'

'In football terms, he's very consistent in his message,' Rosenior said.

'When he is your manager, you know your job. But before we even talk about tactics or motivation or anything like that, it's important to say that he's just a very, very good man. His honesty, his integrity – there's no edge, no side to him beyond what you see. In my experience, that's quite rare in football.

'When you have that, you get people onside very quickly. Not just the players, but the fans and everyone who works at the club. He wants to make you successful and that's very different to just doing a job for somebody. Chris is someone who all the lads respect enormously and nobody wants to let down.'

Sidwell added:

'I've been fortunate enough to work under some of the world's best managers and he rates at the very top. The way he goes about things, goes into every game with thought and in detail, his training methods, the way he keeps the squad together – he has been fortunate in that he hasn't really had to manage the dressing room because it manages itself – but he has been tactically spot on.'

Bruno only had foreign managers to compare to Hughton, even at Brighton. 'The gaffer is my first British manager,' he said.

'The ideas of football are different here from in Spain, but it's been an experience. Gus was very South American, talking a lot. Óscar was quiet but had lots of ideas about football. Sami was so unlucky because we didn't have the right squad to play how he wanted. He couldn't show how he really was. But Chris, how he has changed the club is unbelievable. He takes all the decisions but he is always open to listen to whatever. He'll think about it but even if he isn't going to do it or thinks opposite to you, he will explain why. His door is always open, too.'

Although he is proud to have played for and helped coach the Republic of Ireland, Hughton is a Londoner, born on 11 December 1958 to a Ghanaian father, William, and Irish mother, Christine. 'I was brought up in the East End, in a very multicultural area, and a very working-class area,' he said.

'Although I was born in Forest Gate, I grew up in Upton Park, and the family still lives there. As a child I went to Ghana once, went to Ireland but certainly didn't go regularly, so if I'm looking for an affiliation with either, probably I didn't have that, although there's an Irish part of me and a Ghanaian part. Those were the days when your parents worked, didn't take many holidays and didn't go back home too often because they had mortgages and bills to pay. In those days there wasn't much left over.

'So I was a normal East London kid who played football and wanted to do well at school, because that was the way my mum and dad had brought me up. They were parents of that era who worked hard and wanted the best for you, passed on their values. My dad originally came over to study medicine and then met my mum, they had children and then you've got to support the family. He worked in the post office for forty-odd years and my mum was a dinner lady in my junior school.'

Not surprisingly in view of his background, his political views tend to the left, and he wrote a column in *News Line*, the newspaper of the Workers Revolutionary Party, while at Spurs – even though he passes this off as the idea of 'journalist friends'. 'I've been a member of the Labour Party for thirty years,' he said.

'My beliefs have always been governed by my upbringing, that people have a right to good education, free, high-quality health care and clean, safe social housing.

'I'm not so much a political person but I do take an interest and I believe in a fair, caring and diverse society. But it tends to be who we're playing in the next game that keeps me up at night. This job consumes you, it takes over your life.'

He went to the same school, St Bonaventure's in Newham, as England striker Jermain Defoe, wingers John Chiedozie and Nigel Callaghan, future Leyton Orient manager Martin Ling and Arsenal's Chuba Akpom, who later joined Albion on loan.

'When I was in school there used to be pictures of the gaffer there,' Akpom said.

'I always tried to keep up to date with what he was doing. The kids used him as an inspiration and motivation. I did as well, seeing someone come from the same area and the same school as me to become such a big and successful person. It's nice to be here working with him. I never thought it would happen so soon. It is a bit strange, but I'm glad it has happened, glad that we can both relate.'

Hughton was already on Tottenham's radar at school and started training with them at thirteen, as a left-sided midfield player. When he left 'St Bon's' three years later, Spurs declined to offer him a contract and asked him to stay on as an amateur. He therefore combined training two nights a week and playing for the youth team and reserves with a four-year apprenticeship as a lift engineer – a line of work that prepared him for football's ups and downs.

After two years, Tottenham were impressed enough with Hughton's progress to ask him to turn professional, but he decided to finish his apprenticeship and accept only a part-time deal. He signed on full time once he had qualified and made his first-team debut three games into his first season as a pro. He eventually played in 398 games for the club over eleven seasons, winning the FA Cup in 1981 and 1982 and the UEFA Cup in 1984.

And, as he was keen to point out in the build-up to an FA Cup tie against Arsenal in his first months at Brighton, he had scored twice from left-back in a 5–0 derby win over the Gunners in 1983. A grainy clip of that game shows Hughton starting and finishing the move for the first goal of the game and later playing a pair of one-twos before scoring the second from 15 yards. Both goals were scored from left-back with his right foot, but the big hair and short shorts are also remarkable.

'Some of our players like Anthony Knockaert will look back on these days in twenty years' time and wonder where he got his hair-cut from, or how baggy those shorts are,' he laughs.

'But I look back with fondness because it was a good era to play in. Any era is a good one if that is when you are playing because that's what you want to be doing, that's your passion.

'But it was a good time as regards the relationship you could have with the supporters. Everything you did on or off the pitch wasn't scrutinised and you could possibly drink together after a game, possibly somewhere local and maybe with supporters. But it was different, of course. When I made my debut we only had one sub. Players now can't comprehend that.

'Whenever I see pictures of myself I just see someone at a really enjoyable time of his life and with that will come some funny hair-cuts and very short shorts. Every now and again someone will show me one I haven't seen and that is great.'

He became the first black footballer to represent Ireland, winning fifty-three caps, and also played for West Ham United and Brent-ford. He returned to White Hart Lane as a coach and had played or worked for every Spurs manager from the legendary Bill Nicholson to Martin Jol by the time he left in 2007 – including David Pleat, Terry Venables, Ossie Ardiles, George Graham and Glenn Hoddle. But he names Keith Burkinshaw as his greatest influence.

'As a player, Keith's time as manager was my, and the club's, most successful period for a while,' he said.

'We won two FA Cups, a UEFA Cup and got to a League Cup final, all in four years. And that was Keith. In that era, the way he wanted to play was forward-thinking, and he brought Ossie Ardiles and Ricky Villa from Argentina, which was incredibly brave.

'Later, when I was involved in the coaching, Martin Jol was probably the one I worked closest with. He'd played in England for West Brom and Coventry, but because he'd been out of the English game for a while, although he'd coached and managed in Europe, he relied on me a little. Well, 'relied' probably isn't the word, because he was a very good manager, and very definite about what he wanted. We finished fifth that year, and it should have been fourth, and I think that was the start of the modern Spurs, finishing in good positions in the league, and expecting to. So from the coaching aspect it would be Martin.

'But there wasn't one manager that I didn't learn from. From Christian Gross, although he was only there a year and a half, I learned a lot. He came with a very organised Swiss-German mentality, with a philosophy and structure to his training and put more emphasis on it as a means to give you the best chance of winning games. He was aware that the margins are very fine and you could improve your chances with better, more organised work in the week. Historically, our game was always more physical, direct, high tempo. You put so much into the games that probably the training week was just the build-up to the game.'

He had not always intended to go into coaching.

'When I was about twenty-eight, it hit me that I'd have to do something afterwards and I would like to stay in the game, as a coach. But in my younger years if you spoke to people and asked if they saw me as manager material, probably a large majority would have said no. I wasn't very vocal, although I certainly got more vocal as a defender as I got older. As a defender, you spend a lot of your time organising and being organised. But as a younger player I'd have been one of the quieter ones.'

• • •

Part of every coach's learning process involves getting the sack, and he first experienced it along with Jol in 2007. He moved on to Newcastle, becoming first-team coach and later assistant manager, with former Spurs defender Calderwood his successor as coach. As he had on two occasions at Tottenham, he had spells as Newcastle caretaker manager, including the period immediately after their relegation from the Premier League in 2009.

Following a memorable and potentially disastrous 6–1 pre-season defeat at Leyton Orient, senior players decided that others were not up for a battle to win promotion and Hughton wisely listened to their advice. The local paper, *The Chronicle*, wrote: 'Caretaker manager Chris Hughton is an honourable man doing an honest job, trying to provide the only thing approaching direction as his club hurtles deeper into the mire.'

Hughton did better than that, imposing order on chaos and leading a remodelled team not only to instant promotion but also the title. After his third manager of the month award in November, Newcastle made his job permanent, but that word has little meaning in football. Despite a sound start to the following season back in the top division, including a 6–0 thrashing of Aston Villa, a 5–1 derby victory over Sunderland and away wins at Everton and Arsenal, Newcastle managing director Derek Llambias decided in December that 'an individual with more managerial experience [was] needed to take the club forward'.

Players, coaches, supporters and pundits were naturally outraged that a decent and popular man – who also had an excellent 55.7 win percentage – had been dismissed. Yet he has never displayed any resentment. 'There's a little bit of that in anybody, but it's not something I carry around,' he said. 'It's not nice but any bad feeling you might have was taken away by the reaction of the Newcastle supporters, and that helped. If you feel that you couldn't have done any more, that also helps.'

If Hughton thought that his next job, at freshly relegated Birmingham City, might prove more stable, he was disabused of the notion after only a week when Carson Yeung, the club president, was arrested on suspicion of money-laundering. One positive was an even freer hand to manage as he liked, which was helpful with a Europa League campaign – the legacy of the previous season's League Cup win – to fit into the already-challenging Championship programme.

After a marathon 62-game season, Blues finished fourth but lost to Blackpool in the play-offs, and Hughton accepted an offer from Norwich City to succeed Paul Lambert. The Canaries finished eleventh in his first season at Carrow Road but the board lost its nerve a year later despite being five points clear of relegation with five to play. Norwich went down anyway, losing four and drawing one of their remaining games, the first, and most winnable, 1–0 at Fulham, where the man of the match, in a poetic twist, was the home team's goalkeeper – David Stockdale.

After that, Hughton turned down a number of offers to be assistant manager at various clubs, including some in the Premier League. Instead, he took a course in corporate governance, studying boardroom structures and issues of diversity at the top levels of businesses.

He had seen and experienced racism on and off the field as the only black player in the Tottenham team, and willingly accepts the responsibility of being a standard-bearer for black and minority-ethnic (BAME) coaches, a shockingly under-represented group in top-level football in Britain. 'I'm always conscious of that and it's something I'm very proud to do,' he said. 'When you speak to potential black and ethnic coaches, one aspect that they always speak about is role models in the game. They would like to see more representation at a higher level. And any part that I can play in that, I am delighted to do.'

At times, he has been the only BAME manager in the 92-strong league structure. And, although initially sceptical, he has become a supporter of the introduction in British football of an equivalent of the Rooney Rule in American football's NFL, which stipulates that at least one suitably qualified BAME candidate must be on the shortlist for any coaching position.

'We're in an age of big business and I'm sure there will be future legislation about the workplace,' he told Donald McRae of *The Guardian* in 2017.

'All of the stakeholders in our game appear to have an enthusiasm for change. You see it with the big broadcasters. We're broadcasting English football all over the world, including many African countries. I feel people in the game want to see diverse players and multiracial cultures – which means [black] people in better positions at the stadium, doing the actual interviewing in the boardrooms, because the game on the field is multiracial.'

• • •

The dramatic victory away to MK Dons was followed by another international break and then a home match with leaders Burnley – once again chosen by Sky Sports for the Saturday early kick-off time that never seemed to bring the team much good fortune. Burnley were a solid, physical team, which was no surprise to anyone who had ever seen their manager, Sean Dyche, play for Chesterfield or Millwall. They were playing well, and Andre Gray was repaying the £9 million that the Lancashire club had invested to prise him from Brentford.

The previous evening, Middlesbrough had moved into second place with a 3–2 win away to QPR – a reminder of how costly those two points dropped at Loftus Road might prove – but a win would take Albion back above Boro and to within a point of Burnley. Hughton's men went out to try to get it in front of a 29,683 crowd, 28,050 of whom were home fans, said to be the largest such number to attend the Amex so far.

Kayal and Burnley's notorious Joey Barton immediately began a personal battle for control of the midfield, but Albion got on top first and Stephens put them in front on the half-hour after a Burnley defender could only head Knockaert's corner on into his path.

Dyche claimed that he had seen a weakness in Brighton's defending of set plays and he appeared to be proved right four minutes later as Michael Keane nodded on a corner from David Jones to former Seagulls loanee Stephen Ward. He held off Bruno's attempt to clear and Gray pounced to score from three yards.

Baldock injured a hamstring and was replaced by Wilson before half-time but Albion still went back in front as Murphy ran at the defence before finding Knockaert. The Frenchman sent Ward the wrong way twice before hitting a shot off Keane's heel and over the diving Tom Heaton.

Albion could have scored a third on several occasions and Burnley were lucky not to be reduced to ten men when Barton floored Kayal in a challenge then landed on the Israel midfielder's leg as he jumped over him. The crowd saw it as an intentional stamp but referee Craig Pawson took a different view and Barton escaped with a warning.

Burnley made the most of it with a determined push for an equaliser, and Hemed was replaced by Sidwell as Hughton attempted to gain more midfield control. But Hemed's value in defending set plays had been sacrificed and it was to prove costly in the dying minutes.

The visitors actually had the ball in the Albion goal, if not the net, when Keane met Matt Taylor's corner. Replays showed that his header had been half-blocked by Murphy and had crossed the line before Sidwell hooked it clear, but the officials failed to spot it – as they did a foul by Keane on Goldson before he won the header. It was only a temporary reprieve and seconds later Albion got their marking all wrong from another corner by Taylor, and Keane was unchallenged as he headed in.

Hughton praised his side's performance against 'a top, top team' but knew that it was two more points dropped. 'My biggest disappointment is that we needed to take our chances more,' he said. 'It is frustrating and it was a game we should have won. Burnley have a physicality up front and they can mix up their game, but we could have put the match miles out of sight.'

The relentlessness of the Championship ensured that there would soon be a chance to make up for it and it came away to Birmingham City three days later. Blues went ahead against the run of play thanks to a rare error by Stockdale, who failed to catch a straightforward cross from Jacques Maghoma, allowing Kyle Lafferty to score from five yards. Albion hit back before the interval when Skalák, whose deliveries of set plays was becoming an essential part of the team's armoury, sent over a free kick from the left and Goldson headed his first goal for the club past Tomasz Kuszczak.

And it was Skalák again whose corner from the right was headed in from six yards by Dunk in front of the travelling fans. Hemed was denied what would have been a spectacular third when his overhead volley from a cross by Bruno was palmed away by Kuszczak. And Wilson was unlucky as he raced away late on with Kuszczak up for a corner, his shot towards an unguarded goal hitting Paul Caddis, the covering defender.

Skalák and Dunk combined again six days later in yet another televised game, away to Nottingham Forest. The goal was almost a replica of Goldson's at Birmingham, Skalák's free kick from the left nodded in by Dunk at the far post.

But an almost identical situation was Brighton's undoing as Dexter Blackstock got free of his marker to head in a free kick by Henri Lansbury. Blackstock then caught Goldson in possession and fed Lansbury, only for the Forest man's shot to clear the crossbar by several feet. At that stage, a draw looked a likely and, arguably, a fair result. But too many draws had already been the story of the season.

The City Ground has been the scene of some memorable Brighton matches. A goal there by Gerry Ryan and a penalty save by Graham Moseley on 17 November 1979 against the European Cup holders gave bottom-of-the-table Albion their first away win in the top flight and ended Brian Clough's team's run of fifty unbeaten home games. Leonardo Ulloa's header in the dying seconds of the 2013/14 season put Óscar García's team into the play-offs.

Now they needed another late goal, and Knockaert, on as a substitute, set it up with ninety minutes on the clock. When the Frenchman received the ball from Bruno, there were three defenders barring his route into the penalty area. He danced between two of them, shrugged off another challenge on the corner of the six-yard box and eventually ran into heavier traffic. But the ball ran loose to fellow substitute Sidwell, who hit a low shot into the corner.

It was Sidwell's first goal for the club for over thirteen years. His previous strike had also been late and important, the equaliser in the eighty-ninth minute of a 2–2 draw against Burnley at Withdean on 28 December 2002, his second goal within ninety seconds, both from passes by Zamora.

Having ensured that the gap to second place did not widen, Albion now had the chance to take the initiative with a Friday evening home fixture against Fulham, when a win would take them above Burnley into second place before the Clarets and leaders Middlesbrough played on Saturday.

The match followed what was to become a familiar pattern in games against the Cottagers – early dominance from the Londoners with Albion coming back to win. And how. After a promising opening from Fulham, Hemed scored from a penalty after Richard Stearman had pushed Wilson as he ran into the penalty area. Stearman was, perhaps correctly, aggrieved that Wilson had fallen rather easily, and his vehement protests risked a card from referee Andy Woolmer, who was unmoved.

Hemed got his second before half-time with a header from Knockaert's inswinging free kick, and in the second half Skalák's corner found its way to Bruno, who controlled the ball with his right foot and drove it past Marcus Bettinelli with his left. Hemed completed his hat-trick, only the second in Amex stadium history, when he poked in a deflected shot from Stephens despite appeals from the Fulham defenders for offside. Knockaert, receiving from Kayal, curled a fifth around Bettinelli to make it 5–0.

Burnley and Middlesbrough both managed narrow wins the following day to nudge Albion back down to third place, but Albion had improved their goal difference, which might be a factor, especially with the final fixture of the season being away to Boro. They had also guaranteed a play-off place at least, which had been the staff's pre-season target.

And that goal difference received another boost in the next game as the spring offensive gathered momentum at home to QPR. On Saturday 16 April, the club had released a shortlist of a dozen goals for supporters to choose from when voting for the club's goal-of-the-season award. On the Tuesday, Jiří Skalák forced the organisers to add another candidate to the roll.

Knockaert had already scored a beauty, a free kick over the QPR wall late in an even first half, to prove that the Albion now had more difference-makers than most of their rivals, but it paled by comparison to the Czech's epic first goal for the club.

There seemed no immediate danger to the visitors' goal when Bruno sent a long pass forward six minutes into the second half and QPR defender Grant Hall, a former Brighton youth team product, nodded the ball back into midfield. But Skalák ran onto it and hit it first time from over 25 yards. The ball screamed past the right hand of the diving Alex Smithies and high into the net and the Czech launched a triumphant knee-slide in front of the North Stand.

There were more goals to come. Goldson looped in a header from a corner by Knockaert, who then made it 4–0 with a low shot after some interplay with Wilson on the right.

The same evening, Burnley and Middlesbrough met at Turf

Moor, and it was difficult to know what result would be best to hope for. In the event, the teams drew 1–1, Keane again scoring a ninetieth-minute equaliser. The upshot was that, with three games to go, Albion were behind second-placed Burnley only on goal difference and two points behind Boro, the leaders. And after the next match, all three were level on 87 points, Boro drawing at home to Ipswich while Albion won at relegated Charlton.

Not that the game at the Valley was without incident or difficulty. Home fans were in open revolt against unpopular Belgian owner Roland Duchâtelet and the board, and after only a minute a not-unexpected protest began in the form of balloons and beach balls thrown onto the pitch, which took around six minutes to clear. Needless to say, visiting fans knew how their Charlton counterparts were feeling and were in no position to raise any objection. Indeed, many had joined in their pre-match demonstrations.

Fortunately, the delay did not disrupt the team and, eight minutes in, Dunk volleyed Skalák's long free kick across goal for Baldock to finish coolly. But Charlton had given warning of their abilities at the Amex earlier in the season and levelled six minutes after half-time as the defence went missing and allowed Jóhann Berg Guðmundsson a shot at an empty net.

That forced the visitors to raise their game and Kayal set up the in-form Skalák to bend a shot into the top corner from eight yards in front of the Albion fans in the Jimmy Seed Stand behind the goal. Hemed added a third from a penalty after Knockaert had been crudely fouled by Alou Diarra.

The next evening, the Player Awards dinner was held at the Amex Stadium, and Kayal picked up the player of the season gong after receiving 41 per cent of supporters' votes, ahead of Bruno (36 per cent), David Stockdale and Tomer Hemed. Connor Goldson won the young player of the season vote, decided by club staff. Not surprisingly, Skalák's strike against QPR was goal of the season, collecting 85 per cent of the votes.

The Sarah Watts Inspiration Award, named after one of the club's most loyal and visible fans and a great campaigner during the fight for approval for the stadium, who had died in January 2015 at forty-nine, went to the first response emergency services at the Shoreham air disaster. David Stockdale was presented with his PFA Community Champion trophy for his support for the Grimstone family, and Bruno received a trophy for being named in the Football League's team of the season.

Then it was back down to work at the training ground with two matches to play – barring another trip to the play-offs. Again, the programme for the penultimate weekend was altered to suit live television. Middlesbrough played away to Birmingham on Friday evening, while Albion hosted Derby on bank holiday Monday afternoon. And when Boro blinked first, drawing 2–2 at St Andrew's after leading 2–1, Hughton's men knew that four points from their last two games would mean automatic promotion. Beat Derby, and a draw at the Riverside would be enough.

But when Derby are involved, things are seldom that easy for Brighton.

CHAPTER 7

HOUSE OF CARDS

A record Amex crowd of 30,292 for the match against Derby made for an excellent atmosphere, and the hope was for an early goal to settle any nerves.

It almost came after thirteen minutes when Knockaert sent a free kick over the Derby wall towards an unguarded portion of the net, but Derby defender Jason Shackell had anticipated the danger and got enough of his head to the ball to divert it over the crossbar. And although the team played some ambitious stuff, the goal they craved refused to come. Just before half-time, Dunk played a loose pass that Will Hughes intercepted and, trying to retrieve the situation, the Albion defender fouled Hughes and was booked.

Both teams made changes in the second half, but Derby's paid off first. Andreas Weimann, who had enjoyed purple scoring patches when at Aston Villa, netted almost as soon as he came on, taking a pass from Hughes and shooting hard and low. Stockdale blocked but the rebound fell kindly for the Austrian and although – or perhaps because – he did not hit his shot cleanly, the ball bounced past Stockdale's attempt to recover and went in.

At that stage, with nineteen minutes to go, Albion were a point behind Middlesbrough and a draw would not improve the situation, as they would still be behind on goal difference and require victory at the Riverside to go up automatically. So they still wanted to beat Derby and could ill-afford to concede again.

It was with this in mind that Dunk lunged into a rash and desperate challenge on Craig Bryson with seven minutes to go. As soon as he failed to win the ball, Dunk realised what he had done and held his head in his hands. A second yellow card was inevitable, and suspension for the game at Middlesbrough. And as it was his second red card of the season, he would also miss the first play-off game if it came to that.

Albion still pressed for a goal and, with Stockdale up for a 94th-minute corner, it arrived, substitute Wilson's angled effort hitting Marcus Olsson and looping in. At least the unbeaten run had been stretched to thirteen games, but at a cost. A lap of honour for the players and coaching staff is traditional after the last home match of the season, but this was a subdued affair.

'There's a part of us that's very disappointed today, but that's only because of the levels this group of players has reached and where we've come,' Hughton told the fans over the PA system.

'We've had tremendous support all season – not only here at the Amex, which has been outstanding, but also away from home.

'A lot of supporters throughout the country don't realise that we have some local-ish games, but there aren't many. Our supporters have to travel far and wide every second week and every mid-week – and you as a support have been absolutely outstanding.'

Later, he told the club website:

'If somebody had told us at the beginning of the season that we had to go and win at Middlesbrough in the last game to get promotion, then we would have bitten their hands off. Most challenges we have faced we have risen to this season, and this is going to be a very big challenge but one that we will look forward to.

'They are at home, and that means they will rightly be the favourites, but favourites don't always win football matches. They are a good side and we have got no doubts that it will be a very tough task, but a wonderful challenge for this group of players. We will have a good week and make sure that we do everything right and look forward to a very tough game on Saturday.'

On the eve of the Boro match, Hughton was named Championship manager of the month for April and Knockaert was player of the month, but the only prize worth considering was victory on Teesside. The game had taken on the status of a play-off final – albeit with one side needing only a draw – and the sort of sums usually mentioned in advance of those Wembley occasions began to be brought out. Whoever went up would be an estimated £170 million better off thanks to TV revenue, increased commercial opportunities and parachute payments.

Hughton recalled Greer in place of Dunk, while the main question about the home side was whether the defensively minded manager Aitor Karanka would play cautiously, knowing that a draw was enough, or go out for the win.

The match was deemed important enough for a Premier League referee, Mike Dean, to be assigned to the fixture, but this move was greeted with misgivings by supporters. Many feared that the game would not be refereed by normal Championship standards, and that officials used to the higher echelons unconsciously favour the 'bigger' clubs that they may have visited before on Premier League business – the example of the late spot kick awarded to Derby County by Lee Mason late in the 2–2 draw at the iPro Stadium sprang readily to mind.

At first, the officiating was the least of Albion's worries as Boro made a fast start. Albion were on their heels and conceding free kicks. From one of these, taken by Gastón Ramírez, David Nugent found himself unmarked beyond the far post to knock the ball across goal for Cristhian Stuani, a controversial selection by Karanka, to score his first goal in twenty-two games from three yards out.

And for long periods, a second goal for the home side looked far more likely than an Albion equaliser. Boro had conceded only seven goals at home all season and were confidently repelling any and all attempts by Albion to mount a response. And when they broke, only a block by Goldson prevented Stuani from volleying a second.

'It was agony, horrible, sitting there watching and not being able to do anything to help,' the suspended Dunk said.

'It was a stupid second booking [against Derby] and I think I beat myself up about it for the whole summer. I finally forgot about it when we came back for pre-season and we talked about our goals again. I thought, "Let's do it this year."

'It's got to be up there among my worst moments in football because of how close we were and missing out on goal difference. I was thinking, "If I was out there, could I help?" and it wasn't a good time.'

Hughton's answer was to replace an ineffective Baldock with Wilson for the second half, and now Albion began to gain a foothold. After fifty-five minutes, they equalised with a goal that was uncannily similar to Boro's. Again it was a free kick, bent in by Knockaert, to the far post, where a man was unmarked. This time it was Stephens, heading over goalkeeper Dimitrios Konstantopoulos and in.

Then came the incident that was to define the game in Albion minds, as Stephens and Ramírez closed in on a bouncing ball in midfield. Stephens got there first, touching the ball away from the Uruguayan, whose late challenge brought his leg into contact with Stephens's studs. Ramírez collapsed, writhing on the turf, and Dean, in a decision that can only have been based on Ramírez's reaction rather than anything he had seen, reached for a yellow card.

Ramírez, incredibly, dashed the card from Dean's hand, surely risking dismissal. But instead of sending Ramírez off, Dean looked at a gash on the Uruguayan's leg and now, to the astonishment of the Albion players, showed Stephens red.

Stephens and his teammates stared at Dean in disbelief, but his mind was made up. Instead of being on the back foot, Boro had now been handed a priceless advantage and only a superb reflex save by Stockdale prevented Albert Adomah putting the home side back in front and out of Albion's reach. Hughton went for broke, throwing LuaLua on for Greer, but to no avail and the game finished 1–1.

'There are always going to be big moments in the season that you look back on, Burnley at the Amex, being ahead and conceding two or three minutes into injury time,' Hughton said.

'I always believe, or want to believe, that things balance out. We beat MK Dons at the Amex and got away with a stone-cold certainty of a penalty that Dunky gave away and I couldn't believe we'd got away with it.

'But still to this day Murphy at Bolton was never a sending-off, and neither was Dale Stephens at Middlesbrough – every time I watch it, and particularly the way that it happened with the referee. We found out later that it was the linesman who made the decision, and we looked at it time and time again and the linesman was a considerable way away from the play and at a different angle. I didn't and I don't agree with that one. But at that stage it was still a game that we needed to win at 1–1. We still hadn't done enough. It would have been worse if we had been winning and he'd been sent off and then they'd equalised.'

At the final whistle, Hughton shook Karanka's hand and as the Boro manager turned to blow kisses to the directors' box, he walked into Calderwood's shoulder, which the assistant manager had not made much effort to pull out of the way. Karanka remonstrated with Hughton rather than taking the matter up with the Scot. Albion fans noted bitterly that Ramírez, who had received oxygen after the Stephens incident and left the field on a stretcher, was now apparently fit enough to join Boro's promotion celebrations.

• • •

As Boro rejoiced, the Albion players had to gather their strength for a two-legged play-off semi-final against Sheffield Wednesday, the first match at Hillsborough the following Friday – ominously, Friday the 13th. It would be the club's third trip to the play-offs in four seasons and the previous two were not experiences that the fans or players wanted to relive.

Hughton would certainly be without Dunk in Sheffield, but there was a chance that Stephens's red card could be overturned on appeal, on the grounds of wrongful dismissal and excessive punishment. Video evidence would surely prove that the midfield player had not deserved a card of any colour.

Sadly, but predictably in the light of the club's recent experience of appeals, the FA upheld the decision of the referee at a tribunal on the Tuesday, and Stephens would now serve a three-match ban, ruling him out of both legs of the semi-final and either the Wembley final, if the team won through, or the first game of the 2016/17 season.

Although Albion had finished the season 15 points ahead of Wednesday with a points total that would have guaranteed automatic promotion eight times in the previous twelve seasons, it was difficult to regard them as favourites at Hillsborough. Not only were they without two key players, but Hughton and company had also been fully stretched both physically and psychologically by the Derby and Middlesbrough matches. Wednesday, in contrast, had qualified for the play-offs with games to spare and had had the luxury of being able to rest players. What sort of difference that would make was soon in evidence.

Greer continued in place of Dunk, while Sidwell, Skalák and Bong came in for Stephens, Murphy and Rosenior, and the early signs were promising as Baldock had a shot deflected wide and Hemed hit the post with a header from the corner. When what had looked at first glance to be a perfectly good goal by Fernando Forestieri was ruled out by referee Andre Marriner for offside, it seemed that Friday the 13th might be unlucky for Wednesday rather than Albion.

How premature that was. After thirty-eight minutes, both Hemed and Goldson, who had been receiving treatment for injuries, had to be replaced, by Wilson and Rosenior, with Bruno moving to the centre of defence. And just before half-time, Wednesday scored a goal that counted, Ross Wallace cutting in from the right to hit a 25-yard daisycutter through a crowd of players – including an offside Gary Hooper in Stockdale's eyeline – and in.

Now the Hillsborough crowd was in full voice and the Wednesday players were full of confidence. And it got worse in the second half. Sidwell went down and had to be replaced by Richie Towell and then Knockaert appeared to pull a muscle and departed on a stretcher, leaving Albion with only ten men. In the circumstances, the visiting fans were relieved that Brighton conceded only once more, Kieran Lee taking a pass and turning into the penalty area before shooting beyond Stockdale. Even when a man down, Hughton's men still tried to press forward and Skalák and Baldock went close, but there was no miracle ending and the team suffered its first defeat in fifteen matches.

The following day, Bloom issued a rallying cry. 'Over the last nine months, our players have been outstanding – and they deserve to achieve something on the back of their superb efforts this season,' he said.

'They have made this one of the most memorable seasons in the club's 115-year history. In almost any other year, our points tally would have proved enough for automatic promotion, but on Monday night that counts for nothing.

'Our players were magnificent on Friday night in the most difficult of circumstances. We hardly conceded a chance while playing the last thirty minutes with ten men, having had four key players injured during the game. This has given us a real possibility to progress, and one the players are determined to take.

'We've faced bigger battles, longer odds and tougher tasks in our time, yet still come through to triumph against the odds. We are Brighton, we know the deal: more often than not, we have to do things the hard way.

'Throughout our history we've taken knocks, setbacks and injustice in our stride and come back stronger, time and time again. Let's do that now, players and fans together. This group of players have a belief that they can still achieve our ultimate goal. They know it won't be easy, and they know success never comes easy. It will take huge amounts of spirit and passion from the players and the fans for us to win through on Monday night. Our fans were once again outstanding on Friday, and I implore every single fan to get right behind the players throughout the game. We need you to pack the Amex, turn it blue and white and create a fantastic atmosphere.

'Sing, be loud, make the Amex a bigger cauldron of noise than it has ever been. Don't let up from the first minute to the last – this will be the inspiration that will help the players get the result that we all deserve to help us to Wembley.'

Supporters wondered what sort of patched-up team Hughton would be forced to field in the second leg. In the event, only Hemed and Goldson had failed to recover from the injuries sustained in the first game. Dunk was back and Sidwell and Knockaert, against all the odds, were both in the starting line-up. 'When you saw them the day after the first leg, they had no chance,' Hughton said. 'And they both played.'

There had been plenty of discussion about ways of building the stadium atmosphere. At a previous play-off semi-final against rivals Crystal Palace, every fan had been given cardboard clackers, which attracted criticism. In the end, fans were given flags, and it was clear as the teams came out that it was a well-judged decision as the seats became undulating blocks of blue and white.

From the first whistle, the fans created a bowl of noise that overshadowed the decibel level at Hillsborough, and the players responded, tearing into Wednesday from the kick-off. Sidwell and Wilson had shots blocked on the six-yard line, and Knockaert hit the inside of the near post with a floated free kick after he had been brought down by Glenn Loovens a yard outside the penalty area. Minutes later, from a similar position, he hit the ball low under the wall as it jumped, only for keeper Keiren Westwood to anticipate.

Sidwell was a revelation, driving forward from midfield as he had done at Withdean under Steve Coppell so many years earlier.

Baldock drew a fingertip save from Westwood with a 22-yard effort. Wilson nodded on Skalák's cross but Knockaert headed wide.

Finally, the breakthrough. Daniel Pudil brought down Bruno on the right and Knockaert flighted the free kick into the six-yard area. Bruno got the faintest touch at the near post, flicking the ball past defenders to the far post, where Dunk gleefully volleyed in. Wednesday were rocking and, with only nineteen minutes gone, their lead looked precarious.

'It was very difficult to pick the players up after Middlesbrough,' Calderwood said.

'They realised that the opportunity was still there in the play-offs, but going to Sheffield Wednesday we'd lost two influential players, we knew, but to start the game and lose four to injury was really, really difficult. But the second leg was almost a magical night. It still remains a special match for me. The performance level of the team was something you couldn't help but be proud of.'

As Calderwood says, almost a magical night – but not quite.

With twenty-eight minutes gone, on a rare Wednesday break, Wallace floated in a hopeful inswinging cross from the right that was aimed, if it was aimed at all, squarely at Dunk's forehead. Hooper, with no chance of reaching the cross himself, blatantly pushed Dunk out of the way as he went to head clear and the ball sailed on into the far corner of the net. The defenders waited for the whistle to signal a free kick for Hooper's push, but another Premier League referee, Roger East, had somehow seen nothing wrong and awarded a goal. Albion now needed to score at least twice more.

'The Middlesbrough game was so tough and we still think that refereeing decision was wrong,' Barber said later.

'I can't remember a thing about the drive back, and it took six hours. I came away from the Sheffield Wednesday game really disappointed but not very down because I felt we had a real chance of getting it back. We managed to get two of the four players who had been injured fit, and the first forty-five minutes were the best I've seen us play, an unbelievably good first half. And yet we couldn't get the ball in the net enough times. And there was another terrible refereeing decision.

'I later had a meeting with Mike Riley, the manager of the Professional Game Match Officials Board, and Dave Allison, the head of refereeing for the Football League. I asked: "Are you sure that parachuting Premier League referees into these games is the right thing to do? Because we've now been on the wrong end, in two weeks, of a poor decision by Mike Dean, and a poor decision again by Roger East, and both have had fundamental impacts on the game.

'"Are Premier League referees used to the way Championship games are played? Are they used to the players? If Mike Dean had known that Dale Stephens had never been sent off in his career, had never had a reputation as a malicious tackler of any kind, would that have influenced him towards a yellow card rather than a red? If the referee against Wednesday had been more attuned to the pace and style of the Championship, would he have been in a better position to see the push by Hooper, or would he have known how unlikely it was that Lewis Dunk would miss a header unless he'd been fouled?"

'I didn't criticise, I just asked the question and also questioned the impact that parachuting Premier League referees into top Championship games was having on Championship referees. Was it sending them the message that they weren't good enough? So for two or three reasons they were not the right decisions.'

'I say it was a foul but the lino and the ref didn't,' Dunk said.

'The first half an hour of that game was the best game I've been involved in. Some of the passing and the play was unbelievable and you could see from the Sheffield Wednesday players that they were panicking, but then they scored the goal and it changed the game. We had so much more to do then.'

At first it seemed Albion still might prevail. Wilson took Kayal's pass but could not squeeze his shot past Westwood's right arm. Dunk and Baldock saw further efforts cleared from the jaws of the goal.

With men committed forward, Albion were vulnerable to counter-attacks and Stockdale saved well from a header by Hooper. LuaLua was sent on and Dunk pushed up front, but the ball resolutely refused to run Albion's way, despite twenty-seven goal attempts, nine of them on target, the last one a shot by Dunk saved by Westwood. And seconds later it was all over.

• • •

At the final whistle, Bruno had to be helped off the turf by Stockdale and cried openly. Knockaert hugged him in a vain attempt at consolation. There was a tired lap of appreciation from the players, an acknowledgement of what the team and the fans had been through together.

Bloom congratulated the Wednesday directors and then went down to the dressing room, where he found a predictably sombre mood. 'It was like a morgue,' he said.

'I've never seen a group of people like that. The players were literally on the floor and I felt like that as well. I said a few words, how proud I was of the players that season and how sometimes in life you don't get what you deserve. I also said that what doesn't kill you makes you stronger. I'm sure at the time that they didn't necessarily take it on board but maybe some of them did over the course of the summer. I hugged them, thanked them for what they had done and then left.'

'If there is one word to sum it up, it would be "numb",' Sidwell recalls.

'For what the season took out of us, especially the last part, the back ten games. We had put ourselves in a great position but just had so much bad luck – the Middlesbrough game, the injuries in the semi-final first leg, the home leg when we came out like a steam train and it didn't happen for us – there were a lot of tears.

'A few lads were obviously thinking that was their last chance gone and they would be moving on from the club. The chairman came down and said his words, as did the gaffer. A lot of it probably went in one ear and out the other, but a lot of the lads took on board that emotion, that hurt.'

'At the end of the Middlesbrough game there were tears and there were even more after that game,' Calderwood said.

'If anyone ever tells you that being a professional footballer is easy, then they haven't been unfortunate enough to experience those moments. Results the season before, when we couldn't seem to buy a draw never mind a win, that was difficult. But when you've been so close and deserve to achieve so much more than you actually do, that was cruel. Playing poorly and not winning games is your responsibility, but there was almost nothing more they could have done. Any other year that points total would have been enough. Credit to them that they were able to absorb that and come back.'

Hughton felt a mixture of emotions. 'My take on it was a little different,' he said.

'It was certainly as emotional a changing room as I've been in. We had such incredible bad luck in the first leg. I'd never been involved in a game where one team has four off injured. But we'd stuck in there and got away with a 2–0 that could have been worse. It could have been all done and dusted. And the two injured players that we thought had no chance of making the second leg three days later made the game. So that was incredible. Sidwell and Knockaert both played. In the period that we'd had Sidwell, that was as good as I'd seen him play.

'So yes, the changing room afterwards was bad. But I knew it was going to be an uphill battle with two players that weren't fully fit and after the emotion of the first leg. Wednesday had rested players in the match before the first leg while we were playing at Middlesbrough; they were going into the game on a high while we were dealing with disappointment and had two suspended.

'Of course, the obvious thing was to try to turn it round and get to the final. But what I wanted more than anything was for the lads to put on a performance. Because of what had happened before, I didn't want us to go out with a whimper. So my feeling at the end was one of incredible pride. After what had happened three or four days before, we managed to put on, for thirty minutes, the performance of the season.

'That half-hour was as good as we'd been. And at 1–0, you started to think: "This could happen." And then they got a fortuitous goal, and when that went in I feared it was probably all over, because it was so deflating. So I was incredibly proud that they had put on the sort of performance that they did, in one of the best atmospheres that I've been involved in.

'But in those moments you don't say too much. What you do say is: "You've been a credit to the club and to yourselves all season, and particularly after what happened three or four days ago. And if anything will give you the motivation to do it next season, it will be this." But that's all you say, and it's all you can say, because you know what they're feeling at that moment and it's a part of the game that you sometimes have to go through to come out better at the other end.'

Sidwell shouldered the responsibility of putting on a brave face for the media. 'It's been a long season and we were just touching distance away from doing it,' he said.

'It's a bitter pill to swallow. Their goal was a blatant push. We couldn't have done any more. Especially in the first half. I've never seen a first half like it. We took the game to them. Everyone in there can hold their heads up and be proud, not just for tonight but for the whole season. We pushed the top two for automatic, and now Sheffield Wednesday, to the very brink. Our fans were magnificent.

'Now it will be tough. I don't think we could get any closer to achieving a dream for a lot of them in that dressing room. It has been snatched away from us, but we are professionals. This is our game. We dust ourselves down, go away, have a good summer, re-group – and we know what we have in that dressing room. We go again next season.

'The motivation is to look around and seeing that hurt on your closest allies' faces. And think that we don't want that again. The chairman has come down and congratulated us on our efforts and said that we couldn't have done any more, not just tonight but all season, which is obviously very nice. But that only goes so far. Not many of us will be sleeping tonight. When I signed, I said that everything here is geared up for the Premier League, the infrastructure, everything. We have come very close but next season we need to go that one step further.'

Hooper also spoke to the media after the game, admitting that he had pushed Dunk. 'The ref didn't see it, did he?' he said, admitting that he had spared few feelings for Hughton, his former manager at Carrow Road. 'Yes, he signed me for Norwich and gave me my chance in the Premier League. Obviously I've got to thank him but today we had to win so I didn't really think about it. The main thing was getting to Wembley and we did, getting through and celebrating.'

The noise of those celebrations could still be heard as Hughton, dignified and restrained as ever, faced the cameras. In a cruel accident of timing, it was announced that he had been awarded the League Managers' Association's Championship manager-of-the-season award just as that season finally crumbled to dust.

'It was a tough night,' he said.

'We've been in a period where things have gone against us. But the endeavour that the players have shown in difficult periods, they have shown character all season. It's disappointing and tough that, in the period of the season you want things to go well for us, in and out of our control, they weren't able to.

'I wanted us, if we couldn't go through, to go out fighting and we certainly did. It was a foul on Dunky for their goal and that makes it even tougher. We still feel it was an unjust sending-off for Dale [at Middlesbrough] and we lost a player for three games. But the biggest thing on my mind is how proud I am of a group of players that have been excellent all season and what they have produced has been exceptional. They have to use the disappointment to produce it again next season in a division that, if anything, will be even tougher. And expectations rise.'

And he had appreciated Bloom's visit to the dressing room. 'It was essentially a thank-you for the season. He knows what the players put in. The chairman is a massive supporter, born and bred, and he has invested very heavily in this club and of course he feels it more than anybody.'

Calderón slipped out of the dressing room and walked back down the tunnel and stood on the touchline, staring into the darkened and now empty stadium, seen only by two journalists. When he walked back up the tunnel, it was clear he had been in tears.

'I thought it was maybe the last time I was here,' he said.

'I didn't know anything at that moment but there was obviously a chance that I had played my last game at the Amex. After a couple of years, that was the moment. I didn't expect anyone to see me. It was a bit private. It was emotional. Yes, I was in tears. There were a lot of bad emotions at the time. We couldn't go up, as I think we deserved to after that season. And at the same time it was maybe my last game here. So there were a lot of reasons to cry.'

The next day, Bloom offered Hughton a new contract. The 2015/16 season was over. The new one had begun.

CHAPTER 8

SUMMER 2016

If there was one man who knew exactly how Hughton was feeling after the play-off final second leg, that man was Alan Mullery. In 1978, Mullery – like Hughton, a former Tottenham Hotspur player – had managed Brighton to the brink of promotion to the top flight only to miss out by a hair's breadth.

On the final day of the 1977/78 season, Mullery's talented team had to win and hope that either Southampton or, ironically, Tottenham won the match between the two at the Dell. A draw would mean that Albion and Spurs would be level on points, with the Londoners going up on goal difference.

Brighton did their job, beating Blackpool 2–1 at the Goldstone with two goals from Peter Ward, an own goal by Mark Lawrenson making things interesting in the second half. 'We heard a cheer going round the Goldstone and thought someone had scored at the Dell,' said Brian Horton, Mullery's inspirational captain, who would go on to manage the club himself during the dark Gillingham days. 'But then we found out they hadn't and it was a massive downer.'

Saints and Spurs had played out a tame and predictable goalless draw, with only Sussex-born Southampton striker Tony Funnell making any attempt to score. 'And then in the Sunday papers we saw pictures of Keith Burkinshaw, the Spurs manager, and Lawrie McMenemy of Southampton in the middle of the Dell pitch holding hands,' Mullery said.

Despite the realisation that promotion had not been achieved, there was a pitch invasion by fans at the final whistle of the Blackpool game and Mullery and the players appeared in the directors' box to be acclaimed for what had been an excellent campaign following promotion from Division Three the previous season. Unwisely, he now knows, he grabbed the PA microphone.

'We had just come up the previous season and were full of confidence and just kept the momentum going and it was so very close to being good enough,' he said.

'We had a really good side, as we had to have nearly to get promoted twice in two seasons. So I went in the directors' box and I made a statement. I told all the supporters how good they had been, and I said that next season we would be promoted. Those were my exact words: "I promise you that we will go up."

'That was the most stupid statement I think I ever made as a manager, but everyone was so down after the nil–nil at Southampton and missing out on goal difference. We had played ever so well in both games against Tottenham, drawing 0–0 up there and beating them 3–1 at the Goldstone, and we deserved to go up. I wanted to raise people's hopes and I said that on a whim. I said what I thought would benefit the players and the team. Cloughie [former Derby, Albion, Leeds and Nottingham Forest manager Brian Clough] would do that, Alex Ferguson did it to a certain extent.

'I am a very different character to Chris Hughton – he is a man who thinks before he talks! I'm sure Chris would have started planning again from the second the team lost in the play-offs. Bill

Nicholson at Spurs was more like Chris. He would never say what the team were going to do.

'But I didn't have any doubts. I knew that my players were good enough. I saw everything in them that I wanted and I was confident enough that it would happen. We had Wardy [Peter Ward], who could score goals and Nobby Horton as captain.

'So we went away to Mallorca, played golf and let them go out to clubs because we thought they deserved it. And it built camaraderie among the players, one for all and all for one. They all went together, there were no cliques in the squad, everybody did the same thing. I knew that worked from my days as a player at Tottenham and with England under Alf Ramsey. Chris knows that, as you've seen. He has built a wonderful team spirit.'

'We were such a strong group,' Horton agreed.

'Many of us were experienced, twenty-eight, twenty-nine. But I had never played at the top level, so I was thinking, "Was that my last chance? Will it ever come again?" We'd proved we were good enough for the second level after promotion and now we wanted a chance to prove ourselves at the top.

'You needed to get away, and 30,000 people who went every week felt as bad as we did. The chairman, Mike Bamber, and Harry Bloom, the vice-chairman, were very good to us, we went away to Spain and came back and regrouped. We kept that spirit and kept the belief. We firmly believed we were good enough and we stuck together. They kept the team together although I'm sure they could have got money for Mark Lawrenson and Wardy. To pick ourselves up and do it again was unbelievable.'

'Luckily what I had promised came true,' Mullery said.

'Mind you, it went to the last game of the season up at Newcastle, where we had to win to guarantee promotion. We went up on the

Wednesday before and went to see them play Bristol Rovers that night because I wanted the lads to see the team they'd be playing on the Saturday.

'Unfortunately they won 3–0 and really looked at it, and I said to myself, "Blimey, have I done the right thing?" But the players responded to it. We played golf on the Thursday, did some light training and went through our free kicks and corners on the Friday and went out on the Saturday and were 3–0 up in half an hour. We ended up winning 3–1.

'And it's just as well, because Harry Bloom, Tony Bloom's grandfather, said, "The one thing I want to see in my lifetime is us get promoted to the First Division, and then I will die a happy man." A year and a half after we did go up, he dies sitting next to me on the coach on the way to Stoke. He had a heart attack.

'He was a lovely man, Harry. He was a surrogate father to me. After we'd got to the big league, the chairman, Mike Bamber, wanted to build new stands and I disagreed with him and said, "What we need, Mr Chairman, is better players." He said, "No, no, we've got to build this and improve that" – until Harry said, "Michael, the boy knows what he's doing."

'Tony Bloom is the same. He is not arrogant, he will speak to everyone, but he also believes in what he wants to do, like the stadium, the training ground, which is second to none. We used to train at Hove Recreation Ground. Cloughie once said to me, "Are you still training in the park? Do you still get dog mess all over your boots? I bet you get the apprentices to clean them like we used to".

Despite feeling a sense of relief at getting away with his rash promise in 1978, Mullery admits that he went out on a limb again in 2016. 'I must say that I did say to Tony after the Sheffield Wednesday game that I thought we would go up next season,' he said. 'But I felt more at ease saying that than I had saying that we would go up in '79, when I was risking making myself look an idiot. All we needed was someone to score us twenty league goals, which I thought Chris would find.'

• • •

A board meeting had been in the diary for the day after the Sheffield Wednesday match and it went ahead despite the crushing disappointment of the previous evening.

The nearest photograph to the desk in Paul Barber's office behind the North Stand at the Amex was taken at that meeting, and depicts an optimistic-looking chairman and board of directors sitting around the boardroom table in very businesslike fashion. 'We were determined to send the message that, the day after we lost the chance to be promoted last season, we immediately started planning for the next season,' Barber said.

'We had that photo taken not so much as a historical record, although it has become that, as a symbolic gesture to say, internally and externally: "We're not down, we're not beaten. We're disappointed, we're frustrated at not getting there, but season 16/17 starts today." So that photograph is opposite me every day as a reminder of what we missed out on but also what we committed to achieving. This is such a fine-margin business now that these small things can become significant.'

Bloom set the tone of the meeting. 'We all agreed what a brilliant season Chris had overseen,' he said.

'We had done everything we could, there were no regrets, we got 89 points, which would have got us automatic promotion almost every other season.

'We said that it was the first day of the new season and we would recover quickly because we were so proud of how well the players had done. We didn't look back on errors and things we could have done better because as a board and as a club we felt we'd done everything that we could. And at that moment we were very determined to make next season count and for it to be the one where we got promoted. The aim was automatic promotion. That night Paul Barber and myself and Chris met up and we offered him a new contract and the next day it was done.'

Bloom has played recreational poker for very high stakes and made the later stages of world-level events – and been nicknamed The Lizard for his cold blood at the tables – so he knew all about holding his nerve. And he had made up his mind that the club was not going to sell star players such as Dunk, Knockaert and Stephens. In the case of Stephens, who would be out of contract in summer 2017 and could then leave for nothing, that was a risk even for Bloom.

'I knew this season was key, because we had great players and were going to strengthen the squad too,' Bloom said.

'So we didn't want to lose any of our best players. And I felt I owed it to the other players, and to Chris and the fans, to keep our squad together. It wasn't easy, because we had big offers for some of our key players. Obviously the high-profile one that became a lot more public as the summer went on was Dale Stephens.'

This was a decision based on logic rather than a fan allowing his heart to rule his head. 'Starting to invest in the club and then the decision to take the club on as chairman was from the heart, because financially it didn't make a lot of sense,' he said.

'But everything after that has been from the head, and it needs to be. The heart and the passion is there all the time and it comes out at matches. But financial and budget decisions, those have got to be with the head.

'If you allow the heart to rule the business side, you risk going the way of some other clubs whose owners let their heart rule their head. As a fan, I would rather have someone in charge who was also a fan – but I'd prefer someone who wasn't a fan but knew how to run a business to someone who was a fan but didn't know how to run things properly.'

When the team is playing, of course, things are different. 'On a match day, the responsibility for running the club is very much mine,' Barber said.

'That's what he pays me for. He becomes a fan. In the boardroom he's the first and last with his scarf on. He'll talk about "If only we'd scored this goal or made that tackle," or a refereeing decision. He doesn't ask about the running of the day; he assumes I'm dealing with it.

'That's when you see exactly why he started this journey, a boyhood fan who loves his football, just wants Brighton to win and play well and get to the highest position we can as quickly as possible. He cheers goals, curses if we concede and shakes his head at dodgy decisions. Everything else around the club is almost irrelevant. The food in the boardroom is great, he's very gracious to the visiting directors, but actually everything is about his day as a football fan.'

Bloom grew up watching Mullery's swashbuckling team of the 1970s and early '80s, attending Lancing College before studying mathematics at Manchester University. He went to work in the betting industry and set up and sold a betting website.

Although most articles in the media use his success at poker as a starting point, his wealth is now based on property and investments. The scale of his success in his various ventures can be judged by the fact that he has put an estimated £250 million into the club since becoming chairman in succession to Dick Knight in 2009.

But he had been involved behind the scenes well before then, along with his older brother, Darren, discreetly helping out when necessary without ever seeking the profile that went with an official seat on the board. 'For many years before I became chairman I was investing in the club, with some other people,' he said. 'I gave loans and was a shareholder for many years but wanted to keep in the background.'

When the worldwide recession of 2008 threatened to scupper the financing of the £93 million stadium that Knight and the fans had fought so long to get permission for, Bloom stepped in and became chairman, with Knight moving up to a new position of life president.

The build quality of the stadium, which was constructed to the highest specifications, with padded seats even for away fans, and the training ground, attest to his ambition for the Albion. The ultimate goal was to reach the Premier League and now was the time. 'This was such a good chance because we had such a high-quality squad,' he said. 'It is not possible to have that every season in the Championship without parachute payments. That is the reality.'

CHAPTER 9

REINFORCEMENTS

Hughton did not allow himself the luxury of a long period of reflection or recrimination after the play-off defeat. Armed with his new contract, he set to work almost immediately.

'It was a contract I was very happy to sign,' he said.

'Apart from the obvious, the disappointments and the hard work and how tough it is and all of that, I thoroughly enjoyed the season. I'd had such great backing from the club and the chairman and the players that we'd brought in that it indicated to me that we wanted to go again the following season, and that's what we managed to do.

'I didn't need lifting because it was my responsibility to start planning for next season, so I couldn't afford to be down. I had to play a big part in what was going to happen the next season, recruiting and trying to get things done. So it was probably a bit easier for me because I had no choice but to get on with it. It didn't take long to get over the play-off defeat, two or three days. For the players, it was different, they went away for five weeks, a lot of thinking time. I had to think of other things.

'We'd set a points target where it's worked before and we met all the targets we'd set apart from one. The points tally we had had got teams promotion most years and when you want things to go for you, in those last four games they went against us. But we wanted to be in that position, challenging at the top and pushing for something, again.'

In some ways, the task ahead of him looked more daunting. His team would not take many opponents by surprise this time. And how those players would recover from the disappointment of the previous campaign's ending was anybody's guess. Some hangover would be understandable.

The chief external factor was a division that looked even stronger than it had done twelve months before. Down from the Premier League had come two giants of English football, Aston Villa and Newcastle United, along with Norwich City, Hughton's previous club, who made a habit of yo-yoing between the top divisions. Villa and Newcastle were backed by large fanbases and rich histories, not to mention the parachute payments. Newcastle would, in fact, assemble the most expensive squad ever to compete in the second tier of English football.

Hughton now had to pick up the pieces, but not all of them. Players who would be leaving included Zamora, club captain Gordon Greer, now thirty-five, and, as he had feared, Calderón.

Zamora had scored seven goals in twenty-six appearances, but his presence had meant much more than those bare stats suggest and the goals were all collectors' items in their way. Greer had joined the Albion from Swindon in 2010, led the team to the League One title and into regular contention for promotion to the Premier League as well as earning full Scotland honours, and would be ranked among the club's greatest captains.

The departure of Calderón was a blow, although not an entirely unexpected one, to the fans, who had grown to love a player who was not only a whole-hearted performer on the field but had also immersed himself in Albion in the Community and had been voted the Community Player of the Season by the Football League in 2013. In April, supporters had held a dinner and appreciation evening, 'a celebratory night of thanks for the Basque Country's finest ambassador'.

The marauding right-back had always demonstrated a useful eye for goal and once memorably told the media after needing two bites at a close-range chance to score in a match at Peterborough that he would have 'cut off my bollocks' if he had missed. But arguably his most memorable goal was one he knew little about, when Leeds goalkeeper Marco Silvestri's parry of a shot hit him in the face and rebounded into the North Stand net in Hughton's first season in charge. 'He scores with his face' was his signature chant after that. Now he wrote an open letter to *The Argus* to say farewell.

Hola,

It's been a difficult month for the BHAFC family, but just in terms of results. I'll explain that later.

Last Tuesday, after the defeat in the play-offs, I was told that my career as a Brighton & Hove Albion [player] had reached the end.

Firstly I felt devastated, then sad, followed by a lot of emotions, none of them positive. But I am [a] person who always tries to be positive and in this case I had to do the same.

I started to think about the time when I made my debut, fighting to escape relegation from League One, when we trained in a training ground that wasn't even a training ground and playing games in a stadium that wasn't a stadium either.

And then, when I was leaving the new 'proper' training ground, I said to myself, 'Wow… I have played 231 games, scored 19 goals, now we play in a beautiful stadium, and we are disappointed because we should be in the Premier League. I thought I ought to be proud of having been part of all this.'

So I stopped crying and I started enjoying all these memories. And then I realised that the most important were all those individuals whom I worked, lived, shared experiences with, and my gratitude to them, so…

Thanks first to my family, without them all this would not have been possible. It's going to be difficult to explain to my four-year-old son that Daddy is not playing for Brighton & Hove Albion any more, his first English word was Seagulls, fact! My seven-month-old daughter was born in Brighton, we were sure about this decision.

My wife is now checking all the clubs around Brighton, she wants to live here, we love it: it's not England, it's just Brighton.

I cannot name everyone, because there are too many good people involved. But I want to highlight my teammates. I've been with some very good players but most importantly, good people, they have made me enjoy so much throughout these seven seasons.

Every single day I've enjoyed training and working with them; being so far from home, they have been my family and friends. As I said before I cannot name all of them, because I don't want to leave anyone out.

Finally, but trust me, is a very, very special part of this letter for the fans.

Fans are the real blood of football in general, and clubs in particular. Without you nothing would be possible, and Brighton and Hove Albion has high-quality blood. You are amazing, and you have made me understand that the most important thing is not just winning games, but trying your best to do it.

And you are right, as I said at the beginning of this letter, maybe the results haven't been the ones we all fairly deserved, but you are extremely proud of being Albion supporters, and that's it.

For me, seeing fans waiting desperately for Saturday 3 p.m., to enjoy with their team, doesn't matter the result, that's it. Seeing kids in the school or in the parks with Albion shirts instead of the big clubs and easy ones, that's it. We have done it, and I do feel part of this.

So, just to end, like I said, I will try to remember all those memories, always with a smile in my face, because all of you have created a wonderful fairy tale, but as every tale it has to have an end.

So, many, many thanks and see you soon, because it's not a goodbye, I know I will come back, I have to.

Thanks, gracias, eskerrik asko!

Calde

P.S. If they ask you… Yes, I did score with my face.

• • •

Letting players go is always a hard task for any manager. An easier one for Hughton was to name Bruno as his new captain to succeed Greer, a decision that was well received in the dressing room. 'Bruno is the calmest man ever and that rubs off on everyone else,' Dunk said.

'He speaks when the time is right and always speaks sense and is always encouraging. He is the perfect captain in my eyes because I'm not one for shouters. If someone shouts at me I don't take it too well, so I prefer the way he goes about it. The gaffer is the same way.'

'I think words have more power when you don't talk a lot, and when you say something you try to say the right thing,' Bruno said. 'For me it's harder because I'm Spanish and English is not my first language. But yes, I try to talk more with my actions than my words. Sometimes leaders are not the people who talk more, but the people who do the right things when you have to do them. I try to do that on the pitch.

'My way of thinking is always as a team player. Of course I know how important it is to wear the captain's armband, especially in England, where it means a lot, and so for me it is very special. I'm really proud that the gaffer and the boys wanted me as captain. But I always try to think in terms of the group. If we are where we are, it's because of the group.'

The Barcelona-born right-back had come through Espanyol's youth system, so blue-and-white stripes could be said to be in his blood. But he made only one first-team appearance for the *periquitos*, as a substitute, and moved on to Gimnàstic de Tarragona and then Lleida before helping Almería reach the Spanish top division for the first time in their history. In 2009, Unai Emery, his former coach at Almería, took him to Valencia, where he played in the Champions League and Europa League. He arrived at Brighton on a free transfer in June 2012 under Gus Poyet.

'We were speaking about the club and Gus was telling me his ideas; the club had a new stadium and was planning to build a new training ground,' Bruno said. 'You could have seen that everything was getting better and better. I came because of him, of course, and the ideas he explained to me, because of the city. So of course I knew where I was coming, to a club with big expectations.'

The training facilities, though, were not what he and Vicente had been used to at Valencia. 'But after that it was about the people,' he said.

'You are going to find some people who are not going to take that, to put up with that, but you had players like Vicente, Bridgey

[Wayne Bridge], me, who don't care about that. For us there are more important things than really bad changing rooms, training on pitches that are under water or all mud – for example, how the club is working to get in the right way. You are always going to find some players who complain, "I cannot be here because I am whoever" ... but it wasn't our case. It was much easier than anyone would think.'

He became part of a group of Spanish-speaking players including Calderón, David López, Andrea Orlandi and Leonardo Ulloa. 'Of course, for me it was easier to come to a place where there were lots of Spanish-speaking teammates, you can adapt quicker,' he said.

'But after it makes it tougher to learn English when there are a few Spanish teammates. I was trying to study and spend time with the English players as well and not always the Spanish players. For me it was quite easy to adapt because the English boys were unbelievable and I was happy with both. It was a nice mix.'

Now, with Calderón's departure, he would be the only Spanish speaker on the playing staff, but that was not a concern for a player who had always been keen to adapt to life in Britain.

'For me, since the first day, for me and my family, we knew we were in England and had the same timetables as English people, going to bed earlier than in Spain, eating at different times from in Spain, waking up earlier.

'You have to do that because you are here and you cannot expect everyone to adapt to you. Some of the food, and what you mix with what, is still too much but the rest was quite easy. If you want to enjoy life, you can't keep thinking that you are going to do the same things you did in Spain. You can't properly live the experience.

'I drop the kids off at school and pick them up every day, doing the normal things and speaking with the other kids as well if they have questions. It's a nice community in Hove where we live and it's just a normal life. Our idea was to come and adapt as much as possible and be in the middle of the city, walk around and mix with the people. They love the football club of course, and that makes it such a lovely atmosphere. Even when times were not so good, the fans supported us and for me being around them is so nice.'

Hughton also added to his coaching team. On 6 June, Paul Nevin, who had worked alongside him and Colin Calderwood during their time at Norwich City, filled the gap originally left by Nathan Jones in January.

Nevin, a Londoner, had played for Shrewsbury Town, Carlisle United and Yeovil Town, and also had a four-year spell playing in America. He began his coaching career with Fulham, where he worked as an academy coach and reserve-team manager, and managed in New Zealand. He had also worked for the Football Association as a youth coach and been head of academy coaching at the Premier League since 2014.

'I knew Paul from Norwich, where we brought him in as head of academy coaching,' Hughton said. 'What attracted me to him was his varied background. He'd been at Fulham as reserve-team coach, he'd travelled and managed abroad, and I wanted to use that type of experience.'

The next day, the *Mirror* reported that Crystal Palace had had a £5 million bid for Dunk rejected. And the club announced that Sidwell's loan signing would be made permanent when his contract with Stoke expired at the end of the month, which the midfield player was very happy about. 'When I came back they had put themselves in a great position to get to the Premier League,' he said. 'It wasn't a matter of if they were going to get there, it was a matter of when. I could sense it was going to be soon and I wanted to be part of that.'

Whether it happened this season would depend on the ability of Hughton, Bloom and Winstanley to strengthen the playing squad, and the existing players. They probably knew Hughton well enough by now not to expect a rousing pre-season call to arms, and they were not disappointed. Like Mullery before him, he believed in their qualities.

'The only things I said to them pre-season were the obvious things I would say anyway,' Hughton said.

'What our aims were, which were to get promotion; and that we knew what last season was, that we'd got close and needed to go one step further. But we had good, motivated individuals. They made a decision that they wanted more of it. I can provide them with a platform, but the players have got to be self-motivated. I can lead by whatever example I want but the players have got to generate that motivation themselves. They either have it or they don't.

'They also had a togetherness that had been steeled by the experiences of the previous season. That team spirit was evident when we missed out.'

Hughton added:

'It is easier to have good team spirit when you are winning more games than you are losing. But they work hard at it. They are a bunch of lads that like each other, which helps. When you've got some players who dislike each other, it can become quite a hard dressing room.

'They also make demands of each other. They know what the standards are, which has developed over this period of time. If the first season taught us anything, it was the standards required, for anybody who didn't already know, to do well in the Championship. You looked at Burnley, Hull and Middlesbrough and saw how consistent they were, and what they had to do to keep on dragging out results. Now the players expected the same of each other and they demanded it of each other. And they worked hard at it.'

'I think the manager just trusted us,' Rosenior said.

'He trusted who we are, the spirit of the group and the quality that we had. One of the biggest strengths of the manager is that he doesn't ever change; he is consistent in his message. And so there were no big speeches, there were no talks between the players. We just knew that we would go for it again. That was understood. We have good players, of course we do, but the reason we have been successful is that we don't want to let each other down. And I thought that would see us through. There's a bond there.

'Anyway, look at Leicester. They missed out on promotion when Anthony missed a penalty in the play-off semi-final at Watford and they came back and won the league with, I think it was, over 100 points. That will be our aim, have no doubts about that.'

'One of the boys said to me that as a team we may not be the best, but he didn't want to let his teammates down and I think that was the key,' Baldock said. 'We're a tight-knit group and we feel passionately about the club and I think that has shown. We knew that if we gave our best every time, we were good enough to get where we wanted to be. It was such a fine margin the year before.'

• • •

On 3 July, the club acted to replace Zamora, welcoming back a former goal-scoring favourite for the second summer in succession. They had failed to land Glenn Murray from AFC Bournemouth in January – and who knows how costly that had proved? – but now a loan deal was finally done, Murray signing just in time to join the squad in flying out for a pre-season training camp in Tenerife.

Murray had been largely unknown when he joined Brighton in January 2008 for £300,000. He scored fifty-three goals in 118 league appearances, including twenty-two as the team won the League One title in 2010/11. Poyet made it clear that he did not want to keep him, so the club reluctantly allowed him to leave on a free transfer. He joined Crystal Palace, Albion's greatest rivals, and eventually played in the Premier League for both Palace and Bournemouth.

'I've always been a great admirer of Glenn's, and so has Chris, so that was a very simple one to discuss,' Paul Winstanley said.

'All we needed was to see where he was at physically and mentally and put all those processes into place, to make sure he was the right person for this group.

'And Glenn showed a huge, huge desire to come here, which was pivotal and without that you probably don't get the deal done. A massive desire. He'd seen the wide players we had. I'd been in touch with his representatives for the best part of eighteen months, two years. We tried to get him in previous windows but just couldn't get it done. Either Bournemouth wouldn't do it, or wouldn't let him out on loan.

'Glenn had made it known relatively early that it wasn't working out for him at Bournemouth, but from their point of view they'd invested a lot of money in him and had only got out a handful of games. Glenn still lived in this area and wasn't comfortable so far away. His people represent quite a lot of different players and you're always in conversation so you collect information. You've got to know the "gettables". It's no good chasing a player at, say, Juventus that you can't get.

'That he'd played here was a nice coincidence, but more important was that he was the type of player we needed, especially with the wide players we had. We had no real back-up for Tomer Hemed before, no competition in that area. Tomer had done ever so well in his first season but we relied on him more heavily than we had hoped to. We knew that with our wide players and Glenn's natural instinct for goals, there would be quality crosses and lots of chances and you knew that Glenn would be in there. It was a natural fit and a deal that everyone was keen to do.'

Murray had come to the same conclusion. 'Whenever I join a club, I look at the supply lines, so to say, the wingers,' he said.

'I watched from afar last year, you always watch your old clubs when they're on TV, and everything I saw was positive – Anthony doing what he does, Skally's delivery, I'd seen Solly before his injury, Murph, and it all boded well. Even Kaz I felt could help me score goals.'

Murray still lived near Withdean Stadium and was happy to exchange the 200-mile round trip to Dorset for a twenty-minute drive to Lancing. 'Travelling to Bournemouth was tough,' he said.

'I got a little place down there so I could stay over some nights but then it wasn't going to plan and I didn't feel the need to spend nights away from my family when I wasn't playing on Saturdays. Towards the end I was driving it every day and it was really tough.'

Nor has he ever really solved the riddle of why Bournemouth had signed a player who did not suit their style. 'We did have that conversation,' he said. 'We'll leave it there.'

The deal worked out well. 'It was like Bobby, but without the fitness problems,' Winstanley said.

'Bobby was exceptional, brilliant. He went way above what we thought he could do at the back end of his career and was such a great character as well. When you think back, we delayed it a little too long. We should have done the deal earlier. We would have done Glenn earlier if we could have. But getting him on a loan allowed us

Kazenga LuaLua celebrates his goal against Nottingham Forest in trademark style, 7 August 2015

The pre-match memorial ceremony for the Shoreham aircrash victims, Brighton *v.* Hull, 12 September 2015

Bobby Zamora acknowledges the away fans after scoring his first goal back at Brighton, the winner away to Leeds United on 17 October 2015

Sam Baldock scores against his old club, Bristol City, 20 October 2015

Gaëtan Bong lays down the law against Cardiff City, 23 October 2015

Jiří Skalák celebrates after scoring the goal of the season against QPR on 19 April 2016

ABOVE Lewis Dunk wheels away after scoring at Nottingham Forest, 9 April 2016

LEFT Middlesbrough's Gastón Ramírez writhes on the turf and Dale Stephens's season is about to end with a red card, 7 May 2016

An emotional Liam Rosenior applauds the fans at the end of the play-off final, second leg, 2015/16 season

The strong, silent type: Chris Hughton on the touchline

Bruno – the best beard in football

The band of brothers celebrate Tomer Hemed's goal against Rotherham United, 16 August 2016

Teammates pile on top of opening scorer Sam Baldock at Hillsborough

Anthony Knockaert leaps on Glenn Murray after the opening goal in the 5–0 victory over Norwich, 29 October 2016

Glenn Murray makes his usual celebratory run in front of the North Stand after his favourite goal of the season, his second against Norwich on 29 October 2016

The players raise Anthony Knockaert's shirt after Steve Sidwell's goal at Bristol City, 5 November 2016

Glenn Murray (number 17) glances home the last-minute winner at Birmingham, 17 December 2016

Comeback complete – Lewis Dunk runs to the fans after his winner at Fulham, 2 January 2017

Shane Duffy expresses his delight at David Stockdale's penalty save at Fulham, 2 January 2017

The defenders congratulate David Stockdale on his double save against Sheffield Wednesday, 20 January 2017

Anthony Knockaert dedicates another goal to his late father, Patrick, against Derby County on 10 March 2017

Sébastien Pocognoli runs to the Albion fans at Loftus Road after scoring the second goal against QPR, 7 April 2017

Solly March (right) has just scored the Easter Monday goal against Wigan that won promotion, 17 April 2017

A familiar face in the crowd: Íñigo Calderón reaches down into the tunnel to shake hands with Anthony Knockaert, 17 April 2017

ABOVE Requests to stay off the pitch are politely ignored after victory over Wigan, 17 April 2017

LEFT Tony Bloom in scarf-twirling mode after victory against Wigan, 17 April 2017

ABOVE LEFT No cheering allowed in the press box. Well, maybe just this once. The players serenade the fans after beating Wigan, 17 April 2017

ABOVE RIGHT The players salute promotion in the Amex dressing room. Dunk, Bruno, Ankergren, Bong, Baldock, Skalák, Murphy, Sidwell, Tomori, Kayal, Stockdale, 17 April 2017

LEFT Anthony Knockaert leads the celebrations on the open-top bus promotion parade

BELOW The squad takes the applause on stage during the seafront celebrations

to spend the money we had set aside for a possible transfer somewhere else.'

Murray might have been less than happy if one of his potential supply lines had been cut by a bid of £8 million from Newcastle United for Knockaert, but the club were more interested in strengthening than selling and Bloom stood firm again, as he did when Burnley bid £4 million for Stephens.

There were reports that one possible Albion target was Shane Duffy, the towering Blackburn Rovers centre half, who had impressed for the Republic of Ireland in the European Championships. But many fans discounted these stories. The centre of defence was not an area of the team that had been a weakness. Dunk and Goldson had performed very capably the previous season and Hünemeier would be available in reserve along with promising young players such as Glen Rea in the under-21 team.

Murray was on target, along with Kayal, Hemed and Manu, in the opening friendly, a 4–0 win at Crawley in which Hughton used his entire squad bar Stockdale and Goldson, who had picked up injuries in Tenerife. There were no visible signs of a hangover from the trauma of the end of the previous season, but the next warm-up game, against Championship rivals Fulham at Aldershot, went much less well. Fulham won 3–0 with some ease, new signing Sone Aluko from promoted Hull and exciting teenage full-back prospect Ryan Sessegnon among the scorers.

Fans were worried by such a result against a team they had grown used to beating. 'And rightly so,' Hughton said.

'So was I. Management and coaching is all about doubts and fears and if you don't have them, you can get carried away. There are games or training sessions when I see things I am not happy with, and I think we need to be better.

'It would be lovely if you could look at a player and think: "I will be happy with every single game he plays." But you can't, and those are the things that drive you on every day. You have got to be competitive in this game and if you are ever happy with things, you can guarantee you're getting closer to a time when you're not going to be happy. Managers worry and I'm no different. That Fulham friendly is a good reference, because we were poor in that game and it did concern me because they were a team in our division.'

And the experiment of playing two 'split-squad' friendlies on the same day, Saturday 23 July, was no more successful. The first game, away to Luton with a 2 p.m. kick-off, ended in a 2–1 win for Nathan Jones's new team, Dunk scoring for Albion, while the 5.30 game at Stevenage ended in a 1–0 win to the home side.

Spirits were lifted somewhat by another 4–0 win, away to Oxford United, before a 1–0 home defeat by Lazio in the only home friendly of the summer on 31 July. Murray came closest to grabbing a goal for Albion with a shot on the turn.

Even with Murray's arrival, strengthening the attacking options was seen as the biggest priority in summer dealings, so in early August most fans were happy to hear that a club record fee had been agreed with Tottenham Hotspur for Alex Pritchard – at £4.35 million plus add-ons, potentially double the £2.5 million club record amount paid for Craig Mackail-Smith in 2011.

Pritchard, a former England under-21 attacking midfield player, had impressed on loan in the Championship at Brentford in the 2014/15 season and later at Premier League West Bromwich Albion. He had expected to challenge for a first-team place at White Hart Lane but instead he was made available for transfer.

Hughton saw the 23-year-old as the player to link midfield to a central striker, and supporters saw it as an ambitious move for a player who would improve the team's creativity and add a different dimension to the attack. 'I was looking for a "number 10",' Hughton said.

'I generally go 4–4–2 but also 4–4–1–1. Certainly in the Championship you want a number 10 that you think can really affect the game and score goals. And we saw that in Pritchard. We thought he was very good at Brentford, technically a very good player.'

But newly relegated Norwich City got wind of the deal and gazumped the Albion's offer. Tottenham, to their credit, said they were willing to stand by the deal they had first agreed, but the player, reportedly on the M25 on his way to sign at Lancing, was contacted by Norwich and headed for Norfolk instead.

'I'd spent five days negotiating with my old boss [Daniel Levy at Spurs] to agree terms for Pritchard, and we got the deal done,' Barber told the Supporters' Club AGM.

'We agreed everything with the player and the agent. Then, as the player was on his way to the training ground for a medical, Norwich – with the benefit of parachute payments – jump on the deal and pay the player 50 to 60 per cent more than us. For a 23-year-old on a four-year contract to earn 50 to 60 per cent more, what would you do? I don't blame Pritchard, but that's the sort of market that we're in.

'The approach was illegal – it wasn't authorised by Tottenham – but that's modern football. The temptation to go on the offensive publicly was huge, but it doesn't get you anywhere. What's the point of falling out with a club that you'll probably do business with a few years later? Sometimes you have to bite your tongue and take a longer-term view on these things, however hard it is at the time.'

Winstanley dismisses suggestions that Pritchard might have

changed his mind had he completed his journey to Lancing and seen the facilities on offer before viewing Norwich's more basic headquarters at Colney. 'There were a few darker forces at work there,' Winstanley said. 'Pritchard was well aware of the facilities here because he had trained here with the England under-21s and he had spoken to Chris and myself, everybody and everything was done.'

'I'm not going to lie about it,' Pritchard told Sky Sports.

'I had a good conversation with both clubs and I can only choose one. I apologise for what happened. I'd just left home. I wasn't on the M25, I don't know where that's come from. It's one for the gaffer to talk about, not me. I'm a Norwich player, not a Brighton player.'

Pritchard denied that a factor in his decision was a higher wage offer from Norwich. 'For me it was purely a football decision, and getting to the Premier League, and I'm just here now and can't wait to get started. I think it's the best option for me.'

As it turned out, no apologies were necessary except perhaps to Pritchard from those who persuaded him that his best path to the top flight went via Carrow Road. Ironically, one of those was Brighton-born Norwich captain Russell Martin. 'I know him through a friend and I spoke to him when he was deciding between here and Brighton,' Martin said later in the season. 'I managed to have a little sway in his decision – and I'm not sure if he's happy at me for that! I didn't get a cut either! I spoke to him on the M25.'

But the signing of Reading and Northern Ireland midfield player Oliver Norwood was completed on the same day as the Pritchard deal broke down. Some fans took this to be an indication that the club would finally allow Stephens to leave, especially as Burnley were reported to have made further bids and raised their initial offer. Fans were equally confident that, with Pritchard out of the picture, another player would be signed to replace or compete with Baldock for the number 10/second striker role.

Meanwhile, with twenty-five days of the transfer window to go, there was the minor detail of the beginning of the 2016/17 season.

CHAPTER 10

BACK ON THE HORSE

Anyone looking for omens at the start of what was to prove one of the most momentous seasons in the history of Brighton & Hove Albion might have been very satisfied with the team's goalless draw away to Derby County in the opening match of the campaign. After all, Mullery's promotion team of 1978/79 had also begun their fixtures with a scoreless draw on the road, at Wrexham.

But after a very up-and-down close season, especially in terms of results in friendly matches, particularly the defeat by Fulham, to see Hughton's team almost back to their best, and on a ground which held few happy memories, was also a boost to belief. That was especially true as the team had been without Goldson (knee) and Hünemeier (groin), with Bruno moving alongside Dunk in the centre of defence and Rosenior slotting into his best position of right-back.

After a slow start, Albion began to get a grip on the game and Derby goalkeeper Scott Carson had to save a shot from Murray and a long-distance effort from Hemed. The fact that the 1,500 or so visiting supporters made themselves heard in a normally noisy stadium showed that Hughton's men had performed well, and against a team that was widely expected to challenge for a top-two finish.

The Guardian and *The Sun* both made Nigel Pearson's Rams second favourites for promotion behind Newcastle, as did *FourFourTwo*, who had got Albion's chances so wrong twelve months earlier – this time they forecast yet another tilt at the play-offs for Hughton's men. Ian Holloway on Sky Sports was one of the few pundits to pick Albion for automatic promotion, behind Newcastle.

So avoiding defeat against a probable rival was an encouraging start. 'I remember going to the Derby game and the side hadn't been broken up, and I saw the team pick up where it had left off, playing with a real positivity,' Paul Samrah said. 'I was really heartened. I thought: "All is not lost."'

The management team shared those feelings. 'You don't know how things are going to go,' Hughton admitted. 'But I did then think that it was a good enough performance and that this wasn't a group of players who were still recovering from last year.'

Calderwood, too, had had his doubts. 'It took longer in pre-season to get back to the levels they had before,' he said.

'The first time that I felt we were really going to be in it again was the first league game of the season, when we played away at Derby. And suddenly the team was the one that we'd seen before, giving a very good performance at a difficult away ground.

'Until then and all through pre-season I was feeling more hesitant about our chances than I had been the year before. I think everyone was still suffering, right through pre-season. But in that first game, they became who they were again, a team that would compete.

'They had done the work, and they had achieved the year before. You didn't get the feeling any more that they were trying to prove themselves worthy of being Championship players. That was the legacy of being successful in so many games the previous season. And we told them to look at the history of teams that had gone close, missed out in the play-offs. There was a good chance that the following year they would get themselves up. Leicester, West Brom, there were quite a number.'

The only concern after the draw at Derby was the absence of a goal. Murray had had a good chance but seen his shot saved. But any doubts that 'Muzza' was no longer the prolific scorer of his first spell at the club would soon be dispelled with a triumphant second home debut.

After a 4–0 Capital Cup victory by a much-changed side over Colchester United in mid-week – Elvis Manu scoring an overdue first goal for the club – Nottingham Forest were again the first visitors to the Amex.

Once more the match was moved forward to Friday evening for live TV coverage, and again it was a home win, but a much more convincing one than the year before. Knockaert gave Albion the lead, nipping between two defenders to guide in a cross from Bong on the left from six yards after thirty-six minutes, and Murray put the finishing touch to a header by Hemed after sixty-eight minutes to score his first Brighton goal since 2011.

It was not, however, his first goal at the Amex. He had already established an excellent scoring record there, notching a goal for Crystal Palace on his first return and two for Reading when on loan to the Berkshire club, refusing to celebrate on each occasion.

Now, though, he ran to the fans behind the North Stand goal to revel in his goal-scoring return in the stripes, and any fears that his past at Palace might be held against him disappeared as he was greeted with rapture. Murray was to make that victory run in front of the North Stand many times, a more intimate experience with the supporters than at Withdean, where the seats were across a running track.

'And even further for the away fans,' he said. 'But in that last season at Withdean we were always being shown round the Amex with the future in mind and we could see it going up from where we were training at Falmer. So any time I've come back, even not in a Brighton shirt, it has always felt a bit like home, and it has always been somewhere I've enjoyed playing. You worry about that first goal and for it to come so early on was good. I never really looked back from there.'

He scored a second eight minutes from time with a goal that one studio pundit described as a 'tap-in', but Leroy Rosenior, also in the studio, pointed out how much nous had gone into it. Murray had made space for himself by hanging back as the move developed then darted in to arrive in the right place to score from Baldock's low pass.

Murray claims not to have been concerned about the fans' reaction to his return, but in any case he had no reason to be. Most held no grudge against him for leaving in 2011, even though Palace was his destination, and appreciated his refusal to celebrate goals against the Albion. They were more inclined to blame Gus Poyet for not doing more to keep him after his contract had expired, preferring to pay £2.5 million for Craig Mackail-Smith, a player as uniquely unsuited to Poyet's preferred playing style as Murray had been to manager Eddie Howe's at Bournemouth.

'That was up to the fans and didn't really bother me,' he said of his return to the Albion. 'I am a footballer and want to do as well as I can in my career and I felt it was a good move for me at that stage, moving to a good team that was expected to do well. Whether fans took to me wasn't really in my thinking. But I think the majority welcomed me.

'The circumstances of my leaving were blown up out of all proportion, but I did enjoy my time at Brighton the first time round, even if some people seem to believe I didn't. It holds a special place in my heart, as do all the clubs I've played for. I'd have no reason to celebrate or rub people's noses in it even though I did get a lot of stick that first night back [with Palace]! I wasn't bitter towards the club. I only had fond memories.'

Murray was on target again in the next match, at home to Rotherham four days later. The pre-match news, though, was about the absence of David Stockdale, who had been injured late in the Forest game. That meant a rare first-team start and league debut for Niki Mäenpää. Rotherham were not expected to test him, but in the event he made two impressive saves. By then, though, Albion had netted three times in a comfortable victory. Knockaert got the first after twenty minutes, turning swiftly and hitting a low left-foot shot into the far corner before defenders or goalkeeper could react. Murray hooked home the second from Rosenior's cross, and Hemed made sure with a second-half penalty after Murray had been brought down.

Unfortunately, Rosenior's assist would be his last for some time after he suffered a serious injury late in the next game, an eventful 2–2 draw away to Reading. John Swift put the Royals ahead early on with a free kick that surprised Stockdale at his near post, but the home side gifted their visitors the leveller after only six minutes when Joey van den Berg headed Knockaert's inswinging corner towards his own net, Baldock getting the faintest of touches to claim his first league goal of the season.

That did not deflate Reading, who had the better of the rest of the first half. But Albion started the second well, and Knockaert half-volleyed them ahead from Baldock's pass only a minute into the restart. However, Reading yet again showed that they would be a force by coming back to equalise through Paul McShane, once a Brighton player of the season and credited with a famous winning goal against Palace.

Van den Berg's wretched day continued when he was shown a second yellow card for a foul on substitute Hemed, but after using all three substitutes, Albion also finished with ten men after Rosenior was hacked down by Yann Kermorgant and could not continue.

After the match, Hughton diplomatically described the tackle on Rosenior as 'reckless' but his private thoughts might have been more extreme when he discovered that the unlucky Rosenior had suffered ankle ligament damage and would miss another three months.

Hughton was also asked about the absence of Dale Stephens, the implication being that the midfield player was making himself unavailable in protest at the club's reluctance to sell him to Burnley. 'Dale's fine,' he said.

'There's no doubt he's a little bit short [of fitness], which is normal. He missed a decent chunk of pre-season and hasn't played the number of games others have but he will be fine. One thing I can categorically tell you is he did not refuse to play. Dale has been excellent for us. He's not that type of individual. He trains hard every day, he's a very good professional.'

Whether he would be staying with the club, though, was another question.

• • •

Rosenior clearly would not be fit to start the next Capital One Cup tie away to Oxford United, which a half-strength side won 4–2, and Hünemeier lasted only an hour of his comeback at the Kassam Stadium. Now the club pressed home its interest in Shane Duffy, despite some erratic form on the part of the Ireland defender. Duffy had scored an own goal in Blackburn's 3–0 defeat at Wigan, then two more – and been sent off – in a 2–1 loss at Cardiff four days later. He remained the Welsh club's top scorer for several weeks.

Fans wondered why a reported club record fee of around £4 million was not being spent on someone who could score goals at the right end, and others suggested that Duffy, who had rejected Blackburn's offer of an extension to a contract that had one year to run, might deliberately have sabotaged his own team in that game in Cardiff in order to provoke a transfer. In the circumstances, they questioned the character and reliability of such a player, but Winstanley was not worried.

He said:

'We will always source references on players from teammates, coaches or managers he has played for. If there's a possibility of meeting a player with his club's permission, we will do that too to try to work the player out to see if he will be a good fit. I want to know what his motivation is. What's his social media profile? How does he live off the field, is he married with children, what is his lifestyle?

'Many times we have been interested in a player but I have decided he is not right for us. Many times I have learned from good sources that players have a gambling problem or too many girlfriends or enjoy partying too much. We've always been very conscious of that. What their lifestyle is like. We were keen, and Chris had installed in us as well, that we didn't want anyone who would upset the dynamic of the group. Chris wanted a good mentality and to build a good environment so we always go into a player's character, massively.

'Richie Towell is an excellent character who knew his next step and knew he was never going to come here and play forty-six games but wanted to fight and try and get in. His mentality is sensational, and the way he trains and conducts himself. These are the types of player you want as understudies to what you have got. He needs to play so we can learn more about him, but he's a terrific lad.

'Uwe too. We watched him when Paderborn were relegated from the Bundesliga. We watched him a lot and even in the warm-up you could see what sort of guy he was. He was a driven sort of personality, very motivated – he was their captain and a really strong individual and a superb professional. At twenty-eight, twenty-nine he wanted to come to England and he fitted in well because we actually have so many leaders in the dressing room.'

'We all want to do well in such a highly competitive league, and so if you're choosing between ability and character in a player, then ability comes first,' Hughton added.

'But our first two signings last season were Rosenior and Hemed and they were not only good players but also really good personalities. Anybody coming in after that was very conscious of it. We feel that anyone we're bringing into such a good group, the group will take care of.'

So there was no chance that Duffy would be the type of character to disrupt the squad dynamic, and Winstanley believes that his aberration at Cardiff worked in Albion's favour. 'I think that there were four or five big clubs watching him at the start of the season when he had that nightmare,' he said.

'But we'd seen him forty-one times the previous season. We were so far down the line with him that we knew he wanted to come and had he not had those blips, I think we might have missed out on him and he could have gone somewhere else.

'And as for the problems he had with his game, I remember looking at some clips with Chris on the type of errors he was making, and Chris saying: "I can get that out of him in two weeks." That was just what you wanted to hear, that any faults in his tackling or decision-making could be fixed. And Chris was right, of course. It pretty much did take just two games.'

'When we brought Duffy in, it was a big decision, because we already had good defenders for that level,' Hughton said.

'Connor Goldson had done really well, Hünemeier was very steady, Dunky was the most consistent. But that decision was based on an opportunity that we felt we had to bring in someone even better. You never know until he comes in and plays games, but that was the decision. The fact that we brought in a centre half as our record signing shows what a big decision it was, But we felt we could get better.'

And the wisdom of building a strong group of defenders was to be proved when injuries hit again later in the season. 'I remember Chris saying that if we had the money available we should strengthen wherever we could to give ourselves the best chance because we will get injuries and we will get suspensions,' Winstanley said.

'And you were 95 per cent sure that Duffy and Dunky could become the best central defensive pairing in the division. It was true that we already had Uwe and Connor, who had done unbelievably well for us, but Connor had been injured and we needed to bring someone else in. And Duffy was a good one.'

That was not immediately apparent on his debut, a 2–0 defeat away to title favourites Newcastle. Duffy was the defender closest to Jamaal Lascelles as the Newcastle man got his head to Jonjo Shelvey's free kick from the left, his glancing effort just beating the diving Stockdale. Knockaert hit the crossbar in the second half after a weaving run by Baldock. But Baldock was then shown a second yellow card for a challenge on goalkeeper Matz Sels, ten minutes before Shelvey made the game safe for the hosts from another free kick, bending the ball over the wall and in from 25 yards.

The crowd of 49,196 represented the second-largest crowd ever to watch a Brighton league match, behind only the 52,641 at Old Trafford for the Albion's visit to Manchester United on 6 October 1979, in their first season in the top flight. But the more important statistic was that the team was now down in eighth place, and they had not looked like serious potential challengers to the Geordies.

The endless left-back saga took another turn on 29 August when Belgian international Sébastian Pocognoli joined on a season-long loan from West Bromwich Albion, where his first-team opportunities under manager Tony Pulis had become limited. Thirteen full caps for a leading European national side and 288 club games, including sixteen in the Premier League, brought valuable know-how and experience.

But he was not the extra forward that the fans, and the club, wanted. There was now experienced cover in every position in the team except second striker, where Baldock was unchallenged – a point whose significance was emphasised by the fact that his dismissal at Newcastle meant he would be suspended for the next match, at home to Brentford.

And late in the window the talk was suddenly once again of a possible departure. Burnley had made a sixth offer for Stephens. Again, Bloom stood firm, and this time the player handed in an official transfer request in the final hours of the transfer window. But it was to no avail. Albion were unmoved.

'Yes, the offer was a substantial amount of money, particularly for a player with only one year left on his contract,' Bloom said.

'But at that stage, towards the end of August, we were never going to be able to replace him with a similar player and we had no one else in the squad who could play that role with that physicality. So we agreed with the board and with Chris that we weren't going to sell him.'

The received wisdom with players a year from the end of a contract is to cash in – even for big clubs. But Bloom had held his ground. 'It was a very difficult decision to make,' he admits.

'Of course I understood the financial risk that it entailed, but I was looking at the bigger picture and how big a season this was, and how important Dale Stephens was to us. Chris Hughton totally agreed. Perhaps it didn't look that wise, but looking at how big financially getting to the Premier League would be and how big a difference Dale Stephens would make, the decision was made to keep him.'

As the window closed, Stephens put out a statement addressed to 'Brighton fans' on Twitter:

> This isn't an apology but an explanation that you deserve. Yes I did submit a transfer request earlier today, which I was reluctant to do. The football club have been aware for five weeks I wanted to leave to fulfil my and every footballer's ambitions of playing in the Premier League. I'm twenty-seven years old and recognised this could be my final opportunity to do so, which is why I feel disappointed my chance was taken away. I prefer to give you honesty rather than shy away from my actions now the window is closed. I respect and understand your frustration as this is your football club. I have ten months remaining and will honour my contract.
>
> Regards, Dale.

During the transfer window, Bloom had rejected bids for Dunk, Knockaert and Stephens that might have netted the club around £25 million. It was a statement of ambition and intent, and within days, Dunk would sign another new contract that tied him to the club until 2021.

'It's massive,' Hughton said of Bloom's determination.

'I can't speak for other times but there certainly might have been other periods at the club when those bids would have been accepted. Credit to the chairman. He felt after last season he wanted the squad to be as strong as possible and for us to challenge again. There is no doubt that keeping our best players has enabled us to do that and be in the position we are in. This is a man that invests a fortune in this football club and a fortune of his own money. He should take huge credit for that.'

It was also taken by the players as a sign that the club meant business. 'There had been talk of players leaving but at any club you want to keep your best players and add to the squad and we did that,' Sidwell said. But a big squad, as he knew well from his time at Chelsea, and even after his return to the Albion, brings its own tensions, with players not getting as much game time as they might like.

'It's a sign of the strength of the squad,' he said.

'It's never easy being dropped out of the team or out of the squad. What eases that pain a little bit is when the club are at the top of the league. Then you have to bite your tongue and wait for your chance if the other lads are doing well.

'The gaffer has always done it the right way. He calls you in his office the day before to give you a heads-up. Words can be said but you have got to respect his decision. He does it in the best interests of the team and you've just got to take it and work harder in training the next day to prove that you're worthy of a place in the next squad.

'Squad rotation is important and we have a squad capable enough for the gaffer to do that. He picks and chooses when to do it. It's very easy for the lads who don't play to throw their toys out of the pram and sulk on a Sunday when they go out for training and then it's hard for the coaches to manage them. But to a man in that dressing room, everyone pulls in the same direction and the gaffer couldn't ask for any more.'

Hughton said:

'As a manager, as a person, you have to try and be honest with everyone around you. If I leave a player out, they deserve an explanation. It's about communication, about being clear in what you want. Yes, I'm tougher than I look. You can't survive in this business unless you have a toughness, you need extremely broad shoulders. Every day, there are hard decisions to make, so I'm not as nice as I may seem. But I am honest and I never have any problem telling anyone anything, as long as that is what I truly believe and I have said it for the right reasons.'

• • •

It would have been welcome if the team, inspired by the absence of any departures, had immediately rewarded Bloom's faith with a victory, but football does not follow rules. On Friday 9 September, an evening event for the 1901 Club fans was held at the city's new i360 observation tower, but a technical fault meant that the viewing pod failed to get more than a few feet above the ground. After Saturday's game, that seemed to be an apt metaphor for the club's latest promotion challenge.

They dropped to thirteenth place after losing 2–0 at home to Brentford, and Duffy's Amex debut in the stripes did not go well, not that he could be blamed for a lack of cohesion in front of him. Albion had more of the ball but did little with it. Knockaert nearly fluked an opener when his cross from the right veered too close to goal and had to be batted away by visiting goalkeeper Dan Bentley, but the forwards generally failed to fire.

Unfortunately, Brentford had an in-form marksman in Scott Hogan, who raced onto a pass from Lewis Macleod on the half-hour with Bruno caught out of position. Duffy could not catch him before he shot left-footed between Stockdale and his near post. And Hogan nearly scored an identical goal minutes later, but this time Stockdale saved with his feet.

Albion did create some chances. Murray nodded Knockaert's deep cross back for Hemed to head past Bentley, only for John Egan to hook the ball off the line. And Manu was harshly booked for simulation after a challenge by Harlee Dean that replays suggested had been a foul and a penalty.

But things remained chaotic at the other end, where Bruno and Duffy were on different wavelengths. Stockdale had to save again from Macleod and Hogan, twice, before Hogan got his second after seventy minutes. Albion had just survived a scare when Knockaert had to head off the line from Andreas Bjelland following a corner, but the ball was never completely cleared and Brentford cut through the right of the defence, leaving Hogan to rifle past Stockdale and into the roof of the net.

The move had simply bypassed Duffy, but Hughton was still confident in his ability to integrate his new signing with an unfamiliar goalkeeper, right-back and central defensive partner. And he believed that the team would right itself and challenge again.

'I had no doubts,' he said at the end of the season.

'Did I know roughly where we would be in the table? No, because of the league. You look at teams who are not even in the top six. I always felt we could compete, that we could put in levels of performances, but could I guarantee we'd be in that top six all season? No, you can't.

'The Newcastle game wasn't so bad, because it wasn't that bad a performance. Probably the Brentford one, because it was at home, was more disappointing at the time. It was unusual for us to have two defeats in succession.'

But after that defeat by Brentford, Hughton's work with Duffy was to pay off with a run of seven clean sheets in nine games. 'It took us a few games to get used to each other because we hadn't played together before,' Dunk said.

'But once those few games were out of the way, I think we've fed off each other really well. The first time you line up alongside someone you don't know how you're going to play with them, but you click after one or two games, you know their strengths and weaknesses and where you're going to be. Once you've got that bond, you're flying. Thankfully, I've had good bonds with everyone I've played with.

'Now we know each other's game inside out and what my weaknesses are he's good at and what his weaknesses are I'm good at, so we bounce off each other so well and it's a pleasure to play with him. There has been change to my left, too, which was difficult at times but it's like playing with different central defenders: you play your game slightly differently depending on who's there.'

The team had an opportunity to put the Brentford result behind them only three days later when league leaders Huddersfield visited the Amex. To say that the Terriers were a surprise team was an understatement. Much like Albion the previous year, they had been tipped to struggle, but German manager David Wagner, an old friend and coaching colleague of Liverpool manager Jürgen Klopp, had clearly worked a minor miracle. His team had dropped only two points in its six matches, in a draw away to Aston Villa, and had won at both Newcastle and Leeds.

Hughton made changes, benching Murray and trying Knockaert in the number 10 role that he had earmarked for Pritchard, as well as restoring Stephens to the starting line-up for the first time since his transfer request. Whether as a result of the reshuffle or a desire to show their true mettle, the team gave a much-improved display. However, a goal refused to come. Murphy went through but hit his shot too close to goalkeeper Danny Ward, Kayal sent a screamer just wide, Bruno had a shot blocked, Dunk hit the post with a header, and as the game approached its final stages, Ward seemed happy to waste more and more time, to the frustration of the North Stand and with referee Andy Woolmer apparently oblivious.

So there was extra delight among the supporters when it was an error from Ward, the Wales goalkeeper on loan to Huddersfield from Liverpool, that gifted Knockaert the winner ten minutes from time. Albion worked the ball along the edge of the penalty area from left to right, but when Murphy's pass found Knockaert, the Frenchman's first-time left-foot effort was not especially hard-hit and straight at the goalkeeper. However, the ball squirmed off Ward's glove and as he desperately tried to reach back and recover the situation, his despairing lunge only succeeded in speeding the ball over the line.

The goal had been a freak, but the win was well deserved and it would not be the last time that a team had arrived at the Amex on a good run and with a growing reputation yet been made to look ordinary.

Success, of course, comes from seeing off the teams you are

expected to beat as well as the contenders, and the next opponents, newly promoted Burton Albion, fell into the former category. Nigel Clough's side were to record wins against Derby, Huddersfield, Leeds, Norwich and Sheffield Wednesday during their first campaign at this level, and they did not make life easy for the Albion at their compact Pirelli Stadium either.

Burton were hard-working and disciplined, but although Hughton had to throw 21-year-old Rob Hunt on for his league debut as a substitute for the injured Bruno in the second half, they forced only one save from Stockdale. Their defending, though, was determined and disciplined and they seemed likely to hang on for a point until Knockaert slipped Skalák through two minutes from time and he was brought down by Jackson Irvine. Hemed stepped up to convert the penalty and seal a second successive 1–0 victory.

After a second-string team went tamely out of the Capital One Cup in a mid-week match at home to Reading, the first-choices got back to work again at home to Barnsley, this time shutting out the highest-scoring side in the division in a 2–0 win that, with Knockaert very much on his game, could have been more convincing.

Glenn Murray was back in the side and back on the scoresheet. He had an early shot saved by goalkeeper Adam Davies but he made no mistake in the twelfth minute. Bong had begun the move with a pass from his own area to Knockaert, who ran at the Barnsley defence before sending a diagonal pass to Kayal on the left. Instead of shooting, Kayal cut the ball back for Murray to take a touch with his right foot and drive the ball in low with his left.

It was the type of fast break that would cause problems for plenty of opponents over the season, and another pass from the left, by Bong, gave Murray a chance to double the lead, only for his shot to squirt wide. But he made amends early in the second half, glancing home a header from Skalák's free kick on the left. And a stronger contact with another cross by the Czech might have brought him a hat-trick. Even Duffy came close to scoring, heading over from close range, but the win was good enough to take the team up from seventh to third place, ahead of Reading on goal difference.

Duffy was now settling in and the fans recognised that he and Dunk were forming an almost impenetrable barrier in front of Stockdale, with the Irishman's prodigious leaps making him hard to beat in the air. As a former centre half, Calderwood knew that Duffy would be a valuable acquisition. 'He brought aerial power, authority and a bit more ruggedness, which helped.'

• • •

There was at least one encouraging precedent for a club achieving success by spending on defence rather than attack as Hughton had done. Everton, the league champions in 1984/85, had invested in Gary Lineker for their title defence the following season – but although Lineker became the league's top scorer in 1985/86 with forty goals in all competitions, thirty in the league, Everton finished runners-up to neighbours Liverpool and also lost to them in the FA Cup final.

Manager Howard Kendall then took the counter-intuitive step of selling Lineker to Barcelona for £2.8 million and buying a central defender, Dave Watson, from Norwich for £900,000. Predictably, that affected the Toffees' attack and their top league scorer in 1986/87 was midfield player Trevor Steven, with a paltry fourteen goals, most of them penalties. But they were champions again, while the nation's top scorer, Clive Allen of Tottenham Hotspur, got forty-nine in all competitions but Spurs finished the season empty-handed, and third in the league.

Hughton had looked at the previous campaign and decided that it was not the goals the Albion had failed to score that had proved so costly in the end, but the ones they had failed to keep out, at Bolton, at Derby, at QPR and finally at Middlesbrough. Now, with Duffy and Dunk repelling most attacks, the team was better able to overcome problems that might at one time have looked insurmountable, such as the ankle injury that had forced Kayal off during the Barnsley game and would keep him out until January.

The twin-engine room in central midfield of the Israeli and Stephens was seen as the vital combination without which the team stuttered. And when the next match ended as a drab goalless draw against Ipswich Town at Portman Road, the point seemed to be proved.

Worse still, Stephens's frustration had resulted in a yellow card for dissent then a second for a foul. That meant an automatic one-match suspension and the absence of both first-choice central midfield players for the following game, against Sheffield Wednesday at Hillsborough. Naturally, many fans feared the worst. The team's chance of breaking their duck at the Owls' home looked slim and, after the previous season's traumas there, the omens were poor.

Yet Hughton's men, with Norwood and Sidwell in central midfield, produced what the manager regards as the best away performance of the season, controlling the game throughout. The opening goal was a masterpiece, Dunk making an interception before advancing down the left and playing a superb forward pass to Baldock with the outside of his right foot. Baldock glanced up and then lifted the ball gently over the advancing goalkeeper, Keiren Westwood, who got a fingertip to the forward's lob but could not prevent it dropping in.

'I played that pass off the outside of my right foot because I haven't got a left foot,' Dunk said.

'That was a nice assist. In my youth team days and even earlier than that I was a striker or a winger, but I kept growing and growing and growing and moving further back. The more I grew, the further back I moved. Now I'm six foot four and right at the back so I hope I don't go one step further.'

In the second half, Bong advanced down the same flank and crossed for Knockaert to half-volley in at the near post. An injury-time consolation for Wednesday by Gary Hooper in a goalmouth scramble was insignificant in terms of the result, but the anger and frustration shown by Stockdale and Duffy at the loss of another precious clean sheet when they could have been revelling in the club's first ever win at Hillsborough was revealing.

'When we played that video again not so long ago there were about three defensive players kicking the ball in the net in anger,' Stockdale said. 'People were like: "What's wrong with them? They're going to win, it was the last kick of the game." To us it was a clean sheet gone. Maybe it was missing out on goal difference last season that had affected us so badly.'

'Clean sheets win you games, and with our attackers, I always think we'll win if they don't score,' Dunk said. 'We say that before every match: "Clean sheet, win the game; clean sheet, win the game." If we don't concede, I always think we'll win.'

They were even more annoyed when another late goal in the following match, at home to Preston, that perennial thorn in Albion sides, rescued a point for North End in a 2–2 draw. It was a collector's item in that Duffy was beaten to a header by the Lancashire club's giant Danish striker Simon Makienok. Albion had conceded a ludicrous opener, when Stockdale failed to deal with an ill-advised lofted backpass by Bruno, and Jordan Hugill had pounced. The captain made amends with the pass from which Baldock levelled in the second half, and Murray made it 2–1 with one of his best goals of the season, taking Murphy's pass, turning away from defender Alex Baptiste and tucking a low shot past goalkeeper Chris Maxwell.

Preston's late leveller was a kick in the teeth but normal defensive service was resumed in the next two matches, as the rearguard found itself under pressure from Wolves at the Amex and Wigan at the DW Stadium but held on to record 1–0 wins. Baldock got the winner against Wolves after only fourteen minutes, meeting Bong's cross with a deft near-post header, but hearts were in mouths late on as Stockdale dived to save from Danny Batth and the ball skidded across the face of the Albion goal from a corner as time ran out.

Stephens came off the bench at Wigan to score his first goal of the season, a curled shot from outside the penalty area, to continue a remarkable scoring record against sides from his native north-west, and send the Seagulls into second place behind Newcastle. It was not a great game, but it had a significance that few could have imagined in such a traditionally competitive division: the team would never be out of the top two automatic promotion places for the rest of the season.

• • •

A week later came one of the most memorable performances of the campaign, and one that made the rest of the Championship sit up and take notice. Norwich had led the table twelve days earlier and although they had stumbled at home to Preston the week before, they were still in fourth place, only one point behind Brighton, when they arrived at the Amex on 28 October. Few doubted that Albion would be in for a tough test against a team sure to be in the running for automatic promotion.

Norwich's financial muscle as a relegated club with access to parachute payments automatically made them contenders, as Pritchard had stated when opting for Carrow Road over the Amex. But his appearance was not the only factor to add spice to the fixture. Norwich, of course, had sacked Hughton eighteen months previously, losing their nerve as they hovered above the Premier League drop zone with five games to go but going down anyway.

Now Hughton saw his Seagulls exact a cruel revenge on his behalf, dismembering the hapless Canaries in a 5–0 romp. Murray set the mood early on, taking advantage of a heavy first touch from goalkeeper Michael McGovern after only six minutes, shoulder-charging him aside and turning to plant the ball into the empty goal, albeit with a shot that went in off the near post.

The second was one of the goals of the season, as Bong sent Skalák away down the left, and the Czech produced a beautifully flighted cross with his weaker foot that Murray nodded firmly home despite the attention of two defenders. Just as decisive was Dunk's header at the far post from Skalák's corner before McGovern erred again, miskicking a clearance to the surprised Ryan Bennett. Murray pounced and shot home with the help of a deflection to complete his hat-trick. Finally, Skalák completed a treble of his own – three assists – when he put Knockaert through to dink the ball home and inflict a heavier defeat than any Norwich had suffered under manager Alex Neil in their relegation from the top flight.

Not only had Albion strengthened their grip on second place, they had also improved last season's Achilles heel, their goal difference, to +14.

Characteristically, Hughton refused to glory in victory over his former employers and preferred to dwell on his ironclad defence and the importance of taking three points from a potential promotion rival. 'When you're playing against such a talented team, the basis has to be: can you keep a clean sheet?' he said. 'We defended as a team very well, we restricted them to minimal chances and the team should be as proud about the defensive side as the rest. Irrespective of the opposition, these days don't happen too often.'

But, of course, he could not ignore Murray's contribution. 'Glenn is a proven striker at this level,' he said. 'He scores goals. He worked very hard, the first goal being a great example of that. It was a great opportunist goal. But the second goal was crucial. We were up against a very talented team, but they opened up more at 2–0 and we exploited the spaces.'

As for Pritchard, he had a wretched game, being booked then substituted, to the delight of Albion fans. Afterwards, president Dick Knight spoke to Norwich co-owner Delia Smith, an old friend of his. 'She said: "Would you like Pritchard after all?"' Knight recalled.

The margin of victory established the club's goal difference as worth an extra point, where it would remain all season. Elsewhere in the division there had been an equally unexpected result as Huddersfield gave an error-strewn display as they also went down 5–0, away to unpredictable but talented Fulham. That, it seemed to many, surely showed that the Yorkshire side would not be able to sustain their early promise, a notion they would disprove over most of the rest of the season.

But that looked like a side issue. The table and the team's form, with Murray justifying his return in grand style – even if all nine of his goals so far had come at home – augured well. Amid all the post-match euphoria, nobody could have known that tragedy, personal this time, was about to strike the club again. And yet the aftermath would come to define and cement the spirit in the squad and underpin all that followed.

CHAPTER 11

TOGETHER

As the squad prepared for the next match, away to Bristol City, Anthony Knockaert suffered the grievous blow of the death of his father. It was the second tragedy to strike the popular winger's family. He had lost his 28-year-old brother Steve to a heart attack when he was breaking into the first team at Guingamp. Now Patrick, the father he adored, had been taken ill and Knockaert had rushed to his bedside. He was in time to say farewell before his father passed away on Thursday 3 November.

'Worse day in my life,' he tweeted, 'Daddy just passed away in my arms … You did everything for me, best man in the world. RIP PAPA.' He added in a second tweet: 'Because your dream was to see me in premier league, I promise you daddy we will do it this season for you !!!! LOVE YOU.'

Knockaert remained in France while the squad headed for Bristol, where supporters arriving early for the Saturday evening kick-off were able to avail themselves of a first, a pre-match forum for away fans with Tony Bloom at the Rose of Denmark pub on the edge of Clifton. The best question came from an eight-year-old, who asked: 'When we sing "Tony Bloom's blue-and-white army", do you think: "I'm the man?"'

That brought the house down and Bloom couldn't help laughing along with the crowd, before replying: 'I've never quite thought about it in those terms! It is perhaps a little embarrassing at times. But I think the fans are just showing their appreciation and I appreciate that.'

When fans had walked over to Ashton Gate, they saw that although Knockaert was on the other side of the English Channel, his kit was laid out on one of the dugout seats. The match itself was memorable for two things – Steve Sidwell's opening goal and the celebrations that followed it.

After thirteen minutes, City's Korey Smith, receiving a square pass from Gary O'Neil, was caught in possession in the centre circle by Baldock. Sidwell ran onto the loose ball and, from just inside the Bristol half, lofted the ball goalwards. Goalkeeper Richard O'Donnell, who had been standing on the penalty spot, backpedalled furiously but fell over and was unable to prevent the ball from landing in the back of the net. 'I'd noticed the keeper coming off his line and I thought that I'd have a go at lobbing him if I got the chance,' Sidwell explained later. 'But I didn't expect to do it with my left foot.'

Now, Sidwell turned and rushed to the sidelines, where Bruno had picked up Knockaert's shirt and the players held it aloft in tribute to their grieving comrade. Former Albion player Warren Aspinall, summarising on BBC local radio, said: 'That is what Brighton are all about. That sent shivers down my spine. An excellent thing to do for one of your players who is mourning at home. What they have done is absolutely brilliant. I've got tears in my eyes.'

In France, Knockaert had seen what happened. 'I was in the chapel of rest with one of my brothers,' he said.

'My dad was lying in front of us and it was hard, so hard. I was watching what they did on my phone; a special, intense moment that I'll never, ever forget. They gave me such support. It didn't make me happy, because nothing could, but it made me feel like everybody was with me.'

'It has been a tough week for the group,' Sidwell said. 'Our thoughts are with [Anthony], because football is a fantastic sport that we all love but family comes first. We are lucky that we have a great group of people here, a tight-knit group, and we dedicate that goal and the three points to him and his family.'

The celebration, he said, had been planned 'probably only on the day. Obviously we knew that Anthony wasn't going to be travelling with us, he was in France with his family, and we said before the game that we wanted his shirt, and his kit, all laid out on the bench to show that our thoughts were with him and his family. We said whoever scores, we would celebrate together. We didn't think it was going to be a goal like that but it shows that some things are just meant to be.'

Murphy made it 2–0 seven minutes later. Sidwell won possession in City's half and Murphy exchanged passes with Murray before cutting in from the left and hitting a low right-foot shot that took a slight deflection on its way past O'Donnell and into the bottom far corner. And there was a late, and almost unnoticed, bonus in the return to first-team action of Solly March as a late substitute.

With an international week ahead, some players departed for the training camps of their national sides while Hughton and Bruno prepared to head for Leers, near Lille, to attend Patrick Knockaert's funeral on Tuesday 8 November. But then the other players decided that they wanted to pay their respects in person and support their teammate in his hour of need.

'I think the gaffer was going to go with Bruno, as captain,' Sidwell said.

'That was pencilled in. They asked Anthony first if that would be OK and he said yes. Then the boys caught wind of that and we said, "Let's all go together." Some of us had other priorities – treatment, or international calls or family issues – but we all got together and made the trip out there and it all goes to show the team spirit that goes beyond football.'

Once again, the '#Together' hashtag was proving more than a marketing tool. 'The club arranged a coach, a hotel, everything and it was quite special,' Bruno said. 'Anthony was expecting the gaffer and me but all of us were there and I think it was nice for him to see. We are like family for him as well.'

Knockaert confessed that he was overwhelmed. 'I knew already that this club was special but after that I really thought that this club was amazing and this club will be in my heart for ever because of what they did for me and my dad and my family,' he said.

'To be honest, I don't think another team would have done what they did. Coming all the way from England to France and cancelling training to come to my dad's funeral was a thing that I will never forget and I still don't know even now how to say thank you to them.

'Now for me they are not just some teammates but friends for ever and this football club, I owe them a lot. That's why I give every single bit of my life on the pitch and they deserve it because this club is something special and you cannot see that in any club in the world.'

The insistence on strength of character as a factor in recruitment was paying off. 'I think we've got a squad of superb characters and that means a lot over the course of a season,' Bloom said. 'I'm sure there are moments in training when words are spoken but they are genuinely together as a squad and that means so much. It does get you better results over time.'

Not that the squad was composed of choirboys. 'Of course we have times when we don't agree in training or in games and it must be like that,' Bruno said.

'But when you've got a proper group like we've got, the most important thing is that things you say in training or in games stay there. When we get to the changing room, that's it.

'Sometimes, with Anthony for example – Anthony and me, we've got an unbelievable relationship – but sometimes on the pitch I am shouting at him because I'm thinking he's not doing something he has to be doing or he's shouting at me. When we get to the changing room, it's over. But if you don't have that togetherness, when you come back in, it's not finished and the atmosphere gets worse and worse. We all think we should be playing and we have to play, all big characters and sometimes things happen but afterwards it's all done.

'Anthony has been unbelievable for us for this season and a half. He's our best player; there are no words for him. Everyone can improve, of course, but he's in the right way and he's got a bright future. I just hope everything goes well for him because he deserves it.'

It was that spirit and togetherness, Sidwell agreed, that would help the team fulfil its aims. 'One hundred per cent,' he said.

'If you look at last season, we just missed out but not going up was possibly a blessing in disguise. We were there physically and technically as a team, but mentally we weren't. I think we've gained that this year, we're all together and pushing in the right direction and we just need to get over the line.'

• • •

But one man no longer pushing in the same direction was Colin Calderwood, who was surprisingly announced as the new assistant manager to Steve Bruce at Aston Villa, coincidentally Albion's next opponents. Hughton said he was 'very disappointed, very surprised'.

Hughton and Calderwood had known each other since 1993. 'The year I joined Tottenham as a player, Chris joined as a coach,' Calderwood said.

'He was at the junior end and I was a senior pro, but when I went back there later as reserve-team manager, he had progressed to working with Glenn Hoddle at first-team level. That was when our coaching relationship began.

'When he went to Newcastle, he wanted a bit of help and we won the Championship in 2010. I'd actually left to manage Hibernian in Scotland before Chris got the sack. The next season he gave me a chance to go to Birmingham with him. At first Hibs said no, but eventually in November I did join up with him, and then went with him to Norwich.

'Brighton was a very easy sell. I knew a bit of the history and had seen the development of the club. I was delighted to come and join him, around February time, a month or so after he'd taken the job. Chris had assessed the situation and we sorted it all out.'

The attractions of the new job in the Midlands for Calderwood included the fact that he is a former Villa player, and that he still lived in Northampton, where he had managed from 2003 to 2006. A fifty-mile journey to work along the M1 and M6 to Villa's Bodymoor Heath headquarters was preferable to a 270-mile slog to Lancing and back. Bruce had replaced Roberto Di Matteo as Villa manager in October and was looking for an assistant.

'It was an accumulation of personal things, health-related things and the proximity of Aston Villa and it being the club it is that swayed me,' Calderwood said.

'And I have to be honest and say that the money did make a big difference. There's no shying away from it, the money side does come into it.

'But I didn't want to leave the Brighton situation. The nice thing about the place is that from the security staff up I'd say 85 per cent of the people who work there support Brighton, so they have a feeling for the club. It was a very difficult choice and I struggled for a number of days over it, but I made the decision I did and I'm glad it panned out as it did for Brighton.

'It wasn't popular with Chris, but it's part of a manager's job to calm any turbulence with anyone leaving, a player or a member of staff. And there's nobody better than him. He's never too high and he's never too low. The group is always more important than any individual.'

'I've not done anything sinister,' Bruce said. 'I've taken advantage of a situation, basically. When I heard Colin was interested he shot to the top of the pile. The lure of Villa is that he's closer to home and that is important to him because he's found the travelling difficult.'

And Calderwood admits that he was as certain as he could be that he was leaving a club destined for the Premier League.

'We saw Watford and Bournemouth at Brighton when they went up, and previous times when you play against teams that have gone on to get promoted and you see something in them that makes you understand why they are going to achieve what you think they might.

'The last game I was involved in was at Bristol City, and I thought, "They are damned close." There was a long way to go, but there was something so professional about that performance, capped by the emotion of Anthony Knockaert's situation and the fact that Steve Sidwell scored that fantastic goal. I think that was the moment that I thought they would probably achieve it.'

A compensation package was agreed and Calderwood was given a period of gardening leave to cover the build-up to the Villa match. The fallen Premier League giants were struggling, so Albion were confident, but this turned out to be one of the toughest games of the season.

It began with an early shock as the team conceded its first goal in five games, a glancing header by Nathan Baker from a free kick by Albert Adomah, Albion's old Middlesbrough sparring partner. Hughton's men had to raise their game and it took another goal-of-the-season finalist to draw them level before half-time. Former Villa man Sidwell drove at his former club's defence and passed forward to Murray. He laid the ball off first time to Baldock and wheeled away to the right. Baldock was on the same wavelength and returned the ball into Murray's path and he took a touch and lashed the ball low into the corner from 22 yards.

But if the fans expected Albion, reinforced by the return of Knockaert, to kick on from there, they were disappointed. With ex-Palace strongman Mile Jedinak an abrasive presence in midfield, Villa came again in the second half. Refreshed by the introduction of the talented Jack Grealish – no relation to Albion's late stand-in FA Cup final captain, Tony – they forced Stockdale into a series of saves. He pushed a low drive by Adomah around a post and a header by Jonathan Kodjia from four yards over the crossbar. £11 million man Kodjia had earlier nodded against the bar. There was relief when the final whistle blew with the score still 1–1.

Some fans unhappy at a failure to win were even more disgruntled afterwards when they discovered that Southern Rail, who had been in dispute with the unions for months, had cancelled a number of trains from Falmer at short notice, stranding some supporters who were unable to make onward connections. Earlier in the season, executive director Martin Perry had written to Brighton and Hove's three MPs asking them to lobby for action by the government in ending the dispute, which he estimated had cost the club around £300,000 in lost revenue at the first two home games of the season.

In short, it had not been the evening many Brighton fans had hoped for. But in retrospect, taking a point from this game showed how far the team had come in ability and mental strength over a year. It could have been the equivalent of the Middlesbrough match of eleven months earlier, a damaging home defeat that dented the goal difference as well as the confidence. But the team held on.

The difference from the previous season was in both penalty areas. Now the team had significant weapons at each end of the pitch. The defence took conceding goals personally and Duffy, Dunk and the others not only tackled fiercely and won headers but also repeatedly threw themselves in the way of shots. And behind them, Stockdale was in the form of his life.

At the front, Murray and Baldock were working well as a forward pairing and Murray was as proven a goal-scorer as Zamora but without the complications as regards fitness. His goal against Villa was untypical in that it was hit from outside the box, while he was known more as a predator in the penalty area. But he had already demonstrated the ability to score goals of all types: headers, opportunist strikes and well-timed arrivals to meet low crosses.

'I'm under no illusions – I never will be and never have been someone who dribbles past everyone and bends it in the top corner,' he said.

'It's just not in my make-up. But goal-scoring is a knack, to begin with. And then the more experienced you become, the more you believe in yourself. Some people say you mustn't be afraid to look lazy, by which I mean that defenders have to follow the ball, work together, and I can just stand still and, without moving, end up in space while everyone else is moving around me.

'The second goal against Forest was the opposite, reading the situation and getting there to get the tap-in. But all goal-scorers are different. I remember playing with a guy here before called Fran Sandaza and he was just Johnny-on-the-spot. The ball would just literally hit him in the six-yard box and go in. To me, he was a great goal-scorer because he was always in the right place at the right time.'

And as Murray had hoped, he was getting excellent service from the wide men. 'It was everything I expected and I think Anthony has even surpassed what he did last year,' he said. 'I try to read what they're going to do. Anthony's a bit unpredictable for the defenders as well as us but that's what makes him as good as he is. I make myself available and try to find a pocket of space where he can find me.'

• • •

Before the next match, at home to Fulham, Barber issued a statement regarding the rail chaos following the Villa match. The club includes a transport surcharge in its ticket prices to fund park and ride services and to pay bus and rail companies to allow spectators free public transport before and after matches. Southern had not been delivering the service the club was paying for and now Barber publicly branded their actions 'totally unacceptable. There's no accountability, there's no responsibility and there doesn't seem to be any pride in providing a service to the public. Like so many who rely on the rail network for their livelihoods, our fans have had enough.

'We have one of the best travel plans of any football club in the country. It was a condition of the stadium being built that we put in a sustainable travel plan, which means using trains, buses and fewer cars. Where are the politicians and the government now? Where's the accountability to bring this organisation to account for the poor service to thousands of people in this city, week in week out?'

There was much, much more. Calling out rail companies, though, was just one of many duties for the chief executive, who had been brought on board in 2012. He had worked for the Football Association, Tottenham Hotspur and Vancouver Whitecaps before being sought out by Bloom. One of the attractions of the Championship club, he had said, was that 'the commitment from the owner is off the charts' and, several years later, his appreciation of his employer had only been strengthened.

'Tony has a humble approach – keep your feet on the ground, do things properly, treat people properly and make the money work as hard as you can,' Barber said.

'These are themes that run through every decision that we make. It's not an order or a diktat; it's the way he does things. He wants us to do it similarly, but our own way. This is the overall objective, what you do within it is up to you but let's make sure we do it properly.

'There are so many disciplines and specialisms in a football club. From professional athletes to car park attendants via marketers, cleaners, engineers, salespeople, medics, accountants, groundstaff, cleaners. But unlike in a big factory or university or hospital, you have the huge highs and lows of the results every Saturday or whenever. Ninety minutes affects a whole week. My job is to try to keep everyone somewhere in the middle.

'Of course, you can't guarantee what happens out there on the pitch. But our job is to make it as easy as possible for those guys to go out there and win football matches. So whatever your job is, do it to the best of your ability so that they can win more often. If you're a cleaner, make the dressing room spotless. If they look the part and feel the part, they'll play the part. It's simple Sunday league stuff. If you're the car park attendant, help a player park his car beautifully and him getting out of his car feeling great just might make the tiny percentage difference in him playing better than he's ever played before.'

In return, permanent staff receive free breakfasts and lunches at the stadium and training ground, and all the club's workers, including the 800 or so match-day employees, were offered promotion bonuses of up to 20 per cent. Barber's briefings, either in person or by email, sometimes include news of extra days off and reminders to staff members to enjoy themselves and the team's victories.

But Barber also had to make less welcome decisions soon after he arrived. 'I found that the club was engineered like a BMW but it had Mini revenues,' he said.

'Our cost base was too high. We had strong revenues but the margin we were returning to the football side was too small. We had to stop doing some things that the staff had become used to. Someone came into me one day early on with a scratch on his computer and a purchase order for a new one. I said: "No, we can't do that. It may not look the best but it still works."

'We had to get a grip of our costs. It made me very unpopular at the beginning, internally and externally, but we had to widen the margins that gave us more money in the football budget to build a better squad. When I came in, we had staff numbers as big as Tottenham's. I couldn't compute that. I asked if the figures were right. It was about putting as much money as possible on the pitch to help those guys win matches.'

Barber had grown up as a Tottenham fan, but after five years at the Albion, he admitted that his allegiances had gradually shifted.

'When we played Spurs in the Capital One Cup at White Hart Lane in 2014, I remember going into the directors' box and turning right as I usually did when I was a director there until it was pointed out to me that I was sitting on the left, which my son, who was with me, thought was so funny. And it was the first time I'd looked to the corner of the South Stand to see where my club's supporters were.'

That would be far less likely now. 'My daughter Ellie's entire life has been with me working in professional football,' he said.

'She was never committed in any way to Tottenham or Vancouver, but if you put her in the middle of the North Stand today, no one would doubt her love for this club. She has not just become a football fan but a Brighton fan.

'So I have to live with a Brighton fan, but I've become one anyway. It's been part of my life for five years and the journey has been so dramatic, and painful at times, that you can't help but be drawn in. And I love it here, and so do my family. I've got a son at university in Vancouver, a daughter in Newcastle, but they love coming back to the city.

'It's a special club. There's something about it that gets into your blood. It's partly because of how close it is to the community, partly because the story of the club at times is so heartbreaking but at the same time so heart-warming. So many people care so deeply about it. And it has such a diverse supporter base. I've sat with a leading QC who is a massive fan, as eloquent and articulate about the club as you can imagine, and with a lad with learning difficulties who struggles to put words together in the right order who loves the club with equal passion. And everything in between: you've got artists, writers, actors, musicians, DJs, Des Lynam, a strange rich tapestry. I've never denied being a Spurs fan since I was eight years old but next season I know where I want the six points to go.'

• • •

The staff numbers would grow by one on 24 November as Hughton acted to replace Calderwood. He brought in another experienced man, Paul Trollope, who had been sacked as manager of Cardiff City less than a month before and had been part of the Wales coaching team at the 2016 European Championships. He had previously worked with Hughton at both Birmingham and Norwich and knew his new boss and the division well.

'I'm delighted to be working with Paul again,' Hughton said. 'He's an excellent coach, and since his time with me he's gone on to gain great experience at international level with Wales and in club management with Cardiff.'

Hiring someone he knew and trusted helped Hughton ensure that the transition was as seamless as possible for the players, who had liked Calderwood. 'Colin was a massive part of it here and was very important around the place,' Dunk said.

'If you wanted something, you'd always go to him to take it to the gaffer. He actually brought "Sweet Caroline" in as our dressing-room song – and added a few lines of his own in. He was a good link and got on with everyone, so he was a big loss to us.

'But they recruited well upstairs and brought in Paul Trollope, and he has taken us up another level. His coaching has been a massive help. He is a different character – Trolls is a little quieter than Colin, Colin was a bit more lively around the place – but he inherited the same role and we can always go to him and his coaching has been some of the best I've had in my career.'

'I was at a great advantage having already worked with Chris at a couple of clubs and it's always good to come into something that's working and succeeding,' Trollope said.

'The club had done so well over two years, with a lot of hard work and dedication from a huge number of people. But there had also been an equal amount of dedication from people going back since the Goldstone days to change the club to what it is today, a monumental achievement by everybody. A unity had been created.

'Every successful team needs a successful team spirit and good players, and when I came in in November, I saw both things in abundance: the spirit of the players and the professionalism of the staff Chris leads, but also the quality of the players for this division. They would have deserved to go up the previous year.'

With former Albion player Ben Roberts as goalkeeping coach and Nevin as first-team coach, the backroom team was now complete again. The training ground dynamic was fluid, Hughton said.

'I determine what they [Paul Trollope and Paul Nevin] do and what I want them to do, but I work closely with them. I've been an assistant and a first-team coach, so I know the roles, and what you want is to make a contribution.

'So I don't do all the coaching because I wouldn't want two very good coaches feeling undervalued or underused. On a match day I work a little closer to Paul Trollope as my assistant, which is natural, but he and Paul Nevin are both very experienced coaches who have been around for a while. It's not a case of one does this and only this and the other does that and only that. They both get involved in analytic work, preparation, sessions, going to see opposition.'

Getting points when below its best is supposed to be the hallmark of a successful team, and Albion demonstrated that again in the next match, at home to Fulham. The Cottagers had shown their quality in that pre-season friendly, and impressed again at the Amex, taking a first-half lead through Kevin McDonald's far-post header from a corner and forcing three diving saves from their former favourite Stockdale.

But with points at stake, Albion's steely side came to the fore. And there was yet another spectacular goal for the end-of-season showreel. Stephens headed back a long cross into the danger zone, and when it was nodded out by a defender to the edge of the penalty area, Baldock hit the sweetest of volleys past goalkeeper David Button.

Baldock then saw a close-range shot deflected to safety via a post before providing the winning assist, crossing for Murray to volley home from eight yards as the defenders got their attempt to play the offside trap all wrong.

Baldock was now coming into his own. Few players had divided fan opinion as much as the former MK Dons, West Ham and Bristol City forward. Some despaired at his lack of goals as a front man, and saw him as a good League One player who could not translate his scoring prowess to the higher level. They pointed to his record in West Ham's promotion season, when he was a regular on the team-sheet and scoresheet early in the campaign but played (and scored) far less frequently as the season approached its climax.

Others saw how much space his clever movement and appetite for running created for teammates, especially Murray. Baldock was one of those players whose qualities are most evident when they are not playing and the team fails to function as a result. There was also statistical evidence for his effectiveness in his astonishing record of never having started on a losing Brighton side the previous season.

Fortunately, Hughton and Baldock's teammates were in the latter group. 'I think me and Sam complement each other,' Murray said.

'I think he does do a bit more of the running in the partnership, but I try to pull my weight too. It's the little-and-large combo, but we work off each other and it worked well for a lot of the season.

'When I joined the club, I saw him as a goal-scorer. That's what he is, for me, and has been throughout his career. I know it didn't go quite to plan the first year or so here, but he's definitely rediscovered himself this year and proved that he is a goal-scorer at this level.'

'There is no doubt that there is a confidence factor about scoring goals,' Baldock said. 'Last year I thought I was playing well without getting my rewards in front of goal. But this season I was getting the chances and they were going in and it helps when you score from outside the box.'

Neither Baldock nor Murray could score in the next match, a goalless draw at Cardiff, although Murray did get the ball in the net. It was a poor game until Knockaert came off the bench after seventy minutes. The Frenchman raised the tempo and Murray thought he had won the game and scored his first away goal of the season to boot until the referee – Albion's old friend Roger East – judged that Duffy had fouled an opponent as he nodded Knockaert's corner down for Murray to volley in.

And there was more controversy when Dunk reacted to the crowd holding onto the ball to disrupt Albion's late momentum by throwing it back when they finally relinquished it. He was booked, and the yellow cards were mounting up. A defender collects enough cautions in the course of his normal work without asking for unnecessary bookings, and this was Dunk's eighth of the season and his third in as many games. Bong then got in on the act, collecting a second yellow card of the match for a foul, ruling him out of the next game, at home to Leeds.

The draw was still an improvement on the previous season's calamitous 4–1 defeat, and stretched the team's unbeaten run to thirteen games.

• • •

On 7 December, the club's accounts for 2015/16 were lodged with the Football League, showing a loss of £25.8 million compared with £1.4 million the previous year. But more significant were Bloom's comments in his chairman's statement, in which he emphasised that he and the club were determined to build on the previous season's experience.

'The 2015/16 season was one of the most memorable and exciting in my forty years as a Brighton & Hove Albion supporter,' he wrote.

'The team, under Chris Hughton's astute leadership, gave us a season to savour – and although we twice missed out on taking that final step to the Premier League, it has laid the foundation for our current season. To compete at the top end of the Championship it's important to have a manager who knows how to win at this level and to possess a strong group of quality players. We have both, and while this does not guarantee promotion, it gives us an excellent chance.

'Our increased losses result directly from an ongoing and growing investment in our playing squad, and Chris, Paul Winstanley, Paul Barber and I are very pleased with the squad. Furthermore, on the back of last season, we wanted to retain our key players, and our decision not to cash in key assets has seen player trading go from a profit to a loss.'

There followed the now traditional Friday evening date with Leeds, Sky Sports apparently unable to resist the temptation to single this plum out of the fixture list regardless of the form of either team.

In this case, Leeds were doing well and were in fourth place, having won five of their previous six league games. Albion knew that a win would take them into first place, at least until leaders Newcastle played.

In the end, Leeds, like Huddersfield, failed to live up to their reputation, and Albion were already making most of the running when Kalvin Phillips handled a goalbound header by Dunk from Knockaert's corner. Phillips was sent off and Murray beat former England goalkeeper Robert Green from the penalty spot.

That should have signalled a spell of Brighton dominance, but they seemed strangely inhibited by their man advantage. It took another penalty to provide a second goal as Leeds captain Kyle Bartley tugged Dunk's shirt as they went for a free kick taken by Norwood. Hemed, who had come on for Murray, converted it in characteristic fashion. Although Brighton failed to show the attacking verve of the previous season's 4–0 victory over the Yorkshire team, they had prevented Leeds from mustering a single shot on target. And the league table showed them in first place.

Next was a trip to Blackburn for a meeting of old friends. Former Seagulls Gordon Greer, Elliott Bennett and Craig Conway were now with the Lancashire club, while Shane Duffy was loudly jeered on his return to Ewood Park. He answered the home fans in the most effective way, heading in his first Brighton goal from Norwood's corner. Stephens volleyed home a second from 18 yards after a free kick had been half-cleared before Sam Gallagher, on loan from Southampton, made it 2–1 following some penalty area pinball.

But then life was made easier when former skipper Greer was shown a second yellow card by referee Oliver Langford for a crude challenge from behind on Murray. This was not, as fans speculated, a gift to his old club, although Greer's long service at the Amex and Withdean before that was a factor, as he explained. 'Having played with Glenn, I thought I could read him,' the Scot said. 'It turned out I couldn't.'

The extra space allowed Dunk to get forward and hit a shot that goalkeeper Steele could not hold, Murray nipping in to dink the rebound into the net for an overdue first away goal of the season. Gallagher's second, after a run through an unusually open defence, came too late to make any difference.

• • •

The three points gained at Ewood Park put the team temporarily back on top of the table before Newcastle won at Wigan to reclaim first place the following evening as the lead swung back and forth between the Seagulls and Magpies with matches scheduled on different days and at different times.

Saturday 17 December was another day when kick-off times seemed vitally important, as Albion kicked off away to Birmingham City at 5.30 after everyone else had played. Huddersfield had won at Norwich the previous evening and now Newcastle won at Burton, while Reading, Leeds and Sheffield Wednesday all kept up the pressure with late or injury-time winners. The gap between second-placed Albion and the pack was still five points, but six, or eight, would look even better, and send out a message to their pursuers.

One imponderable before the game at St Andrew's was the decision of the home side's new Chinese owner, Paul Suen Cho Hung, to sack Gary Rowett, the manager who had been doing a sound job in steadily improving the Blues team. Rowett had been replaced by with Gianfranco Zola, the type of big-name former player beloved of rich foreign owners with little clue about the workings of British football and the peculiar demands of the Championship.

Albion's visit would be Zola's first match in charge and although the likeable Italian had failed to prove himself as a coach or manager, players often exert themselves following a change of head coach in order to impress the new man. So the Albion team knew that they could expect something extra from their opponents – or they should have done.

Stockdale, injured in the warm-up but adamant that he could play, was nearly beaten early on. Duffy and Stephens gave the ball away on the right and Lukas Jutkiewicz's low cross was smacked against the far upright from six yards by Maikel Kieftenbeld. And as the team struggled to get out of second gear, it was Stephens again who was robbed by David Davis before the City midfield man crossed for Jutkiewicz to jump early and head Birmingham into the lead seven minutes into the second half. And only a diving save by Stockdale from Jutkiewicz's 22-yard shot on the turn kept the score at 1–0.

But then the game turned thanks to one of those substitutions that most managers will admit only look brilliant in hindsight and are forgotten when, in the majority of cases, they make scant difference. But the introduction of Solly March for Skalák was very much the exception. He came on after sixty-three minutes and immediately began to cause problems for the right side of the home defence. Eight minutes from time, he glided past Robert Tesche and crossed low for Knockaert to volley past Kuszczak and into the bottom corner of the net. It was the first goal since his father's death for the emotional Frenchman, who pointed to the sky.

Instead of settling for a point, Albion went for the kill. Duffy had a header cleared off the line by Jonathan Grounds and with seconds running out, Knockaert took a corner on the right and Murray darted ahead of two defenders to glance a header low past Kuszczak's right hand. Now Murray sprinted away to the fans at the other end and fifteen seconds later the game was over.

To come from behind to win after a largely indifferent performance made a statement to the club's rivals, and the match became one that many players and coaches singled out as pivotal. 'The Birmingham away game, scoring in the last minute – moments like that mould your season,' Murray said. Was his goal celebration the fastest he's run all season?

'Yes, and I'd do it again. You look back and think yes, they were huge points. And I was so pleased that Solly had made it back fully fit and almost back to his best. That's someone I was looking forward to playing with because you could really see the quality he has got while he was trying to get back. In training he can go past people with ease and it was frustrating that he wasn't getting the chance to do it on Saturdays. It's quite a tough injury to come back from, as I know only too well. I was able to give him a bit of support, have a chat before training and try to keep his spirits up.'

March had announced himself on live television and the long hours and weeks of recovery finally seemed worth it. 'The club were great while I was out and my family, friends and girlfriend helped keep me in the right frame of mind,' March said.

'It was tough, more mentally than physically. It took a few months even to start walking again. It was a long process and in some of the early months you are feeling the worst, thinking if you are ever going to be the same again.

'It's always in the back of your mind, but with sports science now, even before my injury there have been quite a few players coming back and performing, so that gave me confidence and hope that I would get back to that level again. There was frustration because you want to be out there playing and helping your teammates, and last season, help us get promoted. And of course it would have been nice if they could have done it without me so I could come back a Premier League player, but it didn't work out that way.'

He had returned via the under-23 team and appeared in the dying stages of the wins at Bristol and Blackburn, getting twenty-four minutes at home to Leeds. But now he looked to be back to his skilful and intuitive best. 'You get a feeling when you're on it,' he said.

'The confidence is there and you just go past someone without a thought. That's what I try to do as much as possible, attack defenders and try to get them on the back foot. And that's when you can take advantage, but it is often without thinking.

'The injury and what happened is always in the back of your mind at the beginning. I wouldn't say it slows you down, but it makes you hesitant at first, mentally. But once you play a few games and get tackled a few times and come through it OK, your confidence grows and you think, "Yes, I'm well, I'm fit, I can still do this."'

Confidence was also a positive factor for Baldock, who opened the scoring in the next match, at home to QPR on 27 December. The London club had lost their previous five games but had been playing better than those results suggested under Ian Holloway, a figure who enjoyed a mixed reputation with Brighton fans. He had been in charge of rivals Crystal Palace when they had beaten Albion in the 2013 play-offs, but had predicted promotion for the Seagulls as a Sky pundit and expressed his admiration for Hughton before returning to management.

His Rangers team played nice football, but were facing an uphill struggle after only eleven minutes when Baldock scored the goal he rated his best of the season. 'It was around that time the season before that we started to falter,' he said. 'So we wanted to get off to a good start straight after Christmas and maintain that good form.'

It was an excellent team goal as well as a fine finish. Murray side-stepped a tackle on the right and passed inside to Stephens. He sent the ball diagonally forward to Baldock, who took a quick touch to kill the ball and then an instant second that sent it away from his marker, Nedum Onuoha. Baldock was now 22 yards out and most of the crowd expected him to take the ball on into the penalty area but instead he looked up and drove a fierce, rising left-foot shot past goalkeeper Alex Smithies's left hand.

QPR could have accepted a sixth successive defeat there and then but instead they took the fight to the home side. Stockdale saved from Pawel Wszołek, then blocked a shot from Massimo Luongo with his feet. But Albion stood firm and extended their lead after Stephens charged into the penalty area and was tripped by Luongo, Murray converting the penalty.

Any chance QPR had disappeared when Baldock fell as he ran for a through ball alongside Onuoha, who was sent off. Knockaert made it 3–0 after cutting in from the right and shooting under Smithies. It was his first goal at home since his father's death and he ran to the dugout to hold aloft a portrait of Patrick. The match ended 3–0, with Albion ending the day on top of the table, two points ahead of Newcastle.

Rafael Benítez, the Newcastle manager, was obviously beginning to regard Albion as a serious threat to his team's title ambitions. Known while at Liverpool for his attempts to play mind games with rival managers, he now suggested that Brighton, rather than his team, would be the side that everyone wanted to beat. 'It will be a boost for them but also more pressure,' he said. 'We have seen a lot of teams playing against us when we were at the top who give 100 per cent. Now every team that will play against Brighton will see it as an opportunity to do something important and there will be more pressure on them.'

But it would not be pressure or a good performance by an opponent that would knock Hughton's men out of first place. A year before, an injury-ravaged squad was stumbling from one disappointing result to another, but now they could not wait for the next match, so the postponement of the home game with Cardiff City, scheduled for 30 December, owing to fog two hours before kick-off was a disappointment. 'It is very frustrating, particularly with the form that we're in at the moment,' Hughton said.

'Unfortunately, the conditions beat us,' referee Chris Kavanagh said after a third inspection.

'The fog is not lifting. We have taken advice from the Met Office and they said the conditions would get worse until eight o'clock. On pitch level, there is a struggle to see one of the assistant referees on the near side. Furthermore, from different vantage points from within the crowd, you would struggle to see different areas of the pitch. I want to see both goalposts and my assistant referees.

'One of the key decisions is crowd safety. If I have come from Brighton or from Cardiff and I've paid my money, I want to see this game and unfortunately the conditions don't allow that at present.'

Newcastle were able to play, beating Nottingham Forest 3–1 to deny Hughton top spot on the second anniversary of his joining Brighton. But the consolation was that the club finished 2016 on a run of seventeen unbeaten games and with the best record of all ninety-two clubs over the calendar year: twenty-eight wins, twelve draws and only five defeats in forty-five league games.

Fans were delighted to note that the worst record over the same period belonged to rivals Crystal Palace.

CHAPTER 12

NEW YEAR 2017

Attention now turned to the always-popular trip to Fulham, a club that Trollope had played for. After a little over a month as Hughton's assistant, he had detected a similarity to the mood in the Wales camp during their successful run to the semi-final of the European Championships.

'Wales obviously have quality players, but it was underpinned with a great team spirit and camaraderie, and certainly in my time being here, I've seen that in this group,' he said.

'Every successful team has a good spirit. Togetherness is a big word here and you can see that strength of character.

'They were so unfortunate to miss out last season, and looking from the outside, 99 times out of 100 the team would have been promoted. Bouncing back from that situation has been a huge positive for everyone; the summer recruitment was very good and added to the strength.

'There's a depth to the group that everyone can see, and there's great competition for places. It's a great place to be and it's testament to the work that's gone on over the last few years. Everyone wants to work in a successful environment and this feels like one of those places at the moment. I see a determination in everyone that we're going to maintain levels through the second half of the season.'

Determination was certainly required at Craven Cottage, as Fulham impressed again in the third match between the teams since summer. The Londoners had an early chance to take the lead from a penalty when referee Stuart Attwell ruled that Bruno had handled after a cross was nodded on by Matt Smith. But Stockdale, on his return to his former club, read Stefan Johansen's kick perfectly and dived to his right to parry. Fulham would fail to convert nine penalties over the season, more than sixty-seven of the other ninety-one English league clubs were even awarded, but that hardly diminished Stockdale's feat.

Fulham, though, remained on top and eventually not even Stockdale could keep out a precisely placed shot into the bottom corner by Lucas Piazon from a pass by outstanding captain Tom Cairney. At that point it looked as though the New Year had brought an unwelcome change of fortune, and not even the introduction of March in the hope of a Birmingham-style transformation of fortune worked.

But within three minutes of Hemed following March off the bench, the scores were level. Referee Attwell could have blown for a foul on Knockaert by Kevin McDonald on the edge of the penalty area, but delayed just long enough for Hemed to run onto the loose ball and tumble over Ragnar Sigurðsson's challenge. Now Attwell did blow, and pointed to the spot. Both Hemed and Murray wanted to take the kick, but the bench opted for the Israeli and he sent David Button the wrong way.

And before Fulham had a chance to regroup, Albion were ahead. Dunk stole possession from Fulham substitute Stephen Humphrys just inside the home half and strode forward before finding Knockart to his right. The winger's shot was beaten out by Button, but

Dunk, who had kept running, lunged forward to head the rebound into the net before running to the 6,000 fans behind the goal, followed by his delirious teammates.

Fulham attempted to get back on terms but without success, and Dunk picked up a soft but not entirely unexpected yellow card for time-wasting. It was his tenth of the season, meaning a two-match suspension, but it was well-timed as he would miss the FA Cup third round tie against MK Dons – which he would have sat out in any case – and only one league game, away to Preston.

Brighton had now played Fulham three times including the pre-season friendly, been outplayed every time, gone behind on each occasion – and taken six league points out of six. Since the home defeat against Brentford, they had been unbeaten in eighteen league matches, fourteen of them victories. 'Our strength this season more than the season before is that we have been able to find a way of winning,' Hughton said.

'There's no doubt that the way we play allows a Knockaert or a Jamie Murphy or Solly March to show their abilities, but we have tried to be a compact side.

'We don't concede a lot of goals and that is a platform to go and win games. The fact that we kept so many clean sheets is testament to the way that the team works and if you've got that then there is an inner belief that you can win a game, or not lose. The difference this season is that in that type of game we've had that little bit extra to go and score where last season we might have ended up drawing.'

The FA Cup match against MK Dons lacked any of the drama of the previous season's away game against the same opponents, a workmanlike 2–0 victory being most notable for a goal-scoring return to action for Kayal after his injury against Barnsley in September. The Albion starting eleven comprised the squad members who had not begun the Fulham match and most, as expected, stood down for the tough trip to Preston. The exceptions were Goldson, who replaced the suspended Dunk, and Sam Adekugbe, who made an unexpected league debut with Bong joining Pocognoli on the injured list. Stephens was also ill.

Albion's poor record at Deepdale led many fans to suspect that this was where the unbeaten run might come to grief, and the team news did little to improve spirits. And so it proved, although both North End's goals in their 2–0 win were preventable. The first followed Paul Gallagher's free kick on the right and at no point did a Brighton player seem to be marking six foot three defender Paul Huntington, who had no problem heading past Stockdale.

Adekugbe played well, and even created a chance for Murray with a cross that the striker headed wide. It was from the other flank that the second goal came, Bruno allowing Callum Robinson to run inside him before trickling a shot beyond Stockdale. To emphasise the way the luck was running, Hemed had a late penalty saved by Preston's Chris Maxwell after the goalkeeper had pulled Murphy back. The prevailing view among fans was that if he was going to miss one, better to get it out of the way when it did not matter.

There was more penalty drama in the next game, a 2–1 victory at home to Sheffield Wednesday on Friday 20 January, a match that had as much incident as the previous season's play-off semi-final. Dunk was back and Pocognoli was fit to start at left-back, while Goldson was at right-back in place of an injured Bruno.

In the captain's absence, Stockdale stepped up to deliver a pep talk in the pre-game huddle. 'I unofficially took it over from Bruno when he was out for one of the games and I spend all week deciding on what I'm going to say, depending on my moods,' the goalkeeper said. 'So if I'm in an inspirational mood it works but nobody has laughed me off yet.'

Knockaert scored twice yet ended up with only a share of the glory. He put the team ahead after thirty-four minutes. Albion broke from the edge of their own penalty area and when Murphy's inch-perfect through pass reached Knockaert, he seemed to have given goalkeeper Westwood a chance with a heavy first touch. Yet the Frenchman kept possession, went past the goalkeeper, checked back and drove the ball into the roof of the net past three covering defenders.

However, just as in the play-off game, Wednesday scored a freak equaliser before the interval. Fernando Forestieri crossed from the left with the outside of his right foot and Norwood's attempted interception only sent the ball towards his own goal. Stockdale would probably have dealt with the situation if Dunk's instinctive attempt to head away had not deflected the ball past him into the net.

Dunk did not seem to enjoy much luck against these opponents at that end, and things seemed no better as Albion defended the south goal in the second half. A Wednesday corner after sixty-four minutes was never fully cleared and when Glenn Loovens shot powerfully from 12 yards, Murray blocked with his hands. He tried to pretend it had been his face, but referee Stuart Attwell correctly showed him the red card.

What happened next is regarded by many as one of the highlights of the season, if not the turning point of the entire campaign. Forestieri took the kick, aiming to Stockdale's right, but the goalkeeper anticipated and parried the shot. Unfortunately, the ball came straight back to the Wednesday striker, who hit it to the other side this time. But Stockdale somehow changed direction and palmed the ball around the post.

Naturally, Stockdale reacted as if he had scored in a World Cup final and his teammates mobbed him before all concerned remembered there was a corner kick to be dealt with.

Down to ten men and with Hemed now a lone forward, Albion were still up against it, defending desperately and relying on quick breaks to try to snatch a winner. And, five minutes from time, it paid off. Sidwell spread the ball wide to Pocognoli, who curved a cross towards the far post that curled away from Westwood. Knockaert slid in between two defenders to half-volley home and the roar from the crowd brought back memories of Dunk's goal in the play-off semi-final.

A frustrated Wednesday now went to pieces. Steven Fletcher butted Stephens after Albion had cleared a dangerous attack and was shown a red card, and he was soon followed to the dressing room by Sam Hutchinson, who was shown a second yellow after launching into a reckless challenge on March.

Murray picked the match out as a key point of the season. 'I got sent off and Stocko makes two big saves and Ant goes down the other end and scores,' he said.

After receiving his red card, Murray had paused at the entrance to the players' tunnel to watch the penalty, punching the air at Stockdale's initial save before going for his early bath.

'I didn't see the second save. I just went down the tunnel after the first one because I thought he'd done his job! I was down the tunnel and someone said: "He's made another one!" He dug me out, Stocko, as he has done, all of us, on many occasions this year. I really do believe that he has been the unsung hero.'

'At the end Muzza gave me a big kiss and said, "Thanks, I didn't see the second one, I didn't see it,"' Stockdale said. 'You're always willing the strikers to score, so to help out in a different way was great.'

• • •

The club appealed that Murray's red card was too harsh, but their appeal was rejected and he missed the rearranged fixture against Cardiff, a game in which the result was more important than the performance. With Murray out, Hughton tried March in the number 10 role, but it was hardly a success.

Nor did the return of Kayal to resume his partnership with Stephens prove as impressive as had been hoped – although his willingness to carry the ball forward rather than pass it square was welcome. Stockdale, in fact, was the busier of the two goalkeepers in the first half, saving well from Junior Hoilett and Sean Morrison.

But Albion improved in the second and Hemed slid March's cross just wide before settling the game in the seventy-third minute with one of his best goals for the club. Norwood, on for the ring-rusty Kayal, played the ball up to Hemed and he turned away from giant Cardiff defender Sol Bamba before hitting a vicious shot between goalkeeper Allan McGregor and his near post from 17 yards.

The victory meant that Albion were on top of the table, two points ahead of Newcastle, but, more importantly, 11 points ahead of Reading and Huddersfield, in third and fourth places.

To illustrate that the club was looking forward on all fronts, they announced two loan transfers – Rob Hunt out to Oldham Athletic and England under-19 defender Fikayo Tomori in from Chelsea – and a major development of the land between the training ground and the A27, to include 600 new dwellings, a school, a park and the first IKEA store in Sussex.

'When we bought the training ground site, we were very conscious that it was in the local plan and was going to be developed,' Martin Perry said. 'Having invested more than £30 million, it was important we protected our investment. The key issue was making sure the flood risk was dealt with on an ongoing basis, so the best course of action was to develop it ourselves.'

That was for the future, but the present involved a tricky FA Cup fourth round tie away to Lincoln City of the National League, who had knocked out Ipswich at Sincil Bank in a replay after a 2–2 draw at Portman Road. Albion did not want to be victims of a giant-killing, but nor did they want to exhaust first-team players or take chances with injury.

Hughton fielded a very similar team to the one that had beaten MK Dons, but included Murray in order to give him match practice after his suspension – which struck some as risky. That was forgotten as Albion dominated the first half. Murray forced an early save from Paul Farman, March hit the crossbar from 30 yards and Richie Towell scored his first Albion goal with a clever first-time finish from a header by Murray.

But Lincoln levelled twelve minutes into the second half when Murray pushed their forward, Theo Robinson, who then collided with Niki Mäenpää. Not only was it a penalty, converted by Alan Power, but Mäenpää was injured and had to be replaced by Casper Ankergren. Five minutes later, Ankergren was picking the ball out of the net a second time after Tomori made his Albion debut one to forget with an inexplicable close-range own goal. Five minutes from time, Hünemeier gave the ball away and Robinson scored with a low shot.

'It was certainly not a result I would have seen coming at half-time,' Hughton said. 'When you concede three goals as poorly as we have, that makes it difficult to win any game. They are all errors.'

However, he had no regrets about making nine changes for the match, although Gabby Logan, presenting *Match of the Day* on the

BBC that evening, claimed that the club would be disappointed if Lincoln drew a Premier League club in the fifth round. She had entirely missed the point that Brighton were no longer a small club hoping for a big-match windfall but an ambitious outfit aiming to play Premier League teams every week.

On the last day of the transfer window, Hughton and Winstanley were busy. They sent Rohan Ince out on loan to Swindon Town, recalled Christian Walton from his loan at Luton Town to cover Mäenpää's injury, brought in Chuba Akpom on loan from Arsenal, a player with Championship and promotion experience gained with Hull City, and also converted Murray's loan signing into a permanent two-and-a-half-year contract.

'I think it was something all parties had discussed at the start of the season,' Murray said. 'It was quite obvious that I didn't have a future at Bournemouth. It had gone well here and it felt the right thing to do in January.'

If the idea of resting players at Lincoln was designed to maximise the chances of a good result in the next game, away to Huddersfield, it manifestly failed. After an autumn dip in form, David Wagner's side were flying once again, having won eight of their previous ten games.

That was no more than a minor worry for fans heading for the John Smith's Stadium, an Amex prototype now showing its age. After all, Albion had played in-form sides before and come out on top. But not this time.

Huddersfield tore into Hughton's team from the off and the midfield of Kayal and Norwood were unable to stem the tide. With hindsight, many wondered why Sidwell had not been asked to bolster a department weakened by the absence of Stephens, who was suffering from a calf injury. Sidwell eventually appeared in the second half, but by then the damage had been done.

The omens were poor from the first minute, when Bruno was caught out of position and had to bring down former Amex loanee Rajiv van La Parra, earning a yellow card. How he avoided a second for a foul on Nahki Wells a minute or so later, only referee James Linington knows. With Aaron Mooy, the Australia midfield player on loan to the Terriers from Manchester City, bossing midfield, the home side poured forward, and scored after only nine minutes when Tommy Smith beat Stockdale at his near post. Linington must have thought he had already done Brighton enough of a favour in allowing Bruno to stay on, so declined to rule Wells offside even though he was standing between Stockdale and any view of the scorer.

Brighton did get another stroke of luck when Mooy's misplaced header sent Hemed through to equalise, but back came Huddersfield and Kayal's tackle became an unintentional through pass to Wells, who restored the lead with a decisive finish. And in first-half injury time, another fortunate ricochet gave Mooy the chance to find van La Parra, and Stockdale, the hero of the Sheffield Wednesday match, turned villain by fumbling his cross onto the head of Elias Kachunga.

But although there was no more scoring, Albion's woes were not over. Dunk, already booked, dived into an unnecessary tackle on Izzy Brown well inside the Huddersfield half and, despite protests that he had won the ball cleanly – not entirely unjustified – he cannot have been too surprised to see a second yellow card followed by a red one.

The only bright spot after that was that Mooy's late 25-yarder hit the post instead of the back of the net, which would have made the score more accurately reflect the home side's dominance. Make no mistake, this was a thrashing, and the home fans' taunts of 'Top of the league, you're having a laugh' were entirely deserved. It also allowed a dangerous challenger to close the gap by three points. And yet on another day, none of the three goals might have been conceded. A different official might have flagged the first offside, and the second and third were the result of rebounds, the third compounded by a goalkeeping error.

But the danger now was that a wobble might become a full-blown blip to rival the Christmas collapse of the previous season. Three consecutive away defeats, two defeats in a row – however you cared to add it up, lose at Brentford three days after the Huddersfield debacle and serious doubts might start creeping in.

• • •

The day of the Brentford match could not have had a much worse beginning when it was announced that routine medical tests had revealed that Connor Goldson had a heart condition for which surgery was advised, ruling him out for the remainder of the season.

'I'm close to Connor and I couldn't believe it when he told me,' Dunk said. 'I was in the hotel with him and I was asked to leave while they told him and it was a massive shock. I can't wait for him to be back and available for selection. It will be amazing for him and a massive relief for him.'

Knockaert, another close friend, said: 'I told him, "Don't worry, when you come back on a football pitch, it will be in the Premier League. We will do it for you." Now, I cannot lie to him – we have to do it.'

Goldson was able to attend the game at Griffin Park, which, in hindsight, might not have been wise for anyone with a dodgy ticker. Hughton seemed to have acted on the lessons learned in Yorkshire up to a point, starting Sidwell, but still playing 4–4–2, with Murphy supporting Murray, and Hünemeier recalled to partner Duffy.

But the first half was another disaster. Skalák failed to track Josh Clarke as the Brentford man set up Spanish playmaker Jota to flick home the opening goal after only fifteen minutes, and with Sidwell and Norwood sitting too deep, pressure came in waves. Seven minutes later, Murray could only backhead Jota's corner to the far post, where Harlee Dean nodded in unchallenged.

Two chances fell Albion's way, but to Murphy instead of Murray, and he headed and then shot wide. And it looked all over in the second half when Jota advanced alone into the penalty area and was upended by Hünemeier. Stockdale, though, made up for his error at Huddersfield, saving his third penalty in succession, Lasse Vibe's kick striking his knee and flying over the crossbar.

Perhaps sensing a change in the wind, Hughton sent on Hemed and Akpom in place of Murphy and Murray to join March, who had replaced Skalák at the interval. Stockdale still had to make another save, from Nico Yennaris, but eventually Albion broke away and got back in the game. Knockaert carried the ball down the right and although his attempted pass to Hemed was cut out, the ball fell for March, who sidestepped two defenders and blasted a left-foot shot past Dan Bentley from 18 yards. That was on seventy-five minutes, and three minutes later the comeback was complete, or so everyone thought, as Knockaert swung the ball in from the right and Duffy powered home a header.

But the drama had just started. First, Dean sliced a cross from March and Bentley had to tip it over the crossbar. Then Akpom headed Pocognoli's cross over the bar from inches out. Next, Tom Field went down with a head injury, necessitating seven minutes of added time. In the fourth of those minutes, Austrian Konstantin

Kerschbaumer, on to replace Field, exchanged passes with Vibe and blasted his first goal for Brentford past Stockdale. Surely Albion were now beaten?

Yet there was still time for Hemed to miss Akpom's low cross from inches out and then, with seconds left, for Norwood to spread play out to Knockaert, whose cross was met by Hemed with a flying header into the corner of the net. Cue pandemonium behind the goal, where the fans included Tony Bloom and Dick Knight.

A point salvaged? Two dropped? An error-riddled mess of a performance? A classic display of raw, never-say-die determination? It had been all of these things and more, but the fans were as exhilarated when they left Griffin Park as they had been depressed at Huddersfield – who were now only six points behind, although it could have been five.

'For me, Birmingham away, winning it in the last minute, Fulham because we were getting our arses kicked but managed to scrape it, and Sheffield Wednesday at home were the main games of the season,' Stockdale said. 'But Brentford was big as well because we were coming off the back of a loss at Huddersfield and you thought they were games last season where we might not have got anything. The mentality to get out of this league was so strong.'

'We could have shut up shop at 2–2 but I wanted to go and win the game,' Hughton said.

'We were a little open and we showed quality to get back in but great character to get what I thought was a fair result. With so little time left, the natural reaction is to think it is going to be very, very difficult. I knew we would have a go. Probably on most occasions it doesn't come, but for us it did.

'There were certainly negatives in the game – we conceded three goals – but at moments like this you've got to look at the character we showed. It's been a tough week with two really tough away games so it was of major importance that we didn't finish these two getting beaten again.'

Rightly, he paid tribute to Stockdale. 'He has made three penalty saves and they have all been pivotal for us,' he said. 'All three have allowed us to go on and get results. Without that save and at 3–0 down, I don't think we come back from that.'

While his saves at Fulham and at home to Sheffield Wednesday had been greeted with roars of delight and chest bumps by team-mates, the Brentford save had elicited only a wave to the crowd from the goalkeeper.

'Your reactions are more extreme the more important the save is,' Stockdale said.

'At Brentford we were trying not to go 3–0 down so I didn't react as if I'd saved the game, but in the end we got a point so it was important after all. Saves are what you're supposed to do, doing my job. Most don't get noticed. But against Sheffield Wednesday, us going up the other end and winning it, it was huge.'

And it emerged that Stockdale's apparently casual wave had been to acknowledge the work behind the scenes of Ben Roberts, the goalkeeping coach. Three successive penalty saves were beginning to suggest that there was more than good luck at work.

'It's a process we go through before every game,' Roberts explained. 'We do a different opposition analysis from the outfield boys. We get all the goalkeepers in and chat during the week and work on certain things. Penalties are one of them.'

The record of likely penalty-takers in the opposition team is studied. 'You can never be certain which way they're going to go, but we've got our own process of what we try to do to force them one way,' Roberts said.

'I don't want to give away our secrets and it's easier said than done and it doesn't always work, but it's important to have something you believe in so that you're not just guessing. You hope you save more than you don't, and Stocko has to some extent proved that in my opinion. It's not rocket science, it's just something we stick to and hope to get more right than we don't.'

All the homework in the world could not, by itself, have resulted in Stockdale's double save from Forestieri against Sheffield Wednesday. That was born of natural agility and reflexes, honed every day. 'I think I have improved over these two years more than the ten previous ones and I think the stats prove it,' Stockdale said.

'Ben Roberts is a big part of that. I try to work on my weaknesses and there are goals we conceded where I thought I could have done better, in footwork for instance. We set out a plan and I just wish we'd filmed the early sessions because there was a massive difference.'

'The morning after Sheffield Wednesday and the double save, we said: "That's as good as it's going to get",' Roberts said. 'The penalty save was decent, he has gone down slightly early, which he was meant to do, because he was expecting a chip, but then the rebound, everyone's heart has gone – but to manage to tip it around the post, that sort of double save will never happen again.'

Roberts had had first-hand experience of winning promotion with Brighton. He had saved a penalty in the shoot-out victory over Swindon Town in the 2004 League One play-off semi-final and kept a clean sheet in the 1–0 defeat of Bristol City in the final at the Millennium Stadium. Although he did not know it at the time, that had been his farewell appearance, as a back injury forced him to retire at only twenty-nine the following year, a premature end to a career that had included FA and League Cup final appearances for Middlesbrough.

His next move marked him out as untypical in the professional football world – not directly into coaching but to live with his girlfriend in Brazil, followed by a backpacking trip around the world, pointedly missing out the usual footballers' haunts of Dubai and Ayia Napa. But after an aborted attempt at a comeback, he was invited to work with Yeovil Town by former Albion teammate Nathan Jones and decided to take a sports science degree at Roehampton, graduating with first-class honours and winning an Adidas Pursuit of Excellence award for his dissertation on the biomechanics of a goalkeeper's jumping technique.

He had been working as goalkeeping coach at Charlton, another of his former clubs, when he was invited to succeed Antti Niemi at Brighton and jumped at the chance. 'It has been fantastic working under Chris and being at a club of this stature,' he said.

'It has changed so much since I was here as a player. When we were in the play-off final at the Millennium Stadium we said that it could turn into this but it has been beyond our wildest dreams.

'It couldn't have gone any better and Stocko has done brilliantly. He has been here three seasons and hardly missed a game or even a day's training. He was carried off against Forest and was out on the training ground forty-eight hours later wanting to play against Rotherham. We wanted to protect him but he told me in no uncertain terms that he was ready to play.

'Niki Mäenpää has trained really hard for two years and in my opinion he has done very well when he has had the chance, but that just shows you Stocko's levels. He has been really good, won us points and been consistent.'

Roberts had shared the despair of the 2016 play-off defeat and had been concerned that the squad would struggle to recover.

'Yes, it was a worry. It took a lot out of us. The boys had done fantastically all season but I think Middlesbrough really hit us, which showed again in the first leg at Hillsborough. Things went against us but I think we'd have turned it around if anything had gone our way. I still think that's the best I've seen us play, that first half.

'I didn't really enjoy the summer. There were a few doubts about, but I think keeping the squad together was huge from the manager and the chairman. I also think from some of the boys who wanted to stay here and felt there was unfinished business. Once the window closed at the end of August there was a real belief and sense of togetherness, a businesslike feeling around the training ground. There have been a few ups and downs but they never deterred us from our path.'

After the shredded nerves at Griffin Park, a straightforward victory was required, and Burton Albion, the next visitors to the Amex, kindly provided it. Dunk returned from suspension and Baldock and Stephens from calf injuries. All three had been missed, while March and Hemed were rewarded for their contributions at Griffin Park with starting places.

Hemed knocked in Knockaert's low cross from the right to open the scoring and Baldock touched in March's ball from the left to make it 2–0. March tumbled rather easily to win a penalty that Hemed dispatched in familiar style.

Marvin Sordell turned past Dunk and forced a good save from Stockdale before Michael Kightly reduced the arrears with a free kick that went in off the post. But Murray, on as a substitute, headed in a fourth from Knockaert's cross to restore the three-goal margin of victory.

CHAPTER 13

ON OUR WAY

The guest of honour at the Burton game was Richard Vaughan, a Plymouth Argyle fan who had earned his place in the history of Brighton & Hove Albion twenty years earlier.

In the final season of the Goldstone Ground, with the unpopular owners of the club showing little sign of wanting either to abandon their suicidal plans to groundshare many miles from Brighton with no realistic plan to return to the city, or to sell to people with the best interests of the Albion at heart, Vaughan, then fifteen, suggested a show of support from fans of all clubs and the idea of Fans United day was born. On 8 February 1997, the old North Stand at the Goldstone was filled with supporters wearing the replica shirts of clubs from all over the UK and even farther afield, and the team was spurred on to beat Hartlepool 5–0.

The fans of other clubs had rallied round in Brighton's time of greatest need and Albion supporters have never forgotten this show of solidarity, even from rivals. They have shared their experiences of the long battles to force out the previous regime and help obtain permission to build the Amex Stadium. Similar events to the original Fans United have since taken place in aid of other supporters' causes including those at Doncaster Rovers and, as events came full circle, Plymouth.

So it was with incredulity that supporters on message boards in 2017 read suggestions from some rivals that the Amex crowds were mainly composed of 20,000 or so bandwagon-jumpers who had simply come along once a comfortable stadium had been built and had had no previous interest in the Albion. 'I can't stand them,' wrote one contributor to a Sheffield Wednesday message board. 'Plastic club, plastic fans' – 'plastic' being the ultimate insult hurled at those not perceived to have suffered long enough in support of their clubs.

This showed an ignorance of history among some, who perhaps believed that football began in 1992 with the formation of the Premier League. Although there were, no doubt, some new fans attracted by the padded Amex seats and its corporate facilities, Brighton had played in the top flight and an FA Cup final and had averaged 20,000 attendances in the second tier several times at the Goldstone, with peak crowds well over 30,000. Reading, in contrast, had not averaged five-figure crowds between 1962 and the opening of the Madejski Stadium in 1998, and had never had a 20,000 average until reaching the Premier League in 2006.

But any ignorance was, perhaps, excusable. In 1992, Brighton were already on the downward slope that would lead to the Gillingham groundshare. Generations of fans grew up regarding Brighton & Hove Albion as a name to be found a long way down the league tables rather than a well-supported club with a reasonably recent top-flight pedigree.

Even when the club had returned to Brighton & Hove, the planning and topographical restrictions on Withdean Stadium meant that the capacity was restricted and its record attendance was 8,691. But when seeking planning permission for the new ground, Dick

Knight was thinking bigger. He had stood on the Goldstone terraces among crowds of over 30,000 and was convinced that the missing 22,000 were still out there.

'I knew that the club had that potential and getting the stadium was key, a stadium that fitted the club's ambitions,' he said.

'And also for the city – it needed to be a stunning-looking advertisement for the city that reflected the style and flair of Brighton. It needed to look good as well as having sufficient capacity. The attitude around the stadium had to be upbeat, and we insisted on it being a community stadium, which the sponsors, American Express, were entirely on board with.

'The stadium had a history before a ball was kicked there because of the role the fans had played in campaigning for it with me and the rest of the board. They came up against so many planning hurdles but the voice of the people spoke, and planning officers, councils and government ministers had to listen to it.

'John Prescott, then the Deputy Prime Minister, played a major role. He could have gone with the public inquiry inspector's report, which came out strongly against building at Falmer and said it wasn't the appropriate place. But by that time the fans had made him aware that there was a strong feeling in favour. He wasn't aware of that until the fans made him aware, by sending him Valentine's cards and persuading every other club to send him bouquets of flowers, to make him aware of our plight.

'So that when he came to a game at Withdean, he told me that he hadn't been aware of the strong support for the stadium until a few weeks before the inspector reported. The fans' campaigns put our foot in the door to stop Prescott slamming it in our face. Instead, he threw the inspector's recommendation out and ordered another inquiry and that was purely because of what the fans had done.

'We had 14,000 fans on our database when we finished at Withdean, where the average capacity was 7,000. If you put aside the new generation of kids who have grown up and are now old enough to go to games, there are probably about 12,000 new fans who have been attracted by the new stadium and the recent successes. 20,000 is certainly a false figure.

'We lost more than one generation of potential young fans when we lost the Goldstone. And we calculated that we missed out on £18 million between the Goldstone and the Amex in gate receipts that we would have got to watch all those promotion teams at Withdean.

'But the fans who used to go were still out there and for me that was proved at the 2004 play-off final when we took over 30,000 to the Millennium Stadium. These weren't fans who turn up to any big event with brand new scarves. You could tell that by the replica shirts. They were old ones, with the Sandtex sponsors' logo, or TSB, or Nobo, from the Goldstone days.

'But even if you say that the stadium has attracted fans, then getting the stadium was down to the fans anyway. And if we'd had the stadium earlier, then we'd already be in the Premier League.

'I was certain that right was on our side. The will of the people was behind us. One of our petitions had over 100,000 names on it. So I felt that it was inevitable that we would be allowed to build that stadium. But Lewes District Council's objections delayed us by about another eighteen months, so much that we ran into the credit crunch of 2008. That was just bloody-mindedness on their part, wasting millions of their council taxpayers' money and costing the club about the same.

'But Tony Bloom had come along and said he would make up any shortfall. Basically, he allowed us to build the stadium immediately rather than having to delay it again. Albion fans have every reason to thank him for that and since he took over he has taken the club forward in a way I knew was possible.

'When I became chairman, I didn't know whether I was living every football fan's dream or whether it would turn out to be a nightmare. At first it was nightmarish, but now we're in a place on the map that we couldn't have imagined twenty years ago. That just fulfilled what I thought was certain if we got the stadium. The infrastructure is there, the fanbase, the right manager, and the right drive at the top of the club, the money and common-sense leadership and know-how.'

• • •

However, there were still frustrations ahead and one of them was the visit of Ipswich Town to the Amex. Roger East was refereeing again, but he could not be blamed for Albion failing to do better than draw 1–1 this time. In fact, he had booked five Town players by half-time, including both their full-backs, which should have been an invitation for Knockaert and March to run at them at every opportunity. Yet too often, safe square passes were the order of the evening.

Things began to go wrong after nine minutes when Tom Lawrence, the Ipswich danger man on loan from Leicester, curled a free kick towards Stockdale and nobody blocked the run of Luke Chambers, who headed in from almost on top of the goalkeeper.

Albion levelled when Bruno was pulled back by Emyr Huws and Hemed was his usual cool self from the penalty spot, although so many players were encroaching that Baldock was almost offside when the ball was struck.

But instead of taking advantage of their reprieve, Albion needed Stockdale's save with his legs from David McGoldrick to reach the interval level. And he repeated the legs-first save from Lawrence in the second half, while Chambers hit the post and McGoldrick went close. Not until late did Albion look anywhere near their best and then Baldock scooped Knockaert's pass too close to goalkeeper Bartosz Białkowski, and Murray's shot on the turn came back off the post.

The gap to third-placed Huddersfield was now down to four points and a potentially testing trip to Barnsley was next on the fixture list. Murray and Murphy returned for Hemed and March, but there were some tricky moments early on, with Baldock booked for simulation and Dunk escaping when Barnsley players and fans yelled for handball – even though Tom Bradshaw, the player leading the appeals, had pushed Dunk to provoke the contact.

In the fifty-third minute, Knockaert resisted a challenge from Barnsley's George Moncur and sent a pass to Baldock, who took the ball on the half-turn and flicked it up before sending a dipping volley over the head of goalkeeper Adam Davies. Adam Hamill came on for the Yorkshiremen and hit a first-time shot over the bar from a dangerous position before Albion scored a second. Baldock began it by covering back and making a clever interception before finding Knockaert on the right. He dribbled past two defenders before crossing low for Baldock to prod home.

It was the first time that Baldock had scored twice for the club and meant that four players were now in double figures for goals, the others being Hemed, Knockaert and Murray.

The result, on a ground where the club had not won since 1991, was a boost after the Ipswich game, and before the next match, a Saturday evening kick-off at home to Reading, there was more positive news – both Newcastle (at home to Bristol City) and Huddersfield (at Barnsley) had dropped points.

There was a minute's applause in the forty-fifth minute for Paul McCarthy, the former Albion captain who had died at the shockingly early age of forty-five. By then, Albion were a goal to the good. An unchanged team began brightly and Baldock curled a shot against the far post with Ali Al-Habsi motionless. But the in-form striker was not denied for long and he controlled Bruno's long forward pass with instep and chest as he charged into the penalty area before blasting the ball high into the net.

Reading's ponderous possession game made little impact until early in the second half, when Roy Beerens's cross was met by Danny Williams, only for Duffy to clear his header off the goalline. That was one of the few occasions on which Reading put any pace into their game. Albion showed how it was done when Stephens sent Murphy racing through to dink the ball over Al-Habsi, and then Murphy ran at the defence before playing Knockaert in on the left and he clipped a fine shot past Al-Habsi.

That set everything up nicely for the long-awaited return match against Newcastle. There was a feeling that the Geordies had beaten a team in flux back in September, before Duffy had settled in, and that leaders Albion would now show their true selves in a genuine heavyweight contest against the second-placed team, a point further back.

And it would indeed be a memorable occasion, if not for the right reasons as far as Albion were concerned. They opened strongly and Bruno forced a good save from Karl Darlow, as did Baldock after Murphy and Knockaert worked a clever free kick that ended with the latter lifting the ball over the wall. With fifteen minutes gone, referee Robert Madley delayed the taking of a corner to warn Newcastle defenders about holding, but Ciaran Clark had obviously not listened, as he grabbed Murray and pulled him to the ground as the flag kick came in. Madley pointed to the spot and Murray scored.

Four minutes later, Pocognoli was unable to continue and Hughton sent on Tomori to play at left-back, an unfamiliar position. He looked uncomfortable early on, but grew into the game and made some excellent challenges. And it hardly seemed to affect the flow of the match, as Darlow had to produce more heroics to keep out a volley from Murray. Stockdale, too, had to be at his best, flinging himself to his right to parry Christian Atsu's first-time shot from 12 yards moments before half-time.

There were further chances for both sides in the second half. Paul Dummett hacked Dunk's header off the line after Darlow had missed Knockaert's inswinging free kick, and Stockdale presented the ball to Yoan Gouffran but recovered to block the forward's shot. And with eight minutes to go, Newcastle equalised with a goal that was replayed on social media all over Europe.

Stockdale cleared a corner to the edge of the penalty area, where Atsu's attempt at a first-time shot was so wayward that the home crowd reacted with laughter. But it died in their throats as the ball hit the heel of Mohamed Diamé and looped crazily towards goal, over Tomori on the line and in. It was a cruel blow and the pain was not over.

A minute from time, Matt Ritchie played a long diagonal pass from his own half out to Atsu on the left. Bruno decided not to try to intercept but to confront Atsu after he had received it. With five defenders behind Bruno, there should have been no danger, but not one of the five had picked up Newcastle substitute Ayoze Pérez, and when Atsu crossed low, Pérez rifled the winner past Stockdale.

'We know the quality Newcastle have got, they showed what they can do with their second goal,' Hughton said.

'But up until the equaliser we had worked out how they were playing and coped with it very well. They threatened because of the quality they have got, but I felt we would hold out.

'You have to pick yourself up quickly in this division because the games come thick and fast. We've got another big game on Saturday, as do Newcastle. We are where we are for a reason, we were very close today. The players have been excellent this season and we need them to go again and continue getting results because this league is unforgiving and you've got to turn things around.'

• • •

There was good news when Liam Rosenior returned to the squad on 3 March, in time for the trip to Nottingham Forest, still full of enthusiasm and belief. 'I am as confident as ever,' he said.

'When I first set foot in the football club, I said we'd get promotion. Because I see not just the facilities, the infrastructure, but also the people, the board, the manager, there's a group of twenty-two really hungry people. Forget footballers, they are hungry to be a success. I just see it in their eyes every day. There is a focus and determination about them which makes me really confident for the rest of the season.'

Rosenior may have been missed on the field, but he had been making his mark on the club in other ways and would be nominated as Community Player of the Year at the EFL Awards in April. He had also fitted well into the wider community, as he explained when supporting the anti-homophobic Rainbow Laces campaign. 'We need to live in a society where everybody is open-minded to other people, and tolerant, and celebrates different kinds of people,' he said.

'We are all different races, creeds, religions, and sexual preference and orientation is just one of those things.

'Living in Brighton, and I've lived here only eighteen months, being in the city and on the beach, people are really inclusive. It's a very liberal place to be and I think this club encapsulates that spirit really well. I am married with four daughters and I wanted to live in a society where they are included and appreciated for who they are.'

Nobody could replace Íñigo Calderón in the hearts of many supporters, but Rosenior was coming close, and when he appeared on the *Albion Roar* radio programme, he impressed listeners with his feeling for the club and his assessment of its prospects.

'I really believe that this club will be strong over the next decade and by that I mean in the top flight pushing in the top half of the Premier League. In terms of infrastructure, philosophy and identity, its sense of personality is very strong. There is a culture, a thought behind everything here, even the way of playing – everything suits the area, the way of thinking and of living here.

'I immerse myself in living in Brighton because it's a liberal, open place where people are respected no matter where they come from, whether they're gay, straight, black, white. That resonates with me. And this football club, in terms of the Community scheme, the women's football team, the academy, the disabled football – the passion for each of those categories is so strong and you feel it. You have to have a sense of who you are and the owner, the manager, we've got that 100 per cent right and you see the results on the pitch.'

He gave a player's view of the recruitment video and his reaction to its depiction of the years of struggle to return to the top.

'How the club has evolved from where it was – the "War Years", the fans' demonstrations – to where the club is now is incredible. I played at Withdean and thought: "Brighton were once a huge club, my dad played at the Goldstone in front of packed crowds" and then thinking: "How did it come to this?" But now to see it go full cycle, there is such a feel-good factor around the place and the fans are fantastic. We feed off it. We all live in the area and we see Brighton shirts in the city and I think it makes a huge difference on the pitch.'

But no sooner had one defender returned than another suffered injury. An unexpected 3–0 defeat away to Forest on what had recently been considered a lucky ground was made worse by a broken metatarsal suffered by Duffy that ruled him out for the remainder of the campaign – unless, that is, the team were to be forced to go through the agonies of the play-offs once more.

The score makes the defeat at the City Ground sound worse than it was. Until the eighty-ninth minute, Albion trailed only to a goal that should have been disallowed. Zach Clough's shot on the hour was deflected in by the forehead of Britt Assombalonga, who was in an offside position, and the defenders protested to referee Oliver Langford and his assistant, gesturing at replays on the stadium big screen that proved their point.

But their appeals were ignored and, try as they might, they could not find an equaliser. And any thought of a comeback ended when Stockdale tried to control an overhit backpass from Rosenior and presented Ben Osborn with an open goal. Clough further distorted the score with a penalty after Dunk was deemed to have fouled teenage substitute Ben Brereton.

It was a travesty of a result and it meant that Huddersfield could close the gap to three points with a game in hand if they could do what Hughton's men had failed to do and beat visiting Newcastle in the evening kick-off.

Fortunately for Albion, the Geordies enjoyed more slices of luck, in this case not a streaky deflection but an indulgent referee – Roger East again – as they won 3–1. After ten minutes, East ruled an innocuous challenge by Nahki Wells on Matt Ritchie worthy of a penalty, which Ritchie converted. Then he decided that Daryl

Murphy had not fouled goalkeeper Danny Ward as he kicked the ball out of his hands before scoring from a narrow angle.

Mooy brought Huddersfield back into the game with another penalty, but 21-year-old Joel Coleman, who had replaced the injured Ward at half-time, then misjudged a long clearance down the centre of the field and allowed the ball to bounce over his head to Dwight Gayle, who tapped it into the empty net.

That setback might have been expected to prompt some humility at Huddersfield, but instead their manager David Wagner tried to put some pressure on Albion in his press conference before the next round of matches in mid-week, when his side would host Aston Villa while Hughton's men went to Rotherham.

'I am totally sure Newcastle United will get promoted,' he said. 'Brighton, we will see. I have heard they have struggled in the past at the end of the season and nobody knows why. But from my point of view my squad is very excited and happy in the dressing room at the moment.'

The players took note of Wagner's comments and filed them away under the heading of 'extra motivation', but Hughton had more to concern him with Duffy out. For the trip to doomed Rotherham, he had the option of playing Tomori in his best position, but instead turned again to Hünemeier.

The German had had a torrid time in the 3–3 draw at Brentford – as had all the defenders – but at Lancing he was regarded as the ultimate professional and the most diligent trainer in the squad. Now his work was rewarded as he stepped into Duffy's place so effectively that the Irishman who had seemed to have made himself so indispensable was barely missed.

'He's done unbelievably,' Dunk said. 'He sat on the sidelines for so long, waiting for his opportunity. He works so hard in training every day. To be ready like he was has been unbelievable and he's been amazing for us.'

Hemed, Kayal and Skalák also came in for Murray, Sidwell and Murphy, and the changes paid off. After Stockdale saved an early shot from Tom Adeyemi with his feet, Albion were largely on top. Baldock had an angled shot saved after a flick-on from Hemed in the first half, and three minutes into the second, Brighton were ahead. Knockaert played a pass through the defence for Kayal, whose shot was blocked by goalkeeper Lewis Price's feet. Baldock's follow-up hit a defender on the line, but the ball fell for Knockaert to bounce a shot into the net.

March made sure eleven minutes from time when he cut in from the right and hit a low left-foot shot from 20 yards that bobbled past Price at his near post, and Baldock and Towell both missed chances to add further goals. It had been a workmanlike performance in the end on a ground where the team had been dismal the previous season. 'We needed David Stockdale to make a couple of early saves,' Hughton said. 'They are a team fighting and they showed that. We had to get through that period and I felt that, if we could, the game would then open up for us. That's exactly what happened.'

Next came a visit from Derby, almost always troublesome visitors to the Amex. This occasion, though, was the exception. Former England manager Steve McClaren was in charge of the Rams for the second time in his career and admitted afterwards that the Championship had moved on since he had last managed in it. His team were poor, and Knockaert skipped through a half-hearted challenge from Julien de Sart before lashing a low left-foot shot past goalkeeper Scott Carson from 25 yards.

Former Amex loanee Darren Bent glanced a header off the turf and over the bar as a warning before the hapless de Sart, trying to interrupt a one-two between Murray and Baldock, only prodded the ball into Baldock's path and he rolled a low shot past Carson. In the second half, old adversary Matěj Vydra bounced a header off the angle of post and crossbar before Murray scored the third thanks to the luck that all successful strikers seem to get on occasion. His shot from Knockaert's cross hit Carson's foot but ricocheted back in off his shin.

McClaren praised Albion and Hughton afterwards. 'I think [we had] a dose of reality tonight in how far Brighton have come,' he said.

'They will go up for certain – physically strong, running, dealing with the ball. Murray was outstanding. He has been a great signing for them, great target, physicality, a real man, a threat.

'In terms of where we need to go, that is the benchmark. It doesn't matter what system we'd have played tonight. It is not about systems, tactics. They were far better than us. We were second best.'

Unfortunately for McClaren, he would not be around to oversee any improvement, as he was sacked two days later.

Albion now faced their last remaining game against another promotion contender, fourth-placed Leeds United at Elland Road, on Saturday evening, while Huddersfield travelled to Bristol City the previous night. Albion fans did not hold out much hope that City, arguably the great underachievers of the division, would be able to do them a favour. After all, they had already lost at home to Newcastle, Reading, Fulham and, of course, Albion. So anyone who watched Sky's coverage expected David Wagner's team to close to within three points of Brighton.

But if results were foregone conclusions, the games would not need to be played and the betting companies would all go broke. And City not only beat Huddersfield, but thrashed them 4–0, with the Yorkshire team also losing influential Jonathan Hogg to a first-half head injury.

That gave Albion leeway in case the worst happened at Elland Road. And it did. The game was even, but Leeds' man in form, former Albion loanee Chris Wood, outshone his Brighton counterpart and former teammate Glenn Murray, at least in the vital area of scoring.

Wood made the breakthrough after sixty-three minutes, stealing a yard on Dunk to head Charlie Taylor's cross past Stockdale. Albion tried to hit back, but Murray's whiplash volley was too close to Leeds goalkeeper Robert Green and his next effort went just wide. Five minutes from time, Souleymane Doukara was brought down in the penalty area by Tomori, standing in for Bruno, and Wood did what had seemed almost impossible in recent weeks – he beat Stockdale from the penalty spot.

The Don Revie Stand had chanted 'You're going to **** it up again', and other voices joined in, insinuating that Hughton's men could be caught or even overhauled and that Leeds would 'hunt down' the Albion. Manager Garry Monk and his squad wisely kept quiet, but a club the size of Leeds has many former players keen to sound off to the numerous media outlets who pander to the fans' prejudices and wishes. And they were echoing Wagner's earlier remarks.

Perhaps they knew that Albion had not been effective recently after international breaks. The home defeat by Brentford and the below-par showing against Villa had both followed these enforced hiatuses. It was essential that the predictors of doom should not be proved right.

• • •

The club's solution to the problem of poor results after international breaks was to take those players not on duty with their national sides on a warm-weather break to Spain. There they could bond, refresh themselves and gather their forces for what looked like a final stretch of eminently winnable games, whatever recent results had shown to those who take results for granted.

The location chosen was Valencia, where Bruno had played for two seasons, and in the hours away from training, the captain led the way in relaxing his men.

'After we had lost at Leeds, it was a perfect time to get away, spend some time just us, the players and the staff, and have a bit of team bonding, get some good training sessions under our belt and it worked,' Dunk said.

'It was a massive help at getting us over the line. We had a bit of golf, had dinner together, just being around each other all day for five days, getting on well. Bruno took us to some nice restaurants. I had one of the best Italian meals I've ever had. It was nice to experience some of what he used to do.'

The climate helped. 'It was sunny and we went on the beach, we went for a dip, and the food was good,' Bruno said.

'I know sometimes English players don't enjoy food too much, but for us in Spain, food is a massive part of our culture. In England, it's not so much. I knew they were going to love it.

'We went to a couple of my favourite restaurants. Nine of us went to an Italian place owned by a family from Napoli. And then all of us went to a typical Valencian restaurant for paella, and that restaurant is the best. They say the guy who makes the paella does it by computer because it's always the same quality, the same flavour. If you went ten years ago and now, it would be the same.

'And on the last day we were there it was the *Las Fallas* festival of fire, and we were walking around the city looking at the burning of the big paper statues and there were small [stalls] selling *churros* and chocolate. The boys loved it. I think they all want to go and play in Spain now.'

Perhaps it was just as well that the team were in Valencia when Martin McGuinness, the former Deputy First Minister of Northern Ireland, died and Derry-born Shane Duffy tweeted: 'More tragic news this morning. RIP Martin McGuinness a true hero for many off [*sic*] us. God bless your family and close ones #ireland'.

Duffy's remark divided opinion among supporters, with some of the more extreme wanting him out of the club, and others agreeing with his view of the late Sinn Féin politician as a man who had been important in the peace process, whatever his earlier role in the Troubles. Most respected Duffy's opinion and his right to express it, although others felt that he might have been naïve in commenting bearing in mind the city of Brighton's direct experience of IRA action, the bombing of the Grand Hotel during the October 1984 Conservative Party conference.

That, though, had happened more than seven years before Duffy, twenty-four, had been born, and his experience of McGuinness must have been mainly as the jocular partner-in-government of Ian Paisley in a peaceful Northern Ireland. Unrepentant, Duffy reacted to one comment on Twitter by replying: 'I'll always stand by who and what I support, it's the way I was brought up.'

Perhaps the best comment came in an extended review of the season by Jason Thackeray on the North Stand Chat forum. 'Duffy's McGuinness tweet was fine with me, not because of what he said but because he said it in the first place,' he wrote.

'This guy isn't scared of anything. Online he's never short of a committed opinion. This translates on the field to a guy who will put his head anywhere, play with a broken nose, head away that brick, take a booking for the team, crank up the fans. Remove one element and you dilute the other. This is an all-or-nothing guy.'

At the time it was nothing, as he recovered from injury. But almost as soon as the Albion party returned from Spain, the omens were good. First, on the eve of the next game, at home to struggling Blackburn, came the news that Goldson's heart operation had gone well. Then it was back out onto the Amex pitch and down to business.

CHAPTER 14

THE HOME STRAIGHT

When Poyet's team won promotion from League One to the Championship in 2010/11, the final season at Withdean Stadium, a miraculous month of March made the difference. Poyet's men won all eight matches they played in that month. Now, with no more games against promotion challengers left on their fixture list, Hughton's team knew that something similar over the seven games of April 2017 might be required if they were to stay ahead of Huddersfield.

Blackburn were first up. They were at the wrong end of the table, but since Tony Mowbray had taken over from Owen Coyle as manager in February, they had begun to develop a mean streak, and they arrived at the Amex on a seven-match unbeaten run. Greer would not face his former club, but Elliott Bennett, one of Poyet's 2011 promotion team along with Murray, and former Albion loanee Craig Conway were both in the team.

Those of the 30,216 inside the ground who had looked only at the table and not the form guide were frustrated as Blackburn refused to buckle. With Huddersfield at home to Burton and heavy favourites to win, three points were surely essential. But as the second half wore on, both games were goalless. A score in either might prove a crucial switch in the momentum of the whole season.

Perhaps it was the tension and frustration boiling over that explained, if they did not excuse, the booing off of Chuba Akpom when replaced by Hemed after fifty-eight minutes.

Then, after sixty-seven minutes, the breakthrough. As Rosenior's cross from the right floated beyond the far post, the ball was nodded forward with a delicate cushioned header by an unusual target man in Knockaert. Murray's nose for a goal had allowed him to make the right run to beat the offside trap and his quality allowed him to take a touch and poke the ball home. The game finished 1–0.

As he celebrated before the North Stand, he gestured as if willing the crowd to calm down. 'It's the supporters' prerogative to get excited,' Hughton said. 'They're there to enjoy the football, enjoy the moment when we win games or score goals. That's probably Glenn's way of saying that we haven't achieved anything yet. We're trying to, we're doing our best to, and we need everybody behind us but we haven't done anything yet.'

'I think everyone was a little bit jittery, including the players,' Murray said.

'I honestly believed it was not a time to be nervous, it was a time to enjoy. And I think if you can relax and enjoy yourself, you can do your best. But if you're uptight and nervous, that's when things start going wrong. Being at the top of the league and fighting for promotion is where you want to be and that's what fans want to be watching. It's when you're at the bottom, that's when the nerves really set in.'

As the fans gathered around the TV monitors in the concourses after the final whistle, the talk was not of Knockaert's rare headed assist but of what was happening at Huddersfield – or rather, what was not happening: their match was still going on, and still goalless. Fingers were chewed as the minutes wore on and still no final score was announced, with everyone fearing yet another late goal for the Terriers, even though they were down to ten men after a second yellow card for captain Dean Whitehead after eighty-eight minutes.

And finally, in the sixth minute of injury time, a goal came – but it was scored by Burton's Australian substitute Jackson Irvine. A final score that would have sounded like an April Fool's joke if it had been forecast now put Albion nine points clear of Huddersfield with six games to play.

After stubborn Blackburn came fast-sinking Birmingham, also at the Amex. Since Albion's visit to St Andrew's in December, the folly of the Blues' owner in replacing Gary Rowett as manager with Gianfranco Zola had become clear. The team was not expected to put up much resistance at Brighton, and they were behind after only two minutes. Knockaert passed out to the overlapping Bruno and Murray swept his low cross past Kuszczak from eight yards.

Pressing home that early advantage was the obvious next step, but instead Craig Gardner almost levelled for Brum with a free kick that cannoned off Stockdale's crossbar, and Dunk had to make a well-timed intervention to block Clayton Donaldson's shot before leaving the field. The defender had felt unwell before the match but played on and was now replaced by Tomori.

'We knew before the game that Dunky wasn't quite right and I was told to be ready,' Tomori said.

'When Lewis went down, I was straight into it. I think I did OK. I'd not played with Uwe before but we've trained a lot together and so know each other's game pretty well. He helped me through the game a lot, always talking to me, and so did Bruno, Bongy and Stocko.'

The strength of the squad was proved by the fact that a pairing of the fourth- and fifth-choice central defenders now saw the team through to half-time unscathed. And the attack began the second half as quickly as they had the first, Murray nodding Bruno's deep cross back across goal for Hemed to chest home from a yard out. This time they scored again six minutes later, Hünemeier half-volleying his first goal in British football with the help of a deflection after Birmingham failed to clear a free kick from Knockaert.

But another deflected goal, by Birmingham's lively Che Adams, whose shot went past Stockdale five minutes from time, suddenly gave the visitors heart and they pressed forward looking for an unlikely second. Stockdale and company held on, however, and returned to the top of the table, ten points clear of third place. A twenty-fifth win equalled the club's best total in a Championship season and Murray had become the first Brighton twenty-goal striker at this level since Mike Small scored twenty-one in 1990/91, a season that ended in a Wembley play-off final defeat by Notts County.

But not everyone was happy. 'Perhaps being a little childish, I shook everyone's hands at the end and then stormed off the pitch,' Stockdale said.

'Because we'd let a late goal in even though we'd won 3–1 and it was deflected. Everyone was happy and jumping about in the changing room because we'd won and I went in to the gaffer and said: "The defending higher up the pitch for that goal wasn't good enough and if we carry on like that we'll get complacent and I've been in this situation before." He said: "No, I agree. If we do it again and it goes to 3–2, what then? It'll be nerve-racking again."'

And it would be, in almost every game, but so high were the stakes now that nerves were always going to be stretched to breaking point. Fortunately, it was not to be the Albion's nerves that gave way.

The following day came the sad news that supporter Paul Whelch had died. Whelch had been one of three people – with reporter Paul Bracchi and accountant Paul Samrah – who in 1995 uncovered the fact that chairman Bill Archer had altered the club's articles of association, scrapping a clause that prevented directors from profiting from the sale of assets if the club were wound up. The main asset, of course, was the Goldstone Ground.

Whelch was the third to pass away of a key group of fans who had worked with Dick Knight to bring the club home from Gillingham to Withdean, then persuade local and national governments to allow the building of the new ground. Former programme editor Roy Chuter died in July 2013 and supporters' club stalwart Sarah Watts in January 2015. 'It was a tragedy,' Tony Bloom said later. 'Paul, Sarah and Roy were all still young and massive supporters and huge driving forces behind our campaigns. The fact that they are not here now to see us in the Premier League is a real shame.'

• • •

The third match in a week was on Friday, as Albion's televised game against Queens Park Rangers at Loftus Road kicked off a weekend in which the contenders all faced potentially difficult away matches. Newcastle were at Sheffield Wednesday, who were coming into form, while Reading would travel to inconsistent and unpredictable Norwich, where anything was possible. Huddersfield seemed to have the easiest trip, to Nottingham Forest, who had upset the Albion so spectacularly but had done nothing since to suggest a repeat was imminent, drawing two and losing three of their five games.

So a first victory at QPR's compact west London ground for sixty years was the Albion aim, and it was soon clear that Hughton's men were going for that win. After Dunk fortunately got away with a handling offence in his own area, both Murray and Hemed had goals correctly disallowed for offside in the first half. But Dunk, although he had declared himself fit, had to be replaced by Tomori again, this time at the interval.

Thirteen minutes later, though, Tomori headed away a cross from the right and the ball dropped into midfield, where Murray and Hemed worked a one-two across half the pitch that left Murray clean through on goal. He feinted to put the ball to goalkeeper Alex Smithies's left then shot into the gap to his right and the Albion fans packed into both tiers of the cramped School End went wild. The pitch-side microphones picked up Hemed screaming 'I love you' as he leapt on Murray in celebration, and the fans probably felt the same.

The second goal, six minutes later, was as unexpected in the identity of its scorer as it was splendid in its execution and, perhaps, fortunate in its origin. Referee Simon Hooper ruled that Murray had been tripped on the right-hand edge of the QPR penalty area, but replays suggested that he had fallen over his own feet, although perhaps a sort of rough justice was done, as a foul on Knockaert a second or two earlier had gone unpunished.

The position of the free kick was ideal for Knockaert to cross or strike at goal with his left foot. When Sébastien Pocognoli came across and, after a conversation with the Frenchman, placed the ball and stepped back ready to strike, few expected anything other than a shot over the crossbar or hit straight at the defensive wall.

Instead, a perfectly struck shot from the Belgian sent the ball arcing over the heads of the QPR defenders and in off the crossbar at the near post. It was the full-back's first goal since scoring for Knockaert's ex-club Standard Liège seven years before and it sparked bedlam behind the goal.

'I had a good feeling before the shot, I don't know why,' Pocognoli explained afterwards.

'I went across the pitch to take it and everybody was probably thinking, "What is he doing?" But it's my favourite place to shoot from and actually at my past club, I sometimes took free kicks and corners. That is my quality but I haven't practised a lot this year but I'm happy.

'I just said to Anthony [Knockaert], "Let me shoot" and we have a good relationship, so he said OK. He tried to explain something for me to do quite technically but I told him I didn't understand what he was saying to me, even in French. I just said, "Please let me take it" and it was a goal and a nice moment. For me, it was one of the best feelings because I don't score a lot of goals.'

In other leagues, the team might have been able to coast through the remaining twenty-six minutes, but not the Championship. QPR had won their previous four home games and now manager Ian Holloway made two attacking substitutions, sending on Luke Freeman and Yeni N'Gbakoto, and the ball was sent repeatedly to the head of the six foot six Matt Smith. Without the height of Dunk or Duffy, Albion were vulnerable, and Smith beat Hünemeier to head QPR back into the game with sixteen minutes still to play.

Some recalled the loss of a 2–0 lead at the same venue the previous season, but this QPR had no Charlie Austin, and this Albion still had eleven men on the field, with Stockdale in fine form, twice saving with his feet from shots inside the six-yard box. And Hughton was taking no chances. Knockaert gave the ball away once too often and was immediately replaced by Norwood, and the final whistle meant that the team had taken nine points in seven days and flung down the gauntlet to their would-be pursuers.

Hughton had said a number of times before that playing before everyone else was an advantage 'if you win' and his words had never rung truer. However nervy the final minutes at Loftus Road had been, the efforts to hang on were worth it as Saturday's results came in. Huddersfield lost 2–0 at Forest, Reading fell apart 7–1 at Norwich and then, in the evening kick-off, Newcastle lost away to Sheffield Wednesday.

Suddenly, after so many weekends of fans looking over shoulders, poring over fixture lists and wondering if and where rivals might drop points, the landscape had altered. Not only was promotion in the club's own hands, but just two wins from five games would now suffice.

'It has been a big weekend, an unusual weekend,' Hughton said.

'Usually if you are looking at the [results of the] teams around you possibly one might go your way, one in the middle and three haven't. So it was certainly a good weekend for the other results but the biggest result was ours at Queens Park Rangers.

'That's how we have to look at these forthcoming games. Our games are the biggest games, because we know if we get the results we need to over these five games then we have looked after ourselves and the others can't catch us.'

Sidwell urged his teammates to savour the moment. 'It's not far away and we had a great weekend with results going for us,' he said.

'It is hard to enjoy it when everything is so intense. You can't look any further ahead than the next game, but I've said to the lads that I've been in this position before and you've got to enjoy it. It's hard to, but you've got to play with a smile on your face because this doesn't happen very often.

'Football is an emotional sport and it is important for me that you don't get very high and don't get too low. You enjoy the good times and get through the bad ones, keep a happy medium. And I've been constantly saying that in the dressing room throughout the season.

We've given ourselves a great opportunity. After what happened last year, all the lads used their experience and took the emotions as an incentive.'

Later, Murray would single out this week as pivotal. 'In April we really produced as a team when our backs were against the wall and when we needed to,' he said.

'We were under pressure from Huddersfield and others around us and then we won three games in seven days and that was a really big week.

'Without a doubt we could feel [Huddersfield] breathing down our necks. Every time we'd come off the field, they'd scored late on or they'd won 1–0 and we'd think: "Jesus, are these going to give up or what? Are we ever going to get the rub of the green?" Obviously we could feel the pressure, but that week in April was huge for us.'

There was an interesting footnote to the weekend's results. Sheffield Wednesday had now done the double over Newcastle, who had done the same to Albion, who had done the same to Wednesday. That, though, was the unpredictable nature of the Championship.

Perhaps of more significance was the publishing of a table of fees paid by Championship clubs to agents during the season, revealing that the £1.5 million spent by Albion put them only in ninth place. Newcastle had paid over £10 million – which was more than Albion had spent on players. It was more proof that Bloom was running his club carefully but without compromising the team's chances of reaching their ultimate goal.

• • •

On the Sunday evening after the victory at QPR, a sizeable Albion party descended on the Hilton hotel in London's Park Lane in good heart for the EFL Awards. And there was tangible reward for the season's efforts. Sidwell was first up on stage to receive the goal of the season gong for his 45-yard stunner at Bristol City.

The presenter asked him whether it was the best goal of his career. 'Seriously? Forty-five yards with my left foot? What do you think? I haven't got any pace so I can't outrun defenders,' he explained. 'That was the only way to score. It was a great moment for me but it was a sad moment because the celebration reflected Anthony Knockaert losing his dad.' As Sidwell recounted the story, Knockaert's eyes visibly filled with tears.

'It was hard to enjoy the goal at the time, there was such a seriousness around it. Not just the goal, but the game, the three points, the victory, were all dedicated to him because he's such a lively character and such a big part of the dressing room and we missed him for a couple of weeks. I know he's up for an award and if he gets it, it's testament to his emotion and his character and his ability as a footballer.'

Stockdale, Dunk, Murray and Knockaert had already been named in the Championship team of the season, but now Stockdale and Knockaert also made the all-EFL team.

Then came the final coup as Knockaert was named Championship player of the season. And it was Hughton, who had been asked to give out the divisional player awards, who had the satisfaction of presenting the trophy to the Frenchman.

Knockaert's win, based on votes from all twenty-three Championship managers – bar Hughton, with votes for your own players not allowed – nevertheless provoked an outcry on social media from Leeds fans, who believed that Chris Wood, as the division's top scorer, had a better claim. But Hughton was in no doubt that the right man had been selected.

'I can see the reasons for anybody thinking someone else should have got it, because they are all top candidates,' he said. 'But we see Anthony week in, week out and what he's produced for us over the season for a wide player, with the number of goals and assists he's got, and his overall play as a team player.'

After the ceremony, Knockaert returned the compliments to Hughton. 'I couldn't be happier than having this manager give me the trophy,' he said.

'He's been so important to me this season after what happened. He's been behind me all the way through. Every time I needed some help, he was there for me. You can see all my performances on the pitch this season that I feel so confident in this team, I feel free to play, he gives me a lot of credit and all his confidence.

'When you have a manager like him, obviously you want to give your life every game. Because if you don't, you regret that you don't do enough for him and that's disrespectful to him. In our team there are players who don't start a lot of games but they still love him because he respects everyone in the same way and for me he's a great guy, he's someone we are lucky to have.'

The award was recognition of a sensational season for Knockaert and his club, which promised to get even better. 'It's amazing,' he said.

'For me and my family it's something special and it's surely a season that I will never forget. The first thing we said to each other when we came back to pre-season was that it was exactly the same goal for us, to achieve the top two or try to get into the play-offs.

'Obviously you always want to finish in the top two before the play-offs and we haven't done it yet. We still need to work hard until the end but we are in a great position now. We always believed in our quality and it hurt a lot last year but it was a good reason to say that we need to get better and do it this season.'

Promotion, he agreed, would be more emotional than it had been with Leicester two years previously.

'Yes, it will be amazing because – I don't know if I said this before to the media – two days before my dad passed away I promised him that we would do it and obviously for me it's so, so important to do it because I don't want to lie to him and it will be amazing and it could be the best season in my life so far.'

In the city of Brighton & Hove, there was more blue and white on display than England white and red during a World Cup. Paul Barber had called for the county to show its colours, and the response was evident everywhere. Shop staff dressed in replica shirts, the *Argus* banner appeared in alternate blue-and-white letters, and every councillor at a meeting of Brighton & Hove City Council wore the stripes.

Easter is traditionally a period when promotion and relegation issues are settled, or at least clarified, but that was not necessarily a good thing for the Albion. They approached the Good Friday and Easter Monday fixtures against Wolves and Wigan respectively knowing that the fans had not been able to celebrate a win at Easter since 2009, when a victory at Colchester had sparked a great escape from League One relegation under Russell Slade.

Even in a season when the laying to rest of ghosts and hoodoos had become common – a first win at Hillsborough, the win at Oakwell, and an overdue three points at Loftus Road – this was still a sobering statistic.

In his pre-match press conference ahead of the Wolves match, Hughton was asked if the open-top bus ride had been booked. Cautious as ever, he replied in the negative. 'No, there's been no talk of that at this stage. If we win enough games.' He did not even seem certain that the club could be promoted by the end of Easter

Monday, let alone Good Friday night, which was possible – if Huddersfield lost at home to Preston before Brighton won at Molineux.

But Hemed, who would again deputise for the still-unfit Baldock, revealed that he had believed in the club's chances ever since he arrived.

'I said from the first day that I came here to go to the Premier League with Brighton. The season before, the team was not so good and maybe people thought it was not the right thing to say because I was new and I didn't know what I was saying. But it's what everyone here has been thinking about every day and we work hard every day to achieve it.

'I spoke to people here and they gave me a good feeling and I think I made the right decision. I saw how huge this club is and from the first day it felt like a Premier League club and also a warm family.

'Now is the moment. We know how important the next month is and we need to leave everything else aside and just concentrate on that. We've been fighting for it all season and now is the moment to finish it. We need to wait a few games and then I can say "I told you so" but not yet. We prefer not to speak about it but it was my target when I came here and I really want to achieve it.

'But we need to stay focused and not to think about it too much, just to think about how to win the next game. Of course we want to finish first but at the start of the season the target was to finish in the first two and all of us would be happy with that. The fans deserve to be there. They give us a push at the right moment and we saw how disappointed they were at the end of the season and this is a chance to give them something back.'

Hughton, though, insisted that burying the memories of the previous season's disappointment had not been his players' main motivation. 'Being in that top group all last season has been the motivation,' he said.

'We enjoyed competing at the top end of the table. That was more of a motivation than last season's disappointment. We have been used to being in this position and that experience has helped us. We've been excited all season because we've been at the end of the table we've wanted to be at.'

On Good Friday morning, Radio Sussex began the day by talking to BBC commentator and Sussex resident Jonathan Pearce for his thoughts on impending promotion and asked listeners and interviewees who they would think of first when promotion was achieved. Many nominated deceased fans.

But promotion was not achieved that day as they and many others had hoped. Huddersfield beat Preston as late as they had lost to Burton, scoring the winner from a rebound after North End goalkeeper Chris Maxwell had saved a 96th-minute penalty taken by Aaron Mooy.

Hughton had not wanted the players to know the result before they walked out at Molineux to deliver yet another determined performance. Wolves were on top early on but Albion soon settled and Hemed hit the bar. Hemed went close again, as did March, and just before the interval the men in blue and white were ahead.

A long kick from Stockdale towards Murray travelled on towards Knockaert – possibly offside when the goalkeeper released the ball – and he took advantage of a slip by defender Kortney Hause, sped down the right and cut inside Hause again before hitting a low left-foot shot that slithered past goalkeeper Andy Lonergan at his near post. 'One of the greatest players to grace the Championship stage takes another bow,' the Sky commentator roared as Knockaert skipped over the advertising hoardings to celebrate with the Albion fans who filled the entire length of the lower tier of the Steve Bull Stand along the touchline.

But once again, the team was unable to have things its own way, and Stockdale was called into action to make three saves in the second half, two relatively routine from David Edwards and Ben Marshall, but the best and most valuable when March failed to track right-back Conor Coady and the goalkeeper had to dive to his right to parry the Wolves man's header, March making amends by blocking the follow-up effort. Too often possession was given away in midfield but, as so often, any failings between the two penalty areas were masked by what happened within them.

Dunk completed the ninety minutes despite a lump the size of an egg on his forehead from a first-half clash of heads, and a limp from a collision in the second, both involving Icelander Jón Daði Böðvarsson. Hünemeier provided able support, and Bruno was impeccable again. 'Stocko made some good saves and we needed our defenders to defend very well,' Hughton said afterwards. 'We've made a habit of hanging on in games when we're under pressure. And we always know that we have quality in the side that can produce something.'

And so it proved. At the sharp end, Murray was tireless and drew fouls at key moments to relieve pressure. Eight minutes from time, Bruno made the latest of a number of cool interceptions, and Hemed's long diagonal ball from deep sent substitute Jamie Murphy racing into the Wolves half. The Scottish winger did not shirk a juddering challenge from Hause, the last defender, and as the ball bounced loose, the alert Murray nodded it forward for Knockaert, who drilled another shot between Lonergan and his near post. It was his fifteenth goal of the campaign, a remarkable total for a wide player, and victory was sealed.

After the final whistle, Knockaert went to the fans again, this time seeking out his brother Simon and giving him his shirt. The victory put the team five points ahead of Newcastle, who could only narrow the gap to four in their late kick-off at home to Leeds, the Yorkshire side snatching a late leveller through Chris Wood. Even former Brighton loanees were helping out.

Not that Hughton's men seemed to need much help. A twenty-first clean sheet of the season meant that a defence that had often been disrupted by injury had still managed to shut their opponents out in half their matches. It was the basis for a timely first victory in an Easter fixture since that win away to Colchester in 2009. Moreover, the result set a new record of eleven away wins in the second tier.

'I would still say that Sheffield Wednesday was our best performance away from home,' Hughton said.

'But at this vital stage, coming to a club that has been on a good run, and for what it meant, to dig a result out as we had to, was outstanding. We more or less reached all our targets last year and still didn't get promoted. We drew a lot of games away from home and that has changed. That has been a big difference to where we are at this moment and where we were at this moment last season.'

One more win would now all but guarantee promotion. Among those reacting via Twitter were Íñigo Calderón and former manager Óscar García, who had recently been linked with the Barcelona job. 'Oh my God, so close, so deserved,' was Calderón's message. García said: 'Only one step more and we get promoted to the @premierleague! Well deserved @OfficialBHAFC!! Really happy for a lot of people!! Big congrats!'

Injured trio Baldock, Duffy and Goldson were shown on social media celebrating with diners at a Sussex restaurant, and leading the singing of Neil Diamond's 'Sweet Caroline', the team's post-match victory anthem.

Albion had now done the double over nine teams, equalling the figure of Gus Poyet's 2010/11 League One champions. If they made it ten at home to Wigan Athletic on Easter Monday, they would be in the Premier League.

On Easter Monday, the [illegible] sports pages ran a [illegible] Hereford that had kept the club [illegible] The writer, Matt Bailey, had spoken [illegible] manager Steve Grant.

Petard, a substitute, [illegible] goal, shooting in after a [illegible] from the post. I thought [illegible]

I've seen the video so many times [illegible] which is good because it was so [illegible] would probably have missed [illegible]

Terry Mayo jumped on the [illegible] everything [illegible] because he was playing [illegible] that because [illegible] it went absolutely [illegible]

The team had been [illegible] amazing and unaffected [illegible] horrible and nervous, [illegible]

CHAPTER 15

UP

On Easter Monday, the day of the Wigan match, the *Daily Mail* sports pages ran a story remembering the 1–1 draw at Hereford that had kept the club in the Football League twenty years earlier. The writer, Matt Barlow, had spoken to scorer Robbie Reinelt and manager Steve Gritt.

Reinelt, a substitute, cancelled out Kerry Mayo's first-half own goal, shooting in after a volley from Craig Maskell had rebounded from the post. 'I thought I was further out,' he said.

'I've seen the video so many times. I was actually quite close, which is good because it was on my left foot. Any further out and I would probably have missed. I just hit it. "Hit the target," I thought.

'Kerry Mayo jumped on my back and yelled: "You've just saved my effing life," his exact words. I don't know where he came from because he was playing left-back that day. The rest of the game was a blur because you're all hyped up realising what it could mean. Then it went absolutely mental after the final whistle.'

The team had been a relegation certainty when Gritt took over in autumn and masterminded the club's great escape. 'The game was horrible and nervous,' he recalled.

'Going 1–0 down was tough having come so far but we regrouped at half-time. There's nothing much you can do in those situations except keep plugging away. We brought on Robbie and changed the system a bit, and he made one hell of a mark on the club's history. It is amazing how one moment can change a career.

'Kerry Mayo was a young lad just about on the transfer list and he was nearly known as someone who sent them down. He came through to have a great career at Brighton, stayed for ten years and got a testimonial.

'If Brighton had gone down at that particular time, with its financial situation and no ground, I don't think it would have come back from that for an awful long time. Thankfully it all ended well and it's great to see how they're doing. To reach the Premier League would be fantastic for the fans and the people who brought the club back from the edge of extinction.'

It was a reminder of how far the club had come in the intervening twenty years, from scrambling for survival at the bottom end of the Football League in 1997 to being ninety minutes from the most glamorous domestic competition in world football.

Well, almost. If Huddersfield, whose match at Derby kicked off after the final whistle at the Amex, were to equal or better the Albion result, they could still, technically, catch up on goal difference. That, though, would require them to make up a deficit of twenty-five goals over their remaining four games and the Albion's three, which was a prospect from the realms of Yorkshire fantasy, or Sussex nightmare. Beat Wigan, and, to all extents and purposes, Brighton were up, whether or not the P for Promotion officially appeared next to their name in the league table by the end of the day's business.

Former players Andrew Crofts, Dean Cox, Gary Hart, Alan Navarro and Robbie Savage tweeted their best wishes, and Bobby

Zamora sent a video message from Dubai, where he was coaching. 'I just wanted to wish Brighton all the best today,' he said.

'A chance to make history, so, to the players, have a great one and do all you can to get promotion. And obviously remember you've got to focus on winning the league. To the club, keep up the great work; you've done tremendously the last few years, just missing out. To the fans, give absolutely everything today, push them on and hopefully there'll be Premier League football at the Amex next season.'

Íñigo Calderón had returned from Cyprus for the Easter weekend with the permission of Anorthosis Famagusta, his new club. 'We said we'd have a whip-round to pay his fine but he said it was all arranged with the club,' Alan Wares said. Calde was introduced to the crowd before the Wigan match, receiving as much devotion as ever – perhaps even more than some of the current players.

'I have felt the love of the fans since the first moment I was here, even if sometimes I didn't know why so much, but at this moment that's not fair to today's team,' he said.

'Today I want to think I am a kind of representative of everyone who has been involved in all this process, because it hasn't just been one year, although this year's team has done the most difficult part, obviously.

'A lot of players before me did very good work, managers too, so maybe I am here to represent all those people, for the players who played at Withdean, Gordon [Greer], Casper as well, and for the fans too. We were without a home, playing at Withdean and with no training ground. When you have known all that, like me, like Glenn, you feel better about today than if you had just come here two years ago. So yes, it is special.'

The match itself was rather less special. The team began slowly, as if content to yield space to a Wigan side who were in the bottom three with games running out but had won their previous two matches. The dangerous Nick Powell, lacking fitness but the scorer of a hat-trick from the bench in their 3–2 win over Barnsley on Maundy Thursday, was again a substitute.

Passes and crosses were underhit as a cautious approach seemed to take hold. But again, the team's weapons forced a breakthrough that their overall play had scarcely merited. Eight minutes before the interval, Dunk hoisted a long ball forward and Dan Burn in the centre of a backpedalling defence misjudged its flight. His attempted clearance dropped for Hemed to touch back to Murray on the edge of the penalty area, and the striker's twenty-second of the season was drilled home.

Murray had the ball in the net again before the interval, but the referee's assistant ruled that the ball had gone out of play before it reached his head. But the lead was doubled anyway 20 minutes into the second half and Knockaert, inevitably, was involved. He bamboozled two Wigan men on the right and his low cross was deflected to March, who sidestepped an advancing knot of defenders and slid the ball between the legs of the unconvincing goalkeeper Jakob Haugaard.

Hemed might have made it 3–0 when Haugaard mishandled, but Jake Buxton blocked his effort and follow-up, and Knockaert had a goal disallowed for offside. The mood in the stands and, perhaps, on the field, was now of relaxed confidence in the outcome – perhaps too relaxed. Powell came on and soon showed his qualities, punishing some lax Brighton play by halving the arrears with a deft header five minutes from time.

Stockdale's fury was evident, and the laxness he had warned against after the 3–1 victory over Birmingham nearly proved costly in the nerve-shredding minutes that remained. 'We were messing about and they got one back and then they had a two-versus-one and luckily didn't pass it,' he said. But eventually referee James Linington blew the final whistle and the club was effectively back in the top flight after an absence of thirty-three years, eleven months and ten days.

Appeals made beforehand by the club for fans to stay off the field were never going to be heeded, and within seconds the pitch was a sea of celebration as the frustration and heartache of the three play-off defeats were finally exorcised. 'I didn't know how people would react because it wasn't mathematically certain,' Bloom said. 'And I wasn't even sure the referee had blown the whistle. I thought there was probably another minute or so and he'd blown for a free kick but that was it. When Knockaert went mad, that was when I knew, and the celebrations commenced.'

Play had been on the East Stand side at the end, and the players now had to force their various ways through the throng. Dunk made it at the expense of his shirt and shorts, eventually striding to the safety of the tunnel in his underwear.

As the news spread that Newcastle had lost 3–1 at Ipswich, bringing the title within three points, the fans chanted the name of Bloom, who waved from the directors' box after discreetly wiping a tear from his eye. Eventually, Barber handed him a blue-and-white scarf and his reserve disappeared as he waved it over his head and then twirled it joyfully, showing as much delight as any of the other fans.

'It all happened naturally and from instinct,' Bloom said.

'For the first two or three minutes after the whistle I was not overly emotional but then it all happened. I looked at the crowds and the magnitude of our promotion finally sank in. This was our moment, we'd finally made it to the Premier League, and so I just lost it for a few minutes. Looking back it looked quite funny but it was just the emotion of the occasion. When I'm at a game it's hard to control my emotions.'

'All I could see in my peripheral vision was my chairman jumping up and down like he'd had an electric prod in his backside,' Barber said. 'It was wonderful.' Behind Bloom stood Alan Mullery, a reminder of the only other day in the club's history to compare with this one.

The volume increased as the players appeared in the press box just above the tunnel, grabbing the PA microphone and belting out songs including 'We're on Our Way', 'We've Got Knockaert' and 'Sweet Caroline' to the sea of blue and white before them. 'When we went up with Reading ten or eleven years ago, that looked like a kids' tea party at McDonald's by comparison,' Sidwell said.

Bloom and Barber had also made their way down and waved again to the fans. 'Twenty years ago we were homeless and here we are on the way to the Premier League,' Bloom said over the PA. 'We want the title and we're going for it.'

Winstanley surveyed the chaos with quiet satisfaction. 'I was very proud watching the group celebrating after promotion, probably the best feeling I've had in my life,' he said. 'Some of the guys were here when we arrived, like Stocko, Bruno, Sam and Dunky, but we brought in Uwe, Beram, Tomer, Duffer, Gaëtan, Séb, Siddy, Knockaert, Skalák, Murph and Glenn.'

Afterwards, Calderón stood in the tunnel where he had wept eleven months earlier. 'It has been a long way through many difficulties, but that is the quality of this club,' he said. 'That's why I did this trip from Cyprus. I had to be here and everything went perfectly. The day they went into the Premier League? I couldn't miss that. And I feel so happy that I made the decision to come. It was a special moment.'

• • •

The tunnel area had been a place of gloom after the previous season's play-off semi-final second leg, with the only sound coming from behind the doors of the visitors' dressing room on the south side. Now it was rowdy and raucous. There were smiles on faces, with players hugging the staff before adding to the cacophony in the home changing room.

Murphy paused to shake Bloom's hand on his way back to the dressing room and say, 'Congratulations, Mr Chairman' as the owner happily surveyed the scene before expressing his relief to two nationally known football writers who are also Albion fans.

'I couldn't compete indefinitely,' he said.

'It doesn't mean that we couldn't have done it next season, but this was the one, after we kept Dale Stephens and the others. I think a lot of people outside the club thought that was it after last season, because it was a tougher division this season than last. And when Huddersfield kept winning, it looked like we might need 95 points. But then, fortunately, they stuttered. And we won five in a row when the pressure was on. Unbelievable.'

Dunk leaned, exhausted but happy, against the tunnel wall. 'We all know it'll be a massive step up but it's just a joy to finally be there and we'll see what we can do,' he said.

'It's a challenge but it's one we accept. We have had ups and downs on and off the pitch but we have stuck together and fought through everything. Togetherness has got us through.

'It is a dream come true for me, my family, everyone. It will be a massive boost for the whole city. We have many, many fans here and it will be a dream come true for them too and I'm glad to be a part of it.

'We have had clean sheets in over half our games, which is massive. They win you games in this league because we are always confident that we can score. Our pockets are waiting for Sergio Agüero and the rest.

'We have gone under the radar but we have always been quietly confident inside our little bubble that we can do it. All the talk has been about Newcastle winning the league and, to be fair, they should have won the league. But we have shown that we can fight and keep fighting.'

The layout of the Amex Stadium is unusual in that managers speak to the written media after games in an auditorium just off the tunnel, and even after the door had been closed behind Hughton, the yells and whoops of delight from the players were still very audible.

'All those memos that went out to stop the fans going on the pitch didn't work,' Hughton chuckled.

'I've been here for two years and four months, but there are supporters out there who have been through all the difficult periods, so I can understand their emotions. When their lad went through at the end, he possibly should have scored and to end up 2–2 after being 2–0 up would have been unthinkable.

'We have shown all season that we can win games in different ways. Sometimes it's not our best performance but we can keep clean sheets and we can score a goal and that is a reflection of a lot of games this season. At Fulham, we couldn't get the ball off them for thirty minutes and to come back and win without playing at our best, and away from home, is a real indication [of that].

'It's the type of individuals we have. We recruited well in the summer, so we had a better team and a better squad. It's my responsibility but it's a team that has achieved. We've been able to rotate in the last period and that is always good for the group. But it is more about the club. When I came here on New Year's Day 2015, we were in the bottom three but it didn't feel like that as a club. It's incredibly well run with a wonderful support base. It was just a question of getting results and then a recruitment process. We recruited good stable individuals and they have grown since then.

'I think most people expected Newcastle to win the title but it's not about beating them. There are really big clubs that are not even in the top six. I know the history of this club. I played at the Goldstone, and I remember the times at Gillingham, but you do have to be reminded of that. There are a lot of people involved in the day-to-day running of the club who were around in those tough times. But it takes an investor and it is outstanding, a wonderful feeling when you have a local investor who is prepared in this day and age to put his own money in when most of the big investors are overseas or consortiums. And I know the supporters appreciate that.'

Bloom himself, normally reluctant to take the spotlight, agreed to speak to the print media on this special occasion, following Hughton into the post-match interview room. He was asked whether the club's progress since he had taken over had made this promotion feel inevitable.

'Days like this are never inevitable,' Bloom said.

'You can get close six or seven times on the spin. I remember Preston were in the play-offs three times and never made it. It gets tougher every year with rich new owners coming in. Everyone has worked hard to get to this position so it is so well deserved by so many people. It didn't go right for us at the end of last season but we've been on the go ready for this moment from the first day of this season.

'I've been a passionate Brighton supporter for forty years. I committed to building the stadium and then the training ground because I love this club. I was in a fortunate position of having made enough money that I was able to, so for me it was an easy decision. I think a lot of other people in the same position would have done the same.

'But you've also got to run the club in the right way and recruit correctly. A lot of other local owners have put money into their clubs and it hasn't worked out well for a variety of reasons. It is important that, outside the ninety minutes when I'm very passionate, like our brilliant fans, the decisions I make for this club have to be rational and unemotional. There are tough decisions in all areas that have to be made every day. You're always going to make bad decisions but hopefully most of the big ones are the right ones.

'We were in a bad position when Chris came in. He needed to get us to stay up and it wasn't pretty and it wasn't easy. But any club can have a bad season. The team spirit is fantastic and Chris has done remarkably well in a very tough league to get the points he has in the past two seasons. We have to strengthen, that goes without saying, but we're looking to do things as we've done, on a gradual basis. We've got a great squad already.

'Thirty thousand people here and many more across the city are all elated that we're now in the Premier League. We were this close to going out of the league twenty years ago and who knows where we would have been if we had ended up in the Conference, without a ground? This is a truly amazing feeling both as a fan and as the chairman and owner.'

Everyone wanted to know about Knockaert. 'We had followed him for a while,' Bloom confirmed.

'We knew he wasn't settled at Standard Liège and wanted to come back to England and we were absolutely desperate to get him. We knew how brilliantly he had done at Leicester and he's done even better for us.

'The past eighteen months have been a pure pleasure watching him. He scores and creates goals, he deservedly won EFL player of the season and I'm so pleased he is at our club. The offer we had for him last summer was relatively easy [to turn down]. He loves Brighton, he loves playing for us and we wanted to keep him, so when those things go hand-in-hand, it was an easy decision. There were one or two more difficult ones. We wanted to keep our main players, the ones who did so well last season, and we set out to do that, and strengthened on top of that and we ended up with a very strong squad.'

The supporters knew that the team were effectively up but stayed behind to watch the Huddersfield game in the concourses and on the big screens in the stadium bowl. Derby's equaliser raised the roof and at the whistle the fans flooded back onto the field. Where some clubs might have fretted about the damage to the playing surface and tried to clear the field, Brighton turned on the floodlights. The players emerged from their lounge to join in the singing, and both Bloom and Hughton spoke from the directors' box.

The tweets of congratulation came thick and fast, from former players and the wider world of football, including Hughton's old Tottenham teammates Jürgen Klinsmann and Osvaldo Ardiles. Former England star Wayne Bridge, a loanee under Poyet in 2012/13, said: 'Buzzing to see @OfficialBHAFC promoted to the

@premierleague. Great club, great fans, great city. Wishing you all the best next season.'

Current England forward Jesse Lingard, who had been on loan from Manchester United the season after Bridge, tweeted: 'Had a great time at your club and see you next season.' *Match of the Day* presenter Gary Lineker said: 'Look forward to introducing you on @BBCMOTD next season.' Zamora said: 'Looking forward to coming to the Bristol City game to celebrate.' The Premier League wasted little time in tweeting a welcome to the forty-eighth club to join its ranks.

'After I'd been in the changing room, and done lots of press, my family were waiting for me and it was lovely,' Hughton said.

'We watched Derby–Huddersfield and, at first, it was difficult because mathematically we hadn't done it. But then it was lovely to be promoted officially with my wife [Cheryl], four children and six grandkids all around me. Most managers dedicate their lives to the job, so it's wonderful for the family to share some success.

'The emotions that you go through in a game are so high for such a long time that I do find it hard to unwind, even when we've won, but the great leveller is the grandkids. They only see *you*, not whether you've won or lost, they don't see the meaning of winning or losing, and they don't change.'

As the fans finally streamed away to Falmer station, they were amazed and delighted to be joined by Dunk, Goldson, Knockaert, Stephens, Stockdale and other players heading out to celebrate in the city centre. Twitter footage showed Baldock and Norwood crowd-surfing inside a packed train, Skalák being carried shoulder-high down Queens Road towards the seafront and players leading the singing again in West Street.

Knockaert conducted his own song, Sidwell looked suitably embarrassed at the fans' version of 'You're Just Too Good to Be True', which includes generous offers of sexual favours to the midfield player, and Stephens joined in when fans sang 'We want you to stay'. After the dramas and transfer request of the summer, he would sign a new contract shortly after the final game of the season.

Hughton was relaxed about his thoroughbred players risking injury being carried through the city and courting hangovers with three games to play and the title to be won. 'When the club and the players achieve what we have this season, everything over the last few days goes with it and it just shows what it means to this group of players and everybody else,' he said. 'We saw the opposite, the disappointment of last season, and we very much saw what that meant. This is the other side of it and everybody has enjoyed it. All of it is understandable, all of it is acceptable, and that is what we are here for.'

As Huddersfield, Leeds and even Newcastle had faltered, Hughton's men had shown the knack of winning when not at their best, responding to that defeat at Elland Road with five successive victories, a sprint finish that had taken them over the line with plenty to spare. Blackburn, Birmingham, QPR, Wolves and Wigan might not have been the most formidable of opposition, but all had posed problems, and the team had overcome them all while Huddersfield were losing to Burton, Leeds to Wolves and Newcastle to Ipswich.

'Everyone looks at key games, but that break in Spain after we lost at Leeds seemed to galvanise everyone,' Trollope said. 'The home wins after that break were expected, but the away wins at QPR and Wolves were special and we pushed forward and the others dropped away.'

'Our form has been exceptional at this stage of the season,' Hughton said. 'That has been a little bit of a difference. We've had a really good spell at the right time.'

One fan posted a picture of Alex Pritchard, looking morose on the bench at Preston after being substituted, alongside an image of Albion players rejoicing. His decision not to complete his transfer from Tottenham to Brighton had not been the only error made by a rival. Rafael Benítez, the Newcastle manager, had tried to heap the pressure on Hughton's men whenever they overtook his team, and the Huddersfield manager and Leeds diaspora had hinted that Albion could be overhauled.

After Wagner's remark, Bruno and company took 21 points out of 24, while Huddersfield had managed only 13. The Yorkshire club and Newcastle had each won two, drawn one and lost two while Brighton were winning five to breast the tape.

'We just ignored it,' Dunk said.

'We've always worried about ourselves. There's been so much talk about everyone else and we've sort of gone under the radar and that's the way we like it. We've had Newcastle in the league and they're a massive club, who have been up there for so long. They spent big money and people were saying they should walk the league. That was fine by us. We didn't want to be the big ones, the main people, we just want to be the underdogs and sneak up on everyone and get promotion like we did.'

'People were doubting us, some saying we were going to bottle it again,' Stockdale said.

'I just want to say to them: "You're welcome." That just spurred us on. Bottlers? Who's bottling it now? Not us, an incredible group of players and staff, from the chairman down. We've still got a job to do. Let's make it seven or eight on the spin. We can reach a hundred points now.'

Supporters of various clubs took this as a barb in their direction. 'After Leeds, some friends may have texted me, saying they were going to replace us and I said "OK,"' Stockdale said.

'Then after Valencia we reeled off five in a row. Hence why I said, "Who's bottling it now?" – not aimed at anyone in particular. People said it was aimed at Huddersfield, Leeds, Newcastle, but I hadn't said any names. People could take it how they wanted to. I don't care, we were promoted. We stayed under the radar. We were the underdog. People saying we'd bottle it? 15 points out of 15 isn't really bottling it, is it?'

The media went to town the next day. Brighton's promotion was the lead story on the front pages of both the *Mirror* and *The Sun*, with photographs of the scenes after the final whistle. In *The Times*, Rosenior profiled his teammates for the benefit of readers who knew little of Brighton's under-the-radar squad. He forecast England places for Stockdale, Dunk and March, that Stephens and Bruno would get even better at the higher level, and that there would be more goals for Murray.

The foreign press also noticed. In Germany, *Der Spiegel* asked Hünemeier whether he had been alarmed by the pitch invasion. 'What we experienced yesterday was perhaps the most extreme and at the same time the most peaceful celebration ever,' he said.

He also revealed that the revelry had lasted until the early hours.

'There was ecstasy all over the city, the streets were full of celebrating fans – and me – and the team went to a club that the football club had hired until four o'clock in the morning. There were a few beers – the English celebrate wildly. But even after filling up, some players are already back on duty.'

Asked to compare the emotions with his rise to the Bundesliga with SC Paderborn, he said:

'I can't compare that. With Paderborn, we had to win on the final day to make the climb perfect, which was an incredible pressure situation – and the more surprising and emotional was the feeling of happiness when we had made it. This time the success was more predictable and in the end a deserved advance for long, hard work.'

Others had nothing to compare this with, and Murphy summed up the way they were feeling. 'Days like Monday don't come around very often, and for most players they don't come around at all,' he said.

'I have been so close plenty of times before and missed out. I was in the play-offs twice with Sheffield United and once with Brighton and didn't go up.

'It is hard to take and there were times you think it will never happen. There was also a Scottish Cup Final defeat with Motherwell when I was younger. I just didn't want to go through my whole career without achieving anything. So to finally get over the line is an amazing feeling.

'The prospect of playing in the Premier League is something I have always aspired to from the moment I left Motherwell as a young kid. It has been a long road, but to get there eventually is just amazing.'

Dunk, the local boy and one-club man, had a longer perspective. 'The celebrations in 2010/11 were good but nothing compared to these,' he said.

'It's promotion to the Premier League and it's where everyone wants to play. From when you're a little boy watching, you want to play in the Premier League and it's just massive and it was great times.

'The fans running on the pitch and mobbing us, that whole day and night was something I'll never forget for the rest of my life. We got the train in with the fans and integrated with them and made it a big day for them and us. That's the way this club has always been, it's a community club and I think it was really fitting for us to do that, instead of just going off and doing it on our own. We loved it, they loved it, so what more could you ask for?'

CHAPTER 16

CELEBRATION TIME

In his press conference in advance of the trip to Norwich, Hughton had warned that everyone would have to get used to the idea of losing more games after promotion. He probably did not mean that it would start with their very first match as a Premier League club in waiting.

There was always the risk of anticlimax after the highs of Easter Monday afternoon and the carousing during an evening that stretched into the very early hours of Tuesday and beyond. Although the players and managers were back in training thirty-six hours later and said all the right things in the days that followed about not wanting to let their standards slip now that the main target of the season had been reached, the same sense of urgency would not be present and, even without intending to, players relax when the pressure is off.

Dunk, March and Stephens had had personal experience of that. They had been present when Albion were Leicester City's opponents at the Walkers Stadium in the first match after the Foxes clinched promotion to the Premier League in April 2014, with the former coasting to a 4–1 win.

The team's performance in their post-party comedown, a 2–0 defeat at Carrow Road, was nothing like as bad as Leicester's had been, and the defence arguably did its job to perfection, preventing the home side from mustering a single effort on target – a stat that would normally have ensured at least a point. However, two shots from outside the penalty area from Pritchard both hit the woodwork – bar first, then upright – and bounced back into the net off the back of the diving Stockdale. He would have done better to watch the shots go past him then pick up the rebounds and otherwise had little to do during the game apart from collecting a few crosses.

'He said he might as well get on the plane home on his own so he doesn't bring us his bad luck,' Sidwell said afterwards.

'Two own goals? I don't think that has ever been seen before, certainly not on Stocko's [part]. But it has given us the kick up the backside we might need to go again, train again this week and then really kick on at home to Bristol City. It's a freak. We've lost the game and we are bitterly disappointed but it's still all in our hands.'

'That's not something I have ever seen before,' Hughton admitted.

'It happens to keepers from time to time, but not usually twice in one game. Obviously there is no blame attached to David at all. He was just trying to make the saves and the ball just came back off him. What I would say is that we were punished for allowing the player to get his shot away by not closing him down on the edge of the box. When that happens you are asking for trouble.'

The defence might have been unlucky to be on the wrong end of such a statistical anomaly but the attack failed to fire in a team showing four changes. Murphy was alongside Murray in place of Hemed, with Pocognoli returning instead of Bong, and Norwood and Sidwell replacing Kayal and Stephens in central midfield. Even so, unlike their hosts, they got three efforts on target.

Norwood created the best chance but Hünemeier's glancing header from the Irishman's cross was too close to Norwich goalkeeper John Ruddy. Murray had a header cleared off the line and Murphy also had a penalty claim turned down when he was checked by Graham Dorrans. But March flitted in and out of the action and Knockaert made less impression than usual and was substituted after an hour. Hughton was unimpressed and had told the players so at half-time. He also cancelled a planned day off for the following week. There were to be no more lax attitudes with the title still up for grabs and two more matches remaining in which to claim it, at home to Bristol City and away to Aston Villa.

The supporters who packed the away seats were denied the title celebrations they had hoped to see, but were in good voice throughout, especially when Pritchard was on the ball. 'You could have gone up,' was just one of the songs, and the most printable, directed at the man who nearly became Albion's record signing. Would they, in fact, have achieved the same feat if Pritchard had altered the team shape, perhaps at the expense of Baldock? Nobody will ever know.

But Pritchard had showed why Hughton and Winstanley had wanted him in August, and picked up Sky's man-of-the-match award. However, struggling to be heard over the ribald chanting of the Brighton supporters at his expense, he admitted that Norwich's victory counted for nothing. 'Brighton have hit their targets for the season and we haven't,' he said, before turning to applaud the hordes in blue and white good-naturedly. His point was well made. The two teams had been a point apart before Norwich's visit to the Amex in autumn, and even after the Canaries' empty revenge, the gap was now 26 points.

Results of the other teams apart from Newcastle were now of only academic interest, but it was noted the following day that

Huddersfield and Leeds again faltered, as if they had brought ill luck upon themselves by talking tough about catching Albion. And there were hollow laughs among many fans when Gastón Ramírez was sent off in Middlesbrough's abject 4–0 defeat at Bournemouth for receiving two yellow cards, the first for simulation.

• • •

The next week began with a day for looking back. First there was the blue-and-white themed funeral of Paul Whelch, attended by board members including Tony Bloom and Paul Barber and directed by Ian Hart, formerly the co-editor of the influential *Gull's Eye* fanzine that had been the first focus for fan discontent in the 1990s. Whelch had been a contributor, and the former whistle-blower had had his photograph shown on the screens at the Amex during the second half of the Wigan match, accompanied by a minute's applause. A school friend delivering a eulogy mentioned how proud he would have been of that happening in the match that guaranteed the club's promotion.

Liam Rosenior had paid tribute after the match.

'I hope his family's proud of him, because if it wasn't for people like him – people who fought for this club to stay alive – we wouldn't have days like this, we [players] wouldn't be here at the fantastic club we're at. So it's poignant that, on this day when we pretty much guaranteed promotion, his face was on the big board as one of the most important games in the club's history is going on.'

'We dedicate this year to everyone who has been lost,' Stockdale said.

'Supporters who worked so hard, Sarah Watts and Paul Whelch – people who spend their lives supporting a club that makes up so much of their lives and they don't get to see the fruits of everyone's labour, their own time and effort. This year is even more special for that reason.'

After the service, fans including many of his comrades from the battles against the previous board and the fight for the new stadium mingled outside the church, including Liz Costa of the supporters' club, Paul Samrah and John Baine, better known in the wider world as musician and poet Attila the Stockbroker.

Dick Knight reflected on the varied backgrounds of the fans who had come together to save the club.

'Liz and Sarah [Watts] became symbols of the campaign, women who were entrenched Albion fans. Sarah was actually more vociferous and radical, and I think Liz had to rein her in at times. At meetings, she was a major contributor and very strong in her opinions. When she said she was going to do something, she did it. It's an absolute tragedy that she didn't see us reach the Premier League, although she saw the Amex, as did Paul Whelch and Roy Chuter.

'Then you had John, alias Attila, a black-clad socialist, poet and troubadour, combining with two city gents in Paul Samrah and Paul Whelch who might never normally have crossed each other's paths. And that just shows the power of sport, and specifically football, to unite people in a common cause. And they were intelligent people, coming up with ideas like forming a political party to fight local elections in Lewes. That resource of different backgrounds and talents not only saved the Albion but has taken it forward.'

Samrah and Baine had been the odd couple at the heart of the fans' protests, eventually sharing PA duties at Withdean. While Samrah chaired the Falmer For All campaign, Baine was more at home leading marches to the home village of despised former chairman Bill Archer. But he had begun to campaign much earlier, getting up on the dugout roof after a home match against Southend United in 1993 to call on fans to rise up against a board that was presiding over decline.

'It was the point where my lifelong left-wing radical politics and activism and my preparedness to put myself on the front line and seeing my football club being destroyed coalesced,' he said.

'First it was incompetence and then when Archer took over it was malice. I knew I was doing the right thing although I'm not going to say it wouldn't have happened otherwise – of course it would, but probably a bit later. But somebody was needed to stand up and actually do it, say I am here, I'm going to take this on. At that time, I was the person. If anyone else had done it before me, I wouldn't have needed to do it.

'The thing I love about Brighton Football Club and my fellow supporters is that people who loathe my politics and everything I stand for in terms of my culture, my music, my poetry, still respect my part in what we've done. I love that because I never just want to preach to the converted. If I had a pint for everyone who says, "You're a commie **** and your poetry's shit but cheers for what you've done for the club mate," or something along those lines, I'd be very drunk indeed. Although, it being Brighton, there are far more who did agree with the politics too.'

'When you look back, it is incredible the amount that everyone did and the way they sustained it so long,' Samrah said.

'But we carried so many people with us that it was never as much of an uphill struggle as it might have been. And we had a lot of luck, with the right party conferences in town at the right time, good weather for all the marches, having the right contacts at Westminster, the fact that the team were playing away to Grimsby on Valentine's Day 2004 so we could nip across the Humber

Bridge and deliver cards to John Prescott's constituency office in Hull.

'We had to do our bit to support the money men, and let them do their bit. They could never say the fans weren't interested or didn't help, because we were and we did. It was a good partnership. We knew what we could and couldn't do. Dick Knight and then Tony Bloom knew they couldn't do it on their own and neither could we.

'Once the decision to let us build the stadium had been given, there was no more work to do so we could sit back and enjoy it, just be fans again. Which is just as well. We got older and had children and have less time. But there is a legacy. Our children and the next generation have a stadium where they can sit and watch football, and the fact that we can fill 30,000 seats without any problem is tremendous. And that is despite the fact that we lost a generation of fans.

'There have been a fair few knocks since we got to the Amex: Shoreham, saying goodbye to a few of the campaigners and that all puts play-off defeats in a proper perspective, but we have got through everything, still united, and we hope that will continue when we're in the Premier League and probably no longer winning most home games.'

Then in the evening was the annual player-of-the-season dinner at the stadium, which was an even more enjoyable occasion than usual. 'We are still buzzing,' Kayal said on arriving.

'Last season we were unlucky and this is a big, big achievement for everyone – the players, the fans. It still feels like a dream. In Israel, the press was crazy, among the family and friends emotional messages and texts.

'Everyone knows it was my dream from when I first left Israel and went to Scotland, to be in the Premier League. We are waiting for the fixtures to come out. When you see Arsenal away and then you are coming back to Man U at home then you need to go to Chelsea, you know you are in the big league with the biggest clubs in the world. It's something special for all of us.'

Stockdale, Bruno, Dunk and Knockaert were all presented with awards to mark their selection in the Professional Footballers' Association Championship team of the year.

'It's been my best season so far,' Dunk said.

'Being promoted and getting named in the PFA team of the year has been huge and something I'll remember for the rest of my life. From the start of the season, we came in and had meetings and set promotion as a goal. If we hadn't believed it, we wouldn't have done it. There's been many games this season where we haven't played so well and we've won and that's what gets you over the line. And if your peers vote for you, it means you're well thought of from the outside and it's a nice feeling.'

Significantly, after his dismissal at Huddersfield, he had received only two more yellow cards and avoided a three-match ban for fifteen bookings that many had considered inevitable.

'After missing the Middlesbrough game, it was always in the back of my mind to stop the silly ones and thankfully I've gone nine games without getting booked. I've closed my mouth. I've been told so many times, "Keep your head together, don't do anything stupid," and finally I think something has clicked in my brain. You want to play every game and if you're doing stupid things like that, you can't be up for selection.'

March, still only twenty-two, was young player of the season for the second time. Sidwell again stepped up to receive the goal of the season trophy and, in another echo of the EFL awards, Knockaert followed him on stage to collect the top prize as player of the season.

It was barely noticed that Newcastle were playing Preston, clinching their own promotion with a 4–1 victory.

March had also received international recognition with a recall to the England under-21 squad, celebrating with a well-taken long-range goal against Denmark, cutting in from the right and shooting across the goalkeeper into the top far corner. It reminded Albion fans of arguably his best strike for the club, in a pre-season friendly at home to Norwich. 'When you're out of your club team for that long, people might forget about you and you're completely under the radar,' he said. 'Obviously I was off the under-21 scene but you keep hoping. I wouldn't say I was surprised to get the call again but I was hoping and I was pleased.'

England had used him on the right, while Hughton had played him on both sides as well as in the number 10 role at home to Cardiff. But what did March prefer? 'I change my mind on this myself,' he said, 'but on the whole I think the right, so that I can come inside and shoot on my left. The Denmark goal wasn't quite as good as the one against Norwich but still a good strike. But I'm happy anywhere at the front.'

March had returned to the Albion squad to find that he had extra competition from Knockaert and Skalák but was happy just to be fit again.

'The competition among the wide men here keeps you on your toes and you know that you need to play well to get in and then to keep your place. To play games, you have to perform. You want to get touches in the game and make things happen, but the way the game goes you can be out of it for minutes at a time. That's when you have to keep focused.

'The crowd getting behind you and singing your name makes a big difference. It lifts you, I don't know how, but it gives you more energy, it lifts you massively. And we're going to need that next year. But scoring the goal that eventually took us up, although I didn't know it at the time, was the best moment of the season. It was on my right foot so I have to admit I just closed my eyes and hit it and when I opened them it was in the net – happy days. When Huddersfield drew, it sank in and it was a nice feeling.'

Although injury would force him out of the England under-21 squad before the summer's European Championship finals in Poland, he had the consolation of knowing that he was now a Premier League player.

'A Premier League player? That will really hit home when the fixtures come out and we see who we're playing. In the days of Withdean, you wouldn't have seen the club being in the Premier League now. But it's amazing and credit to everyone like Dick Knight and the chairman who made it happen.'

Wednesday 26 April was the twentieth anniversary of the last game at the Goldstone, and the event was remembered in an event at the Komedia in central Brighton's North Laine entitled 'Build a Bonfire' – a fan song that had become the title of a book by Steve North and Paul Hodson, who co-hosted with Alan Wares and Ady Packham of the *Albion Roar*.

Attila the Stockbroker began the evening of readings, music, stand-up and interviews with a poem entitled 'From Hereford to Here'. It spoke of:

A glorious end to twenty years
Of struggle for our dream.
The Albion in the Premier League
And we all played our part.
We're more than corporate football, us.

We're football's beating heart.
With sheer determination
Without a hint of fear
We made the noise which brought the boys
From Hereford to here.

'The event was commemorating twenty years since the last game at the Goldstone but also, in a way, celebrating us, the fans,' Alan Wares said.

'Tony Bloom rightly gets a lot of credit for where we are now, as do Dick Knight, Chris Hughton, Paul Winstanley, the players. But we're also cognisant of the fact that none of this would have been possible without what we did twenty years ago.

'Matt Francis [the club's England wheelchair international] got up on stage in his wheelchair and said: "You've got to realise that you didn't just save an old and cherished club; you left a legacy for a generation – opportunities for people who otherwise wouldn't have had them, in the form of Albion in the Community."

'It was the fans talking about the fans. And I think we owe ourselves a debt of gratitude. Dick led us, the flock was looking for a leader and he came along. We knew where we wanted to go, we were just looking for someone to lead us – and give us a bag of money.'

Now the players knew all the fans' songs, and had proved it by singing them from the press box after the Wigan match, including 'We're on Our Way', which had become the unofficial promotion anthem. 'That is our song of the season, even if, I think, Sunderland sang it first,' Wares said.

'But very few of these things are original. Sidwell does look genuinely embarrassed by his song.

'Liam said that vocal support absolutely makes a difference. It doesn't just make us feel good; it genuinely has an effect on them. If they want us to make some noise, who are we to refuse? Jason Thackeray said that when Hemed's penalty went in at Fulham, he felt the stand bouncing, but when Dunk headed in, he thought it was going to collapse. The build-up to the Sheffield Wednesday play-off game was so loud that it actually hurt. The trouble with the Bristol City home match was celebrating a win before it had happened.'

• • •

The mood at the training ground during the week before Bristol City's visit was positive, and the sense that the title would be secured in the televised match on Saturday evening was palpable. The Championship trophy would be at the Amex stadium in readiness for a post-match presentation, and a party mood would reign in the stands. Blue-and-white flags and streamers were being provided, and the fans would be ready to applaud the players' lap of honour.

All but forgotten in all this were City, who had shown their qualities only occasionally during a largely disappointing season, beating both Fulham and Huddersfield 4–0. Lee Johnson, their manager, who had made his professional debut as a player for Albion in December 2000, scoring in a 2–0 victory over Cardiff City in a Football League Trophy tie at Withdean, had watched the Norwich match on television.

'Every panel member had said Brighton would go and win [against us] by three or four, by four or five,' he said.

'Everyone is expecting Brighton to win, and win comfortably. You hear on the media circuit people talking about it being an easy three points. That gets the anger and aggression going in everybody because they want to prove they are good players. It makes you feel we have got to go there and prove what we are about.'

And that was before results elsewhere on Saturday afternoon left City needing a point to be mathematically safe from relegation. As their players went back to the dressing room after their pre-match warm-up, they looked at the flags waving around the Amex and their expressions spoke of their determination to spoil the party.

Then goal-scoring legends Zamora and Peter Ward were introduced to an Amex record crowd of 30,338, and Ward quipped that they might come on in the second half if there was no score. When Murray pulled an early chance horribly wide after a defensive miscue, you suspected that the joke might end up not seeming so funny after all.

That impression increased as the match wore on. City looked focused while the men in stripes played at an exhibition pace, over-confident that goals would come. Hopeful high balls were easily dealt with by City's giant defender Aden Flint, and Jiří Skalák's low shot after twenty-eight minutes, saved by Frank Fielding, was to be their only effort on target until far too late.

And after forty-three minutes, the visitors showed how it should be done. Matty Taylor's cross, in contrast to so many of Brighton's, was perfectly aimed for Josh Brownhill to nod in his first goal for the club from six yards.

Albion still had forty-seven minutes to prove their title credentials, but Murray's late header, also dealt with by Fielding, was as close as they came, and it would all have been over long before then but for Taylor's miss from six yards or Stockdale's excellent save from City substitute Bobby Reid.

'We limited a very good side to very few chances,' Johnson said, and praised his former club.

'It's certainly a club I look up to and Chris is a manager I look up to. I think the club is one we can model ourselves on. They got promoted through working hard, having a good manager and getting top players in. It's what dreams are made of for a club like this – no parachute payments but outstanding work being done behind the scenes and at the tip of the iceberg.

'It's a great city, a great place. It always had the fanbase and the history and they had to give it a facility that was worthy of that history. They have put a fantastic stadium together and deserve to get promoted. And I hope they do it as champions. I think they will. They are the best team.'

That feeling, though, was not reflected in the home dressing room. The mood had been positive among the fans while the squad had taken a post-match lap of honour, but the players' faces looked more like those of a relegated team going through an unwanted ritual.

With the disappointment still fresh, Sidwell said:

'It has put a massive dampener on the whole season, if you ask me. I know we have next week but more hopes were pinned on this game, no disrespect to Bristol, with it being a home game and the form and record at home. The celebrations should have been better out there. The lap of honour should have had a trophy.

'We have another chance at Villa Park next week, but it's going to be very tough, especially after two defeats. With it being their last home game, they will be wanting to end on a good note for their fans, so we need to go there with the right frame of mind and each and every one of us needs to be at the top of his game.

'That is two defeats back to back, and I think that has only happened once before this season; we pulled together after that and we will have to do it again.'

He was at a loss to explain the flat performance.

'We've trained well and prepared well and didn't take the game for granted, but it just didn't happen from start to finish. I'm not sure when we had our first shot on target, our first corner, it was one of those games where we lacked that spark and energy.

'Some people are saying we got promoted too early with three games to go, but I don't think so; there is no sense of that in the camp. We are not talking about the Premier League at the moment; our celebrations have been and gone. We prepared all week for this but it wasn't to be. We get three bites at the cherry and we will need the third one.

'I don't think there were nerves – I think we have had bigger games this year where we have needed to grind out a result. Maybe it was the whole party feel. I can understand they wanted it to be a day for everyone to enjoy and we have let them down. I can't put my finger on why it has happened, but it has – and we need to dust ourselves down and get back on track. We have one more game to go and we will give it our all.'

• • •

Aston Villa, tough opponents at the Amex in autumn, represented the final challenge, and there was a boost for all concerned when Connor Goldson joined the players for the pre-match warm-up in the Birmingham sunshine.

'We all care about each other and what Connor has been through, we were all so worried about him,' Rosenior said.

'But we knew how strong he is as a person as well as a player. Football ability doesn't matter at a time like that, it's your character that is so important and Connor's character and his mentality is so strong that we know he'll come back better than ever. And he's a good guy as well, which gave us motivation to make sure that his next game would be in the Premier League.'

Villa, in their final home game, were in no mood to be upstaged on their own pitch by the visitors and gave as good as they got in the first half. Henri Lansbury headed wide and Scott Hogan, who had scored twice for Brentford at the Amex, had a shot saved by Stockdale after a poor backpass by Pocognoli.

Newcastle had gone ahead in their match at home to Barnsley after twenty-three minutes and were 2–0 up on the hour, so Albion could not afford any slip-ups, and after sixty-four minutes they got the goal they craved. Baldock was felled by Nathan Baker, who was sent off, and Murray scored from the penalty, his twenty-third and final goal of a memorable season, and ran to the fans, reprising his goal celebration from the Withdean years. He had another chance when a short backpass presented him with the ball but he unselfishly tried to find Baldock instead and James Chester intercepted.

Against ten men, the best defence in the division would have been fancied to hold out. But a minute from glory, it was all snatched away. Jack Grealish hit a shot through a crowd and Stockdale took his eye off the ball as Dunk lunged across to try to block and it went past him into the corner of the net. There was pandemonium on Tyneside, where Newcastle finished 3–0 winners, and stunned silence among the visiting fans at Villa Park.

At the final whistle, Bruno, who had been substituted, came back on to pick the prostrate Stockdale off the Villa Park turf, not just performing a captain's duty but also returning a favour from a year before, when the goalkeeper had lifted his skipper after the play-off semi-final second leg.

'They are difficult moments,' he said.

'Stocko didn't deserve this at all. He has had an incredible season for us. But in the tough times is when you have to be by the side of your teammates. When I was lying on the pitch [at the Amex],

Stocko said to me, "Next season we are going to be up," and I'm never going to forget that.

'We don't deserve to leave here feeling like this. It's such a shame. We had three chances to be champions and we didn't manage it. It is so, so cruel that they score right at the end with ten men. But we will realise we have had a spectacular season. What has happened leaves a bitter taste in the mouth. But we will evaluate what we have done, we will put it into context. We have been working week after week for two years to win promotion.'

That context was clear. Bruno and his men had proved themselves beyond doubt one of the two best teams in a highly competitive Championship. They had been first or second since October. When it truly mattered and promotion was on the line, they had held their nerve and won those five crucial March games in succession.

They had hit their pre-season target thanks to an irresistible combination of team spirit, resilience, hard work and no little skill, led there by an inspiring manager, backed by a dedicated coaching and backroom staff and supported to the hilt by the chairman and board. The fans had responded, the average home attendance of 27,996 being the highest in the club's history.

They had finished eight points ahead of third-placed Reading, and, in the end, twelve ahead of Huddersfield. Leeds had not even made the play-offs. There was a kind of justice in the fact that Fulham, so impressive in three games against the Albion, had grabbed sixth place.

The positive stats had piled up: fewest defeats in the division (9) and the most home wins (17), the joint-best defensive record (40 goals conceded), and most clean sheets among the ninety-two clubs (21).

Stockdale led goalkeepers in all four divisions with twenty shut-outs, and Murray had equalled the club record of goals in the second tier, first set by Bill Curry fifty-seven years previously. 'Glenn's goals can't be underestimated,' Baldock said. 'He scored such a lot of important goals, often in narrow victories. He has done so well and taken us over the line.'

Mullery put the achievement in perspective:

'After the disappointment of the play-offs in 2016, it just shows the character in the players, to be in the top two for most of the season. As for the three games after we'd won promotion, I think it's human nature to think: "I've done enough." As a manager, yes, you want them to go out there and win the title, but sometimes when you've achieved what you've set out to, over forty-three games beforehand, it's all taken place and you're there. It's about human beings and human nature.'

It was true that, at the beginning of the season, everyone in the Brighton camp would gladly have accepted automatic promotion in second place behind Newcastle, the clear favourites. Nevertheless, they knew that the title had been theirs for the taking and that they had handed the trophy to the Magpies, and feelings remained raw in the immediate aftermath of Villa Park.

'I was unbearable on the drive back, replaying all the ifs and buts and misses in my head,' Barber said.

'Ellie could have gone back in another car with my wife but was in the car with me and she regrets that. When I got home, I felt as low as I had felt in football, lower than after Middlesbrough or Sheffield Wednesday, which was ridiculous. We had a lot to look forward to, we'd been promoted, we had a trip booked to the USA which Tony was funding, we had a promotion parade and after-party the next Sunday, we'd already had a great day and night after Wigan.

'I'd been home about two hours when I got a call from Tony and he said he felt the same, and asked: "How can that be?" I said: "I don't know, but I'm angry, disappointed and I feel physically sick." He said: "So am I. Let's talk tomorrow." But the next day I took the dog for a walk along the seafront, I remembered we'd been promoted, bumped into a few people who were also disappointed but OK and by the evening I was over it. Tony called and he was too. I spoke to Chris and he was the same. We had a fantastic few days in Las Vegas and came back to the promotion parade and that was so amazing that any disappointment was completely blown away.'

• • •

Open-top bus rides along the seafront had always been the club's traditional way of celebrating promotions. Some feared that the loss of the title might make this one a damp squib. They need not have worried. Despite an indifferent weather forecast for the Sunday of the parade, the sun shone and the atmosphere in the city hours before the start of the parade was like Cup Final Day or Super Bowl Sunday, minus any concerns about the result. In a nod to Brighton history, a flotilla of mods on blue-and-white scooters cruised up Church Street, parkas festooned in club emblems and flags streaming. A Belgian chip shop offered blue-and-white striped mayonnaise.

Bruno had sensed that the whole city was waiting for a party. 'Now it's just crazy,' he said.

'Normally English fans are different from in Spain. They don't bother you like in Spain. Here people respect the players. But now some people cannot stop themselves saying something. They are really happy so of course I understand.

'Some people that I didn't know were fans, who I've seen often at the kids' school, are saying things like "We are just over the moon."

I say I didn't know they were fans and they say: "Yes, we go to every match, we've got season tickets." So I say: "You didn't say anything to me about it in the last three years?" And they say: "We didn't want to bother you," and that's great.'

The team, media and guests boarded the buses by the statue of Steve Ovett, another Brighton sporting hero famous for beating rivals over a distance – and sometimes easing off at the end. Some were struck by the fact that it was the same starting point for the seafront marches in which fans had walked to the conference centre to lobby delegates to the annual conference of the governing Labour Party to give planning permission for the new stadium.

John Baine, who had been at the front of those marches, was now happy to be a face in the crowd along Kings Road. 'There are people from other clubs taking the mickey out of us, saying that we were celebrating finishing second, as if there's really that much difference between finishing first or second,' he said.

'Some people were really cut up that we missed out on winning the title, but I was only mildly irritated, because I was at the Riverside a year ago and I know the contrast in emotions between what we have achieved and what happened last season. People were saying we were "tinpot" because we were having this party, but we weren't celebrating coming second, we were celebrating the glorious culmination of twenty years of struggle to save our club.'

The convoy moved off into crowds that were already large enough to slow progress before the buses had even reached the nominal starting point at the Palace Pier, and the players' bus shook as the team bounced up and down on the top deck. The 'No Standing in the Upper Saloon' notice was honoured in the breach rather than the observance. At one point, Knockaert and Baldock were showering fans on one side with beer while on the other, Sidwell, March,

Knockaert and Murray played a cross between volleyball and head tennis with fans who threw footballs up from the pavement. Some of the players wanted to get out and walk and talk with the fans but were held back by security.

'It was great to see the fans' passion at the parade,' Bloom said.

'Among so many tens of thousands of people, I spotted one Manchester United shirt and one Aston Villa shirt and the rest were all in blue and white. So many people, young and old, all sharing celebrations with the players, it was an amazing experience. I am aware of what it means to our fans because I am one of those fans. They have been through so much over the past twenty years and it was our fans who were the driving force to get us permission to build the stadium. Without the fans, we wouldn't be here today. They have been so great for so long.'

Hughton said:

'These are moments that everyone – coaches, staff, players – have to remember and savour because for some, that might be the only bus parade that they ever get to go on. Some may go on to great success and have other moments like that, but others may not, for whatever reason. I have been there and those are the times that you have to enjoy, particularly as a player. They deserved it and if anybody wasn't sure what it meant to the city of Brighton, then they found out on that day.'

It took the buses more than ninety minutes to travel the two miles along the seafront to Hove Lawns, where a concert-size stage had been erected. In the VIP area, former players Kerry Mayo, Gary Hart, Michel Kuipers, Ian Chapman and, from further back, John Templeman, mixed with city councillors and players' families. Mark McGhee, once in charge of the Albion and now Scotland assistant manager, was there too, hoping to have a chance to tell Murphy that he had earned a first call-up to the Scotland squad. Darren Bloom hugged Dick Knight. 'We did it, mate,' he said.

Police initially estimated that 60,000 were there, but many more had watched the bus ride and the figure was revised upwards to 100,000, making it easily the best-attended of any of the club's promotion celebrations over the years. Knockaert modelled next season's kit, becoming the first player in Albion history to wear a Premier League shirt. 'I guarantee 100 per cent we are staying up next season,' he said.

Bruno bowed to the crowd. 'This club went through tough times and we are where we are because of you,' he said. Backstage he admitted: 'It felt like being a rock star.'

Then, one by one, the players came out to be hugged by Bloom and presented with their runners-up medals. Kayal's had to be fitted over a blue-and-white jester hat, while Dunk and Goldson strutted out from opposite sides and performed an elaborate NBA-style celebration. Knockaert almost danced across the stage. Hughton, last out, just managed to dodge a champagne shower. Then the players took a team selfie with the flag-waving fans as a backdrop and Norman Cook, alias Fatboy Slim, played a DJ set at a reception afterwards for players, coaches, directors and guests.

Cook, of course, was a dedicated fan who had invested during the Withdean years, describing one of the perks as 'the most expensive parking place in history'. The record label he appeared on, Skint, had been both the team's shirt sponsors and an apt description of the state of the club.

'He was happy to help financially but he never wanted to be a director,' Dick Knight said.

'And he did help out, several times. The legal fees kept on coming and Norman supplied money, as did the other directors. But he was very generous, as was Billy Brown, whose family live in Henfield and came to Withdean even though his family had boxes at Arsenal and Chelsea.

'Norman was very high-profile, and would wear the Skint Albion shirt at mega gigs all over the world, and that kept the club and our struggle in the public eye. Norman had two gigs at the Amex, the first non-football event there, as I had always promised. He's a lovely guy and a genuine Albion fan. He'd done a gig in Amsterdam the night before the Wigan game that finished at 5 a.m. and flew back in time for kick-off.'

'I loved every moment of it,' Rosenior said.

'When you've achieved what we've achieved, you can see how happy it's made so many people. I've played in an FA Cup final, been promoted to the Premier League before, but nothing comes close to this.

'You couldn't even describe the feeling, and it gives us the motivation to do well next season. This club has got so much potential; it's got a big fanbase and we want to make sure we stay a Premier League club. There's so many good people at the club and you see how much it means to them.

'The fans are the most important people at any football club. They're the lifeblood of the club and I saw fans from the age of five to eighty out supporting us. I want to say thank you to them, and hopefully they continue to support us. All we try to do is our best for them.'

On the following Thursday, Bloom and Hughton were awarded the freedom of the city of Brighton & Hove. Hughton had had to be persuaded that he, as a Londoner and relative newcomer, deserved the award. 'The chairman is local, Brighton born and bred,' he said.

'We can see where he went to school [Lancing] from the training ground and sometimes when players come to sign, I tell them that. His family have been involved for three generations and he has pumped a fortune into this club. What the chairman has done is such an incredible single act. He's employing me to do what I've done, but nobody's employing him. So I can understand him getting it. I accepted it on behalf of the whole club. I am the manager but I have so many people under me who have also worked hard for what we've achieved.'

Bloom, in fact, expressed similar sentiments in his acceptance speech. 'This award is not just for me but all the amazing hard work and dedication of all our staff at Brighton & Hove Albion and all of our amazing fans,' he told the assembled councillors.

'The scenes when we were promoted and at the victory parade where 100,000 of our fans turned up shows how much our football club means to the city of Brighton & Hove. I'm very proud to be chairman and owner and to realise the dreams for all of our fans and all of the people in the city.'

Hughton also accepted graciously. 'Ninety-nine per cent of my life is about football, but it's also about family life and living,' he said.

'I thoroughly enjoy living in Brighton & Hove, it's a great bargaining power for the club. We have a wonderful facility our chairman provided for us, but we also have a wonderful city to live in, which we hope will be a big pull next season. Thank you very much, it's something that's very humbling, particularly for somebody that has only been here for just over two years.'

And the honours kept coming. Eight days after the parade, Hughton received the League Managers' Association's Championship manager-of-the-season award for the second successive season, to loud cheers from his peers. And he presented the LMA's special achievement award to Danny Cowley, the manager of Lincoln City, who had beaten Albion in the FA Cup.

Finally, there was time to take stock before planning again. 'There have been so many highs and lows over the past two seasons,' Bloom said.

'The biggest individual low was the 1–1 draw against Sheffield Wednesday. On the one hand I was so proud of the players and of the fans. I think that first half was the best I've ever seen us play and I've never heard the fans so vociferous. But at the end of it all we were still in the Championship.

'The highs? Sidwell's goal, one of the best I've ever seen from a Brighton player, and then the celebration with Knockaert's shirt that showed the togetherness of the squad. Glenn Murray's last-minute goal up at Birmingham, Stockdale's save and Knockaert's 85th-minute winner against Sheffield Wednesday, Lewis Dunk's goal against Norwich that put us 3–0 up against a big team who were a promotion rival at that time. That was when I had a really good feeling that we were going to do it.

'Being in the away end at Brentford, when all three goals came straight at me, including the equalisers from Duffy and Hemed. The other moment I really, really knew this was going to be our season was the end of the Blackburn game. We'd won 1–0 and Paul Barber gave me a nudge and said: "Huddersfield and Burton are still nil–nil." I smiled and two minutes later there was a big cheer that went up from the North Stand and I was thinking to myself: "Is it a cheer for a nil–nil, or could it possibly be for a late Burton winner?" And of course it was the latter and we were almost there.

'But if I had to choose the most memorable moment of the season, it has to be after the Wigan game. It was key, absolutely critical, to get promotion this season, because there was no way we were going to keep all our players if we hadn't and the Championship is only going to get tougher. The financial loss last season was £25 million, the loss this season if we hadn't got promotion would have been £30 million. Those aren't the sorts of numbers I'd be able to or would want to carry on indefinitely. And we'd done it.'

'Now we've got another challenge ahead of us and that is keeping the spirit that we've had and the values that we've got and carrying them into the Premier League,' Barber said.

'Because I think that could make the difference in a league where some clubs – not all of them – have lost that special connection that they had with their communities. Tony and I do six fans' forums a year around Sussex and for Seagulls Over London and we've got to keep doing them, maybe even more if there's now more demand. They are very important for keeping our feet on the ground.

'Tony is not going to change, so we shouldn't change. It's going to be tough because the players we bring in may be more famous, but then our existing players are going to become more famous as well. But they should still stop to sign autographs as they always have. That's what makes us what we are. We're the same football club playing at a different level. And that's important. We've come a long way since the Goldstone and Gillingham and Withdean, but we are still Brighton & Hove Albion.'

APPENDIX 1

2015/16:

Friday 7 August	Nottingham Forest (h) 1–0 (LuaLua 50)
Saturday 15 August	Fulham (a) 2–1 (Baldock 30, Hemed 90 pen)
Tuesday 18 August	Huddersfield Town (a) 1–1 (Kayal 1)
Saturday 22 August	Blackburn Rovers (h) 1–0 (LuaLua 35)
Saturday 29 August	Ipswich Town (a) 3–2 (LuaLua 10, Hemed 12, 67)
Saturday 12 September	Hull City (h) 1–0 (Hemed 5)
Tuesday 15 September	Rotherham United (h) 2–1 (Hemed 27, Stephens 67)
Saturday 19 September	Wolverhampton Wanderers (a) 0–0
Saturday 26 September	Bolton Wanderers (a) 2–2 (Stephens 31, Murphy 35)
Saturday 3 October	Cardiff City (h) 1–1 (Stephens 38)
Saturday 17 October	Leeds United (a) 2–1 (March 14, Zamora 89)
Tuesday 20 October	Bristol City (h) 2–1 (Baldock 53, Zamora 82)
Saturday 24 October	Preston North End (h) 0–0
Saturday 31 October	Reading (a) 1–1 (Murphy 51)
Tuesday 3 November	Sheffield Wednesday (a) 0–0
Saturday 7 November	MK Dons (h) 2–1 (March 5, Murphy 19)
Sunday 22 November	Burnley (a) 1–1 (Zamora 1)
Saturday 28 November	Birmingham City (h) 2–1 (March 17, Zamora 47)

Saturday 5 December	Charlton Athletic (h) 3–2 (Wilson 50, Zamora 83, Hemed 85)
Saturday 12 December	Derby County (a) 2–2 (Wilson 22, van La Parra 75)
Tuesday 15 December	Queens Park Rangers (a) 2–2 (Stephens 53, van La Parra 55)
Saturday 19 December	Middlesbrough (h) 0–3
Saturday 26 December	Brentford (a) 0–0
Tuesday 29 December	Ipswich Town (h) 0–1
Friday 1 January	Wolverhampton Wanderers (h) 0–1
Tuesday 12 January	Rotherham United (a) 0–2
Saturday 16 January	Blackburn Rovers (a) 1–0 (Zamora 3)
Saturday 23 January	Huddersfield Town (h) 2–1 (Zamora 30, Wilson 66)
Friday 5 February	Brentford (h) 3–0 (Knockaert 27, Hemed 43, Murphy 90)
Saturday 13 February	Bolton Wanderers (h) 3–2 (Murphy 11, Hemed 43, Kayal 58)
Tuesday 16 February	Hull City (a) 0–0
Saturday 20 February	Cardiff City (a) 1–4 (Stephens 55)
Tuesday 23 February	Bristol City (a) 4–0 (Murphy 8, Baldock 21, Hemed 56, Little og 75)
Monday 29 February	Leeds United (h) 4–0 (Hemed 18 pen, 28, Cooper og 22, Dunk 38)
Saturday 5 March	Preston North End (a) 0–0
Tuesday 8 March	Sheffield Wednesday (h) 0–0
Tuesday 15 March	Reading (h) 1–0 (Wilson 25)
Saturday 19 March	MK Dons (a) 2–1 (Hemed 56 pen, 62)
Saturday 2 April	Burnley (h) 2–2 (Stephens 30, Knockaert 45)
Tuesday 5 April	Birmingham City (a) 2–1 (Goldson 29, Dunk 48)
Monday 11 April	Nottingham Forest (a) 2–1 (Dunk 27, Sidwell 90)

APPENDIX 1

Friday 15 April	Fulham (h) 5–0
	(Hemed 29 pen, 34, 79, Bruno 54, Knockaert 87)
Tuesday 19 April	Queens Park Rangers (h) 4–0
	(Knockaert 45, 84, Skalák 51, Goldson 73)
Saturday 23 April	Charlton Athletic (a) 3–1
	(Baldock 8, Skalák 55, Hemed 90 pen)
Monday 2 May	Derby County (h) 1–1 (Wilson 90)
Saturday 7 May	Middlesbrough (a) 1–1 (Stephens 55)
Friday 13 May	Sheffield Wednesday (a) 0–2
Monday 16 May	Sheffield Wednesday (h) 1–1 (Dunk 19)

LEAGUE APPEARANCES:

Bruno 46, Stockdale 46, Stephens 45, Kayal 43, Hemed 40 (4), Dunk 37 (1), Murphy 31 (6), Rosenior 27 (4), Baldock 25 (3), Goldson 22 (2), Greer 20, Knockaert 18 (1), Bong 13 (3), March 13 (3), Hünemeier 13 (2), Wilson 11 (14), Zamora 10 (16), Calderón 10 (7), LuaLua 9 (9), Skalák 8 (4), Crofts 5 (12), Ridgewell 5, Sidwell 4 (12), van La Parra 4 (2), Ince 1 (11), Manu 0 (8), O'Grady 0 (3), Forster-Caskey 0 (2), Chicksen 0 (1), Holla 0 (1).

LEAGUE GOALS:

Hemed 17, Stephens 7, Zamora 7, Murphy 6, Knockaert 5, Wilson 5, Baldock 4, Dunk 3, LuaLua 3, March 3, Goldson 2, Kayal 2, Skalák 2, van La Parra 2, Bruno 1, Sidwell 1, Own goals 2.

APPENDIX 2

2016/17:

Saturday 6 August	Derby County (a) 0–0
Friday 12 August	Nottingham Forest (h) 3–0 (Knockaert 36, Murray 68, 82)
Tuesday 16 August	Rotherham United (h) 3–0
	(Knockaert 23, Murray 26, Hemed 58 pen)
Saturday 20 August	Reading (a) 2–2 (Baldock 8, Knockaert 46)
Saturday 27 August	Newcastle United (a) 0–2
Saturday 10 September	Brentford (h) 0–2
Tuesday 13 September	Huddersfield Town (h) 1–0 (Knockaert 80)
Saturday 17 September	Burton Albion (a) 1–0 (Hemed 88 pen)
Saturday 24 September	Barnsley (h) 2–0 (Murray 12, 48)
Tuesday 27 September	Ipswich Town (a) 0–0
Saturday 1 October	Sheffield Wednesday (a) 2–1 (Baldock 26, Knockaert 73)
Saturday 15 October	Preston North End (h) 2–2 (Baldock 54, Murray 65)
Tuesday 18 October	Wolverhampton Wanderers (h) 1–0 (Baldock 14)
Saturday 22 October	Wigan Athletic (a) 1–0 (Stephens 68)
Saturday 29 October	Norwich City (h) 5–0
	(Murray 6, 60, 73, Dunk 64, Knockaert 84)
Saturday 5 November	Bristol City (a) 2–0 (Sidwell 13, Murphy 20)

Friday 18 November	Aston Villa (h) 1–1 (Murray 45)
Saturday 26 November	Fulham (h) 2–1 (Baldock 52, Murray 79)
Saturday 3 December	Cardiff City (a) 0–0
Friday 9 December	Leeds United (h) 2–0 (Murray 23 pen, Hemed 82 pen)
Tuesday 13 December	Blackburn Rovers (a) 3–2 (Duffy 16, Stephens 61, Murray 79)
Saturday 17 December	Birmingham City (a) 2–1 (Knockaert 82, Murray 90)
Tuesday 27 December	Queens Park Rangers (h) 3–0 (Baldock 11, Murray 53 pen, Knockaert 69)
Monday 2 January	Fulham (a) 2–1 (Hemed 74 pen, Dunk 75)
Saturday 14 January	Preston North End (a) 0–2
Friday 20 January	Sheffield Wednesday (h) 2–1 (Knockaert 34, 85)
Tuesday 24 January	Cardiff City (h) 1–0 (Hemed 73)
Thursday 2 February	Huddersfield Town (a) 1–3 (Hemed 20)
Sunday 5 February	Brentford (a) 3–3 (March 75, Duffy 78, Hemed 90)
Saturday 11 February	Burton Albion (h) 4–1 (Hemed 12, 57 pen, Baldock 47, Murray 83)
Tuesday 14 February	Ipswich Town (h) 1–1 (Hemed 29 pen)
Saturday 18 February	Barnsley (a) 2–0 (Baldock 53, 68)
Saturday 25 February	Reading (h) 3–0 (Baldock 35, Murphy 56, Knockaert 80)
Tuesday 28 February	Newcastle United (h) 1–2 (Murray 14 pen)
Saturday 4 March	Nottingham Forest (a) 0–3
Tuesday 7 March	Rotherham United (a) 2–0 (Knockaert 48, March 79)
Friday 10 March	Derby County (h) 3–0 (Knockaert 5, Baldock 43, Murray 78)
Saturday 18 March	Leeds United (a) 0–2
Saturday 1 April	Blackburn Rovers (h) 1–0 (Murray 67)
Tuesday 4 April	Birmingham City (h) 3–1 (Murray 2, Hemed 48, Hünemeier 54)
Friday 7 April	Queens Park Rangers (a) 2–1 (Murray 58, Pocognoli 64)

Friday 14 April	Wolverhampton Wanderers (a) 2–0 (Knockaert 45, 82)
Monday 17 April	Wigan Athletic (h) 2–1 (Murray 37, March 65)
Friday 21 April	Norwich City (a) 0–2
Saturday 29 April	Bristol City (h) 0–1
Sunday 7 May	Aston Villa (a) 1–1 (Murray 64 pen)

LEAGUE APPEARANCES:

Stockdale 45, Knockaert 44 (1), Dunk 43, Bruno 42, Murray 39 (6), Stephens 33 (6), Duffy 31, Baldock 27 (4), Sidwell 26 (8), Skalák 24 (7), Bong 24, Hemed 20 (17), Murphy 20 (15), Kayal 17 (3), Pocognoli 17 (3), Norwood 16 (17), Hünemeier 11, March 9 (16), Rosenior 9 (1), Goldson 4 (1), Tomori 2 (7), Akpom 1 (9), Adekugbe 1, Mäenpää 1, LuaLua 0 (3), Manu 0 (2), Hunt 0 (1), Towell 0 (1).

LEAGUE GOALS:

Murray 23, Knockaert 15, Baldock 11, Hemed 11, March 3, Duffy 2, Dunk 2, Murphy 2, Stephens 2, Hünemeier 1, Pocognoli 1, Sidwell 1.

INDEX

INDEX